Making Identity Count

Making Identity Count

Building a National Identity Database

TED HOPF *and*
BENTLEY B. ALLAN

OXFORD
UNIVERSITY PRESS

OXFORD
UNIVERSITY PRESS

Oxford University Press is a department of the University of Oxford. It furthers the University's objective of excellence in research, scholarship, and education by publishing worldwide.Oxford is a registered trade mark of Oxford University Press in the UK and certain other countries.

Published in the United States of America by Oxford University Press
198 Madison Avenue, New York, NY 10016, United States of America.

Library of Congress Cataloging-in-Publication Data
Names: Hopf, Ted, 1959– editor. | Allan, Bentley, 1983– editor.
Title: Making identity count : building a national identity database / edited by Ted Hopf and Bentley Allan.
Description: New York, NY: Oxford University Press, 2016. | Includes bibliographical references and index.
Identifiers: LCCN 2015031647| ISBN 978–0–19–025548–0 (pbk.) | ISBN 978–0–19–025547–3 (hardcover) | ISBN 978–0–19–025549–7 (ebook)
Subjects: LCSH: National characteristics—Political aspects. | National interest. | International relations—Philosophy. | Constructivism (Philosophy) | World politics—21st century.
Classification: LCC JZ1316 .M35 2016 | DDC 327.101—dc23 LC record available at http://lccn.loc.gov/2015031647

CONTENTS

PART THREE   CONCLUSIONS

ACKNOWLEDGMENTS

Thanks are due first and foremost to the National University of Singapore's Faculty of Arts and Social Sciences for providing the funds that made this volume possible. Craig Jenkins and the Ohio State University's Mershon Center for International Security Studies provided early encouragement, even if we had to decline our very first grant.

The project benefitted from a presentation at the Institute for Qualitative and Multimethod Research Workshop at the Maxwell School, Syracuse University. We would like to thank Colin Elman for the invitation and all the workshop participants, especially Nahomi Ichino, Jay Seawright, Jim Mahoney, and John Gerring, for their comments. Bear Braumoeller and Eleonora Mattiaci provided us with invaluable assistance multiple times. Brian Pollins' feedback and enthusiasm have been inspirational.

Students in Bentley Allan's *Constructivism* course test drove the methods. Special thanks are due to Karen Reitman, Hannah Kronick, Jarrett Olivo, and Michael Hur for always asking the right questions. Students in *Discourse Analysis II* at the National University of Singapore Summer School for Social Science Research also forced us to clarify our thoughts and helped refine the method. Thanks are due to Luke O'Sullivan and Tobias Hofmann for inviting us to teach and for allowing us to coopt the course for our purposes. We also thank Vijayalakshmi Rehunathan and Aloysius Tan Yong Cheng for their continuous administrative support throughout the project, and beyond.

We must also thank the authors that appear in this volume for their hard work. Special thanks are due to Srdjan Vucetic and Jarrod Hayes for their comments on our chapters.

Finally, we greatly appreciate the excellent copyediting and final production efforts at Oxford University Press, in particular Prabhu Chinnasamy and Brendan Frost. We are grateful to David McBride and two anonymous reviewers of the original manuscript for their support and constructive criticisms.

PART ONE

INTRODUCTION

Making Identity Count

Constructivism, Identity, and IR Theory

TED HOPF

Constructivism, despite being one of the three main streams of international relations (IR) theory, along with realism and liberalism, is rarely, if ever, tested in large-n quantitative work.[1] There are many reasons for this, but the most important ones are methodological. Constructivists almost unanimously eschew quantitative approaches, assuming that variables of interest to constructivists defy quantification.[2] Quantitative scholars mostly ignore constructivist variables as too fuzzy and vague, not least of all because constructivists have told them for 20 years that they are fuzzy and vague! And the rare instances in which quantitative scholars have operationalized identity as a variable, they have unfortunately realized all the constructivists' worst fears, viz., reducing national identity to a single measure such as language, religion, or ethnicity, thereby violating one of the foundational assumptions of constructivism: intersubjectivity.

Quantitative reductionism examines identity not by recovering meaningful identities from the subjects themselves, but instead by choosing which identities matter and then coding subjects for their presence or absence. Constructivists, on the contrary, argue that identities are socially constructed through interaction among agents, and so their recovery must be inductive in order to "let the subjects speak." This "ethnographic sensibility" is lost in quantitative reductionism.[3] We think that ethnographic sensibility and quantitative concerns with replicability can be fruitfully combined, yielding a large-n intersubjective database of national identity that can be profitably used by quantitative scholars. In this volume, we present the first step of this project: examples of transparent, replicable reports on national identity that can be used as the basis for quantitative operationalizations of identity, inductively recovered.

This is critically important because identity is an obvious alternative explanation for war, peace, cooperation, and conflict. Constructivists argue that identity relations explain both enduring rivalries and security communities, cooperation on security and non-security issues, and failure to reach such agreements. In this volume, our dependent variable of interest is acceptance of the prevailing Western global hegemony of liberal democratic capitalism. We offer this as just one possible variable of interest, given the many other outcomes in IR for which identity relations might be relevant. We also limit ourselves to the national identities of the United States, the United Kingdom, China, Russia, Japan, Germany, France, Brazil, and India in 2010.[4] Our ultimate aim is an intersubjective national identity database of all great powers from 1810 to 2010.

This is a "plausibility probe," in the Ecksteinian sense, a test drive of our method for recovering discourses of national identity in an economical way.[5] In previous work on identity and foreign policy, I took years to look at thousands of texts; we have reduced that to dozens of texts requiring about 200 hours of work.[6] By sampling across texts that are more elite, such as leadership speeches, newspaper editorials, and textbooks, and more mass, such as newspaper letters to the editor, bestselling novels, and blockbuster movies, we hope to capture the range of discourse in a society. The volume also explores the theoretical implications for beginning to test constructivism in a serious and systematic manner.

But this volume is also more than just a plausibility probe of a method; it is also a theory-building exercise. We use the identity reports on the nine countries in the volume to test a constructivist account of hegemonic transition. We hypothesize that identity relations are crucial to understanding whether Western neoliberal democratic hegemony is likely to be challenged by a rising China. We conclude that the mass and elite distribution of democratic identity in the world among the countries is a significant barrier to Chinese authoritarian capitalism replacing Western hegemony, and observe that China's rise could even reinforce Western hegemony, since its own national identity accepts neoliberal market principles as fundamental to what it means to be China.

In what follows I explore how national identity might contribute to a more comprehensive theory of international hegemony, the main empirical focus of this volume. I review how much the variable of identity in the constructivist IR literature has already contributed to offering solutions to a wide array of world politics puzzles. I then critically analyze how identity has been theorized, conceptualized, operationalized, and measured by quantitative IR scholars. I conclude with some findings about national identity from the chapters in this volume.

I. Identity, International Politics, and Hegemony

Since the seminal work of Alexander Wendt, IR scholars have recognized that behavior in the international system is not driven solely by the distribution of power, but also depends on the "distribution of identities."[7] That is, patterns of cooperation and conflict depend on how states understand themselves and others in the international system, rather than solely on institutional or material factors.

An identity is how one understands oneself in relationship to another. Any individual or state has multiple identities because its identity is different in interaction with different others. So, an individual's identity as a daughter is evoked when interacting with her mother, but she is a mother to her daughter, and so on. Similarly, a state's national identity changes depending on with which other state it is interacting. So, what it means to be France is different when interacting with the United States, with Germany, and with Francophone Africa. Discourses of national identity contain multiple elements of identity. These discourses are generated both by ruling elites at the level of the state and in society as a whole, as well as in interaction with other states.[8]

Despite this revolution in theory, many scholars carry on as if intersubjective social relations and identities do not matter. This is a serious problem in the literature since it ignores a leading theoretical paradigm and leads to systematic omitted variable bias in most large-n treatments of international conflict. Indeed, as Wedeen argues, "even scholars sympathetic to constructivism have been slow to apply its lessons, in part because the coding work entailed in generating a large, constructivist-oriented data set would be difficult to do."[9] It is our aim to fill this gap.

Neorealism, for example, claims that states balance against power, except when they do not. At those times they do the opposite, and bandwagon.[10] After World War II, for example, the world did not balance against the United States, despite the fact that it produced half the world's GDP and was the world's greatest military power. Nonetheless, European states bandwagoned with the United States in order to balance against inferior Soviet power. In order to address this embarrassing indeterminacy Steven Walt invented balance of threat theory.[11] He introduced additional objective variables to explain when power is threatening, and when it is not. So aggregate power, military power, and the offense-defense balance in military technology were added to neorealism as auxiliary hypotheses to save neorealism from its empirical "mispostdictions."[12] But Walt also required a fourth element: perceived offensive intentions, a subjectivist variable of the first order which he never theorized. Constructivist IR would reconceptualize offensive intentions as identity relations among states. So, European states did not balance against the United States because they understood themselves as democratic capitalist states closer to US identity than to the authoritarian communist identity prevailing in the Soviet Union. One could re-present the run-up to World War II from a constructivist perspective as well. We could hypothesize that French and British identities were closer to Nazi Germany than they were to the Stalinist Soviet Union. This is just a hypothesis, but a large-*n* database of all great-power national identities would allow scholars of any stripe to test whether identity relations are a better predictor of alliance choices, and balancing and bandwagoning, than the objectivist variables on offer from realism, and make sense of what balance of threat might actually mean by threat. It would be important to know, for example, if Russia and China are allies of identity, as nondemocratic capitalist states, and so will ally against the United States, even in the face of realist concerns over the objective threat to Russia of superior proximate Chinese power. In this case realism would predict Russia's search for allies against China, the proximate threat, especially given Russia's lightly populated Far East.

Neoliberal institutionalists have explained how states learn to cooperate under anarchy by positing the objective conditions under which states will go for long-term cooperative gains over short-term payoffs in strategic choice environments that look like prisoners' dilemmas.[13] A constructivist hypothesis would be that states are more likely to cooperate the more closely they identify with each other, rather than against each other. In other words, leading with a cooperative move in the face of a possible sucker's payoff is more likely if two states already understand themselves as similar, whether allies, friends, democracies, modern, civilized, Catholic, or something else.

Neoliberals have also offered a rationalist solution to the puzzle of cooperative regimes outlasting the distribution of power that gave rise to those institutions in the first place. So, the International Monetary Fund (IMF) and World Trade Organization (WTO) should have long disappeared with declining US power, but instead they have persisted. Keohane offers a transactions cost explanation, viz., states cannot rationally invest the time and effort in the construction of a new set of cooperative rules with unpredictable results, and so instead rationally settle on what already exists.[14] A constructivist hypothesis would be that institutions persist because regime members understand themselves as members, and so most often automatically cooperate without reference to the many institutionalized sanctions that await them if they defect. Moreover, we should expect more sustained and consistent cooperation among particular groups within a regime, based on their identity relations. So, for example, within the WTO, the same objective behavior by France and Russia, say, restricting grape exports from Germany citing a health and safety exception, will be understood automatically by Germany as an action within the rules when emerging from France, and a violation when adopted by Russia.

For many, mostly realist, IR scholars, states adopt and adhere to norms because they are in their rational, often material, interests to do so. They follow the "logic of consequences," or Max Weber's *Zweckrationalität*.[15] Constructivists do not believe there are such things as objective material interests; all interests are implied by a state's identity in a particular context. Instead, there are three additional logics a state might also follow: First, states might follow the "logic of appropriateness," or Weber's *Wertrationalität*, or value rationality. They adopt and follow norms because to do so is consistent with their identities. Second, they may follow a logic of affect, i.e., do what produces affective feelings, whether aversive or attractive, toward other states.[16] Third, they may follow a logic of habit, doing what they do unreflectively and automatically, again based on internalized identity scripts.[17] If true, we should expect to find many empirical examples of states adopting norms that contradict their material interests, but resonate with their identities. For example, states might adopt an antislavery norm once they understand themselves as civilized, modern, and/or Christian, despite having to forego material gains as a consequence.

One area of abiding concern in the quantitative conflict literature is "enduring rivalries," or examples of two states locked in conflict for years, or even decades. None of the candidate explanations has proven very convincing over the population of cases. Geography, balance of power, the types of interests in dispute, regime type, alliance relationships, etc., have all failed as general explanations for the maintenance of hostility between pairs of states.[18] A constructivist hypothesis would be that identity relations between these states account for their durability. Beyond the not so interesting, but still promising, possibility of states understanding each other as enemies, other possible understandings could be empire v. empire, Jewish v. Muslim, modern v. primitive, civilized v. uncivilized, and so on. Constructivism could also suggest how enduring rivalries end; they do so only after identity relations change, i.e., when one or both states come to understand themselves, and so other states, differently. So, for example, one could argue the Cold War enduring rivalry between the United States and the USSR began to end when Moscow under Gorbachev began to understand the USSR as a normal social democratic great power, rather than a Communist superpower.[19]

On the flip side of enduring rivalries are enduring amities, or special relationships between two states, such as Israel and the United States, or among a few states, such as the Anglosphere, or across a large number of states, such as the European security community. The constructivist hunch here is that these states, whether bilaterally or multilaterally, have identity relations that make the use of force against one another virtually unthinkable. It is obvious by now that these states understand each other as friends and allies, but more interesting is the origin of these identities; how, for example, the Anglosphere was originally forged in a racial Anglo-Saxon identity, and only later, much later, evolved into a more de-racialized identity relationship of democratic English-speaking friends and allies.[20]

Constructivism can also contribute testable hypotheses to the treaty ratification literature. It is a core finding of qualitative work that domestic ideas and national identities influence whether or not a country will support the adoption of particular international norms.[21] However, statistical studies do not test this hypothesis because such data are not available. Frank argues that there is an international social basis of environmental treaty ratification but he is not able to test a cultural variation of this directly or control for domestic cultural explanations.[22] Von Stein includes no cultural or identity variables in her tests.[23] We would hypothesize that whether or not a country identifies with capitalist modernity would be an important predictor of environmental treaty ratification, as would the centrality of scientific ideas to a country's identity.

Most germane to this volume is a constructivist alternative to hegemonic stability theory. The most prominent early theorists of hegemonic international order offered primarily materialist explanations, while relying on subjective reasons for the failure of their theories to offer adequate accounts of the empirical record. Constructivism can theorize, as in the case of threat perception in the balance of threat theory, those subjective reasons left untreated by materialist accounts.

Charles Kindleberger, for example, concluded that the crisis of hegemony in the 1930s could have been avoided had the United States only recognized its material interests in succeeding Britain as the global lender and market of last resort.[24] A constructivist hypothesis would be that the United States didn't understand itself in a way that would imply any material interests in the hegemonic role Kindleberger's materialist theory prescribed. We can tell a similar story about Stephen Krasner's theory. He argued that as power is concentrated in a single state, as in the rise of Britain, and then the United States, an open global trading system results; hegemonic decline begets closure.[25] But Krasner acknowledged historical anomalies for this theory. British decline in the late 19th century didn't result in British closure; The US rise in the 1920s and 1930s didn't result in openness. And US decline in the 1970s (and afterward) didn't result in closure. Like Kindleberger, Krasner explained the anomalies with subjective variables. The City of London's role as global financier prevented British closure; the parochial interests of US finance prevented adopting a hegemonic role; the strength of US multinational corporations and finance has prevented closure until today. Duncan Snidal saved hegemonic stability theory's materialist account, but only by cleverly reversing its argument. Hegemonic decline may reduce the hegemon's material interest in providing a public good of free trade, but other states' interests in the provision of that good necessarily rise as the hegemon declines, and their free-riding is no longer possible if the good is to be produced.[26] Once again, however, the key here is whether this "k-group" actually understands its interests in the way prescribed by the materialist model.

A constructivist alternative to Kindleberger and Krasner would be that the predominant discourses of national identity in declining Britain, and the rising and declining United States, did not imply the interests that the materialist theory predicts. A constructivist assessment of Snidal would explore the discourses of national identity in the candidates for his k-group, which today would include China, Japan, Germany, the United Kingdom, France, Brazil, and India. We would expect that states who understand themselves as capitalist or liberal would constitute the necessary k-group that will perpetuate Western neoliberal hegemony. If, however, a state like China constitutes an alternative economic model, perhaps one of state-led growth and strategic protection, a sufficiently large k-group could not form, and neoliberal hegemony would end. This is what the empirical chapters of this volume explore.

II. Identity and Constructivist IR

We have confidence that identity should be included as an alternative explanation in many areas of world politics because constructivist IR theory has already demonstrated its empirical validity in a wide variety of domains.

A predominant discourse of national identity that includes European as its most important element has accounted for a wide range of crucial outcomes in international politics. Adler and Barnett have shown how collective identities have undergirded the construction of security communities, or anarchy-free zones, in world politics, in particular in Europe for the last 60 years.[27] Alternatively, Neumann and Welch have shown that a European failure to understand Russia and the Soviet Union, and the Ottoman Empire and Turkey, as European has resulted in their ostracism from Europe for centuries.[28] It has also been shown that the stronger a state's European identity, the more commitment that state has to a broadening and deepening of the European Union.[29] Scholars have shown that the political and economic trajectories of the 15 post-Soviet republics can be explained by the strength or weakness of their European identities.[30]

The adoption of particular EU norms, such as abolition of the death penalty, or the granting of equal rights to sexual minorities, has also been explained by the relative predominance of a European identity in states being considered for EU membership.[31] Jelena Subotic has shown that Croatia's greater willingness to suffer the domestic political and economic costs of pursuing EU membership in the 1990s than Serbia in the same period is explained by the greater weight European identity had in Croatia as opposed to Serbia, which had a competing Slavic identity that resulted in a greater attraction for Russia than for Brussels.[32] The Soviet decision in 1955 to effect a rapprochement with Tito's Yugoslavia can in part be explained by a Soviet Slavic identity that made the Slavic Yugoslavia one of Russia's little Slavic brothers, and hence more worthy of trust.[33]

Another predominant discourse of national identity, race, also accounts for a broad range of important outcomes in international politics. Racialized identity has become an important alternative to the democratic peace. Maria Fanis has shown, for example, that the peaceful resolution of crises between Britain and the United States in the 19th century had nothing to do with each side identifying the other as democratic, but rather centrally with each side identifying each other as on the same side of the racial divide against others.[34] The Anglosphere, a special community consisting of the United Kingdom, the United States, Australia, New Zealand, and Canada, was also constructed not from collective democratic identification but rather from a shared understanding of each other as racially Anglo-Saxon.[35] Zoltan Buzas has shown that American racialized identity helps explain legislation aimed against Japanese foreign direct investment in the United States in the 1970s and 1980s, while British and Dutch foreign investments were both far higher.[36] The United States pursued a multilateral strategy of alliance-building in Europe after World War II because of a racial identification with Europe that was absent in Asia. US attention to East Asian security needs was performed only on a bilateral basis.[37]

One might expect that a great-power identity would be commonplace among states with the material wherewithal to be judged as objectively powerful. This is trivially true. What matters is precisely how being a great power is understood by that state. In fact, in some cases, as for Russia and Turkey noted above, other great powers never accorded them equal status as fellow great powers. In the postwar Soviet case, Soviet elites did understand the USSR as a great power in a more conventional sense, but without the addition of other elements of that discourse, most importantly its identity as "vanguard of the world revolutionary process," we could not understand why most of the Cold War was not cold, and yet did not entail direct conflict between the two superpowers. Instead, it was acted out in the decolonizing world, with 20 million deaths.[38] The most interesting postwar great-power identities are perhaps in Japan and Germany, which, as Katzenstein and Berger have shown, include a commitment to an economic great-power identity, but shorn of conventionally corresponding military might and political influence.[39]

Constructivists have shown that a civilized national identity accounts for a variety of outcomes, as well. For example, Price has shown that such an identity explains general revulsion for the use of chemical weapons. Tannenwald argues it has spawned a post-Nagasaki taboo on the use, and contemplation of use, of nuclear weapons. Martha Finnemore has explained the expansion of armed intervention on the behalf of human rights to an expansion of the collective identity of civilized beyond Christian Europe, to non-Christian Europeans, to all of humanity.[40]

None of these findings would have been possible without a theorization of identity that privileged the inductive recovery of prevailing intersubjective structures. Since individual decision-makers are ultimately responsible for making the choices that matter in world politics, it is tempting to attribute causality to discrete decision-makers; this would be a big theoretical and methodological mistake. First, a decision-making approach assumes that the beliefs of each prime minister or president are unique, and must be treated as such. Constructivism instead assumes that such beliefs are themselves social products of intersubjective structures that are quite enduring, and so promise to explain relations between and among states across decision-makers and regimes. Constructivist work on identity, although research-intensive, is theoretically parsimonious. Once one has uncovered a prevailing discourse of national identity, one can expect that discourse to both persist over time and explain a broad range of outcomes, regardless of who is making foreign policy in that state.

For example, the Sino-Soviet split persisted across Communist Party General Secretaries Khrushchev, Brezhnev, Andropov, and Chernenko because the Soviet Union understood itself as the vanguard of the world revolutionary process. China's claims to that same identity made it impossible to effect any kind of rapprochement. Only with the coming to power of Gorbachev, and the empowerment of a Soviet identity of normal social democratic great power, did Sino-Soviet identity relations become amenable to a détente between the two enemies.[41] Soviet "adventurism" in the developing world lasted from 1955 to 1985, across four Soviet General Secretaries. It was spurred by the Soviet vanguard identity described above, and so persisted until Gorbachev's endorsement of a new Soviet identity that abandoned this vanguard role. But what about the ten years between the end of World War II and the Soviet military aid to Nasser's Egypt? During this period, nationalist leaders in the decolonizing world were understood by Soviet elites as imperialist lackeys, rather than potential allies. This was because Soviet identity at the time was one that understood the Soviet Union and socialism to be insecure, and so only other communist allies could be trusted, such as the people's democracies in Eastern Europe and Mao's China. All others were understood as potential enemies. With Stalin's death a new discourse of Soviet identity, one that had been preserved at the societal level, was empowered; this discourse understood the Soviet project as fundamentally secure, and hence that allies need not be Soviet clones. This simple change reversed the default from "who is not us is against us" to "who is not against us is potentially with us."[42]

Finally, Germany's Nazi past is a significant other for the construction of German national identity today. It implies a thick and rich collection of relationships between Germany and all the rest of Europe, let alone Israel, the Middle East, and the rest of the world in general. Looking at individual

German chancellors and foreign ministers and their beliefs would be meth-odologically nonsensical and hardly parsimonious. Looking at each individ-ual German bilateral relationship with another state is unnecessary, so long as we have performed the discursive analysis necessary to generate an identity topography for Germany at home.[43] For constructivists, idiosyncratic leaders are just that, idiosyncratic. If they appear, they disconfirm the constructivist hypothesis that discourses of national identity, and not individual leaders, explain foreign relations. In this way, constructivism is as falsifiable as any approach to IR.

III. Identity and Quantitative IR

There are several ways in which quantitative IR scholars operationalize iden-tity that does violence to constructivism's commitment to an intersubjectivist ontology and an interpretivist epistemology. First, they do not let the subjects speak for themselves. They do not investigate how subjects themselves under-stand and practice their identities. Instead, they assign identities to these sub-jects based on some "objective" label they apply before they do their research. Second, they operationalize the concept of identity in ways that make it most easily amenable to measurement, rather than remaining true to the conven-tional methodological convention of developing measures that faithfully cap-ture how a variable is theorized, conceptualized, and operationalized.[44] This second problem violates not only constructivism's ontological and episte-mological priors, but even the methodological rules of mainstream positivist social science.

Third, in a partial improvement over the first two approaches, quantitative scholars use surveys to ask subjects their identities. The problem here is that the survey questions are specified in advance, limiting the choices subjects have, in fact, forcing subjects to choose identities they may never have even considered in the first place, and foreclosing their own answers to the question. What good, for example, does it do to find out that a majority of Russian respondents reject the market as a basis for their economic system if we do not know that when Russians see the word market, or *rynok*, they think of two things: a bazaar and the reign of disorder, violence, and economic collapse that characterized Russia of the 1990s after the Soviet collapse? We offer a solution to this problem in our concluding chapter, viz., using discourse analysis and ethnography to specify survey questions in the first place.

It is to address these shortcomings in quantitative research that we propose to create an intersubjective national identity database so scholars in that tradition can avoid these problems in the future.

Objective, A Priori Assignment of Identities

Errol Henderson, for example, when trying to determine if different religious identities account for more conflict between two states, simply assigned countries religious identities based on whether their populations have been coded for having different religious affiliations.[45] Missing here of course is any concern about whether the people so coded actually understand themselves as Muslims, Catholics, Christians, Jews, or whatever, let alone whether it was these identities that caused any conflict with states coded differently on the religious dimension. Perhaps, as is demonstrated above, other dimensions of national identity, such as modernity, or civilization, or capitalism, account for hostility across differences. Presuming that it is ethnic identity that matters, there is widespread use of the "ethnolinguistic fractionalization index" in the quantitative conflict literature. It just assigns ethnic identities to individuals and groups within and between countries, and then claims to assess whether ethnic identity plays a causal role in violent outcomes.[46]

The vast literature on the democratic peace exemplifies the problem of assigning identities to states. States are awarded democracy scores based on Polity IV or Freedom House, many other objectivist variables are controlled for, and the regression coefficient emerges that demonstrates a positive association between two democracies and peace between them. The problem here is that scholars who have actually unpacked the democratic peace, that is, performed case studies to see if it is democracy or democratic identity that stays the hands of democratic leaders when contemplating violence against another democracy, have almost unanimously found democratic identity has less to do with the outcome than advertised. Vucetic and Fanis have found a racial Anglo-Saxon white identity that matters; Ido Oren has found that elites change the identities of their adversaries from democratic to authoritarian after they get into conflict with them, as the United States routinely has done during the Cold War. Frederic Schaffer, meanwhile, in his investigation of the meaning of democracy in Senegal, finds that contrary to Western academics, Senegalese believe they are democratic if there is a fair distribution of goods after an election, but their concept of *demokrasi* doesn't include such indexical features of Polity and Freedom House scores as secret balloting, alternation in power, or free elections.[47]

In an important exception to these disconfirmations of the democratic peace by constructivist work, Jarrod Hayes has demonstrated that democratic identity can cause peace between two democracies, but only if the public and at least a significant part of the elite of that country understands both itself and the other state against which it is contemplating hostility as democratic. In the case of the United States and India in 1971, for example, while President Nixon and his national security adviser Henry Kissinger were hoping to punish India for its conduct against Pakistan, they were unable to frame India as a threat to US security. The US Congress, the chattering classes, and the public all perceived India as the aggrieved democratic party in conflict with an authoritarian Pakistani regime.[48]

Whether constructivism confirms or disconfirms the democratic peace is not as important as the fact that in order to credibly test the hypothesis that democracies do not fight each other because they understand each other as democracies, it is first necessary to empirically establish just how states do understand each other. What are the identity relations between and among states?

Reduction of Identities to What Can Be Easily Measured

In a work designed to differentiate between cultural difference and geographical contiguity as alternative causes of war between states, Henderson reduces cultural similarity to religious similarity, again objectively assigned, and ethnic similarity to language, again objectively given.[49] Biddle and Long hypothesize that human capital and cultural values explain the military advantage of democracies but their operationalization reduces culture to "primary religious affiliations."[50] Goldstein, Rivers, and Tomz attempt to control for the effects of common culture on trade levels, but operationalize this as "whether they share a common language" as stated in the *CIA World Factbook*.[51] In a particularly egregious instance of this problem, Sambanis, in an effort to explain civil wars, reduces identity to a conflation of religion and ethnicity, and then declares that all other civil wars are not cases of identity, as if the only identities that matter to people are the two he has assigned.[52] David Laitin, in his extraordinarily rich book on post-Soviet identities, openly apologizes for reducing national identity to language usage. "Language, because it is relatively easy to monitor and measure, is particularly kind to social scientists seeking a window on identity shift." He goes on to acknowledge that his work is "only one aspect of cultural change" and awaits investigation of "other cultural realms."[53] Claiming to "address a series of problems with existing conceptions of identity and ethnicity" in the literature, Gartzke and Gleditsch "distinguish between shared and different culture by religion, ethnicity, and language."[54] Of course, three a priori objectivist variables are better than one or two, but they don't capture a constructivist theorization of national identity. In an effort to distinguish between interstate conflicts caused by interests and those caused by identities, a distinction, by the way, that no constructivist would accept, since identities give rise to interests, scholars reduce identity to objectively assigned ethnic categories.[55] Of course the most famous case of conceptual reductionism is Samuel P. Huntington's identification of civilizations as religions.

Retrieval of Identities from Survey Research

In an effort to gauge the effects of identity on relations among states, a team of authors asked the same 60 questions to respondents in the United States, Norway, Bulgaria, and Hungary. While interesting differences emerged, there is no way to say whether this is a valid measure of the identity terrain in those countries, as the respondents were forced to answer questions formulated by scholars, not offer their own ideas about identity.[56] In an effort to assess the relationship between identity and European integration, Matthew Gabel reduces national identity to materialist or postmaterialist values based on available data from the Eurobarometer survey.[57] While of course it is interesting to know what the association is between these values and support for the EU, it does not capture national identity.

Discourses of National Identity from This Volume

By way of contrast with how identities have been treated in the quantitative IR literature, in the chapters that follow we find that the eight countries analyzed in this volume have salient national identities that would be omitted absent a discourse analysis of a broad range of relevant texts. Besides recovering missing identities, discourse analysis also allows us to distinguish between those identities held by elites versus those reflected among the masses. We can also go beyond merely noting the presence or absence of an identity like democracy or capitalism by assigning a valence to it. Surely, it matters if capitalism is part of Russian national identity, but the masses largely reject it, while the elite lauds it. The very fact of an elite-mass split on national identity matters enormously, if we are concerned with how stable a national identity is, and if we would like to know what kind of national identity might be empowered if a regime changes, either through elections or less democratically.

What I offer here are just a few of dozens of findings with significant implications for the foreign relations of these eight states as reflected in their domestic discourses of national identity. A predominant aspect of German national identity, its rejection of its Nazi German past, has significant consequences for German foreign relations with Europe and the Middle East in particular. The fact that the Japanese masses understand Japan as peaceful, but elite discourse ignores this characterization of Japan, surely matters to Japan's foreign relations in the region. While the Chinese elite identifies negatively against the United States, largely on strategic grounds, Chinese masses identify with the United States positively, largely on cultural grounds. Both Hindi and English Indian discourses consensually understand India as democratic, but the Hindi discourse contains both Asian and Western models of economic development, while the

English discourse identifies only with the West. French national identity combines a consensual understanding of France as both democratic and anticapitalist. The United Kingdom consensually identifies positively with the United States. Brazilian elites and masses identify positively with Europe, against the United States, and not at all with Latin America. The United States understands itself as a state whose own national security is threatened by events occurring all around the world, and does not identify itself with, or against, any other country.

It is striking that none of the eight countries investigated in this volume treated its ethnic, religious, or linguistic identity as significant to its national identity. This implies that all the quantitative social science literature that has reduced national identity to these three variables is not using a valid measure of national identity. These findings alone make the need for an inductive recovery of national identity obvious. Indeed, the discourses of national identity performed in this volume uncover aspects of a country's identity that cannot be discovered through any kind of a priori specification of what identities matter, a reduction of identity to ethnicity, religion, or language, or through specifying a survey instrument whose questions have not been formulated according to the kind of inductive work recommended and practiced in this volume.

Notes

1. TRIP 2011, pp. 27 and 47.
2. On the possibility of a fruitful combination of both interpretivist/ethnographic and neopositivist social science sensibilities, see Hopf 2007 and Wedeen 2010.
3. Schatz 2009.
4. We choose these countries on objective grounds: they are nine of the ten largest economies in the world. Apologies to Italy. We will include it in the future.
5. Eckstein 1975.
6. Hopf 2002 and Hopf 2012.
7. Wendt 1999.
8. For a critical review of identity, see Lebow 2012, esp. pp. 24–39.
9. Wedeen 2002, p. 724.
10. Waltz 1979.
11. Walt 1985.
12. They are auxiliary, and not ad hoc, hypotheses, in Karl Popper's sense, because they are productive, in that they go beyond just explaining the particular case that has not corroborated neorealist claims, but also offers testable hypotheses for many additional cases. Popper 1959, pp. 61–63.
13. Keohane 1985.
14. Keohane 1985.
15. March and Olsen 1998.
16. Ross 2006.
17. Hopf 2010.
18. Goertz and Diehl 1995 and Diehl and Goertz 2000.
19. Herman 1996 and Brown 2013.

20. Vucetic 2011.
21. Keck and Sikkink 1998.
22. Frank 1999.
23. Von Stein 2012.
24. Kindleberger 1973.
25. Krasner 1976.
26. Snidal 1985.
27. Adler and Barnett 1998.
28. Neumann 1996; Neumann and Welsh 1991; and Zarakol 2011.
29. Risse 2010.
30. Abdelal 2001; Tsygankov 2001; and Hopf 2002a.
31. Checkel 2001.
32. Subotic 2011. One could hypothesize that the current political turmoil in Ukraine is largely the product of a country whose identity is split between European and Slavic/Russian/neo-Soviet identities.
33. Hopf 2002.
34. Fanis 2011.
35. Vucetic 2011.
36. Buzas 2013.
37. Hemmer and Katzenstein 2002.
38. Hopf 2002 and 2012.
39. Katzenstein 1996 and Berger 1998.
40. Price 1997, Tannenwald 2007, and Finnemore 2003.
41. Luthi 2008 and Hopf 2009.
42. Hopf 2002 and 2012. For equally, often disastrous application of US identity in the developing world, see Hartz 1955, Packenham 1973, and Shafer 1988.
43. Katzenstein 1996, Berger 1998, and Jackson 2009.
44. Sartori 1970.
45. Henderson 1997. Rummel does the same for religious conflict within states (Rummel 1997).
46. Fearon and Laitin 2003; Cederman and Girardin 2007.
47. Fanis 2011, Vucetic 2011, Oren 1995, and Schaffer 1998.
48. Hayes 2013.
49. Henderson 1997.
50. Biddle and Long 2004, p. 536.
51. Goldstein, Rivers, and Tomz 2007, p. 51.
52. Sambanis 2001.
53. Laitin 1998, p. 368.
54. Gartzke and Gleditsch 2006.
55. Rothman and Olson 2001.
56. Larsen et al. 1995.
57. Gabel 1998.

References

Abdelal, Rawi, *National Purpose in the World Economy* (Ithaca: Cornell University Press, 2001).

Adler, Emanuel and Michael Barnett, eds., *Security Communities* (Cambridge: Cambridge University Press, 1998).

Berger, Thomas, *Cultures of Antimilitarism* (Baltimore: Johns Hopkins University Press, 1998).

Biddle, Steven and Stephen Long, "Democracy and Military Effectiveness," *Journal of Conflict Resolution* 48:4 (August 2004), 525–546.

Brown, Archie, "Did Gorbachev as General Secretary Become a Social Democrat?" *Europe-Asia Studies* 65:2 (March 2013), 198–220.

Buzas, Zoltán I. "The Color of Threat: Race, Threat Perception, and the Demise of the Anglo-Japanese Alliance (1902–1923)." *Security Studies* 22.4 (2013): 573–606.

Cederman, Lars-Erik and Luc Girardin, "Beyond Fractionalization: Mapping Ethnicity onto Nationalist Insurgencies," *American Political Science Review* 101:1 (February 2007), 173–185.

Checkel, Jeffrey, "Why Comply? Social Learning and European Identity Change," *International Organization* 55:3 (Summer 2001), 553–588.

Diehl, Paul and Gary Goertz, *War and Peace in International Rivalry* (Ann Arbor: University of Michigan Press, 2000).

Eckstein, Harry, "Case Study and Theory in Political Science," in Nelson Polsby and Fred Greenstein, eds., *Handbook of Political Science* (Reading, MA: Addison-Wesley, 1975), 79–138.

Fanis, Maria, *Secular Morality and International Security* (Ann Arbor: University of Michigan Press, 2011).

Fearon, James D. and David D. Laitin, "Ethnicity, Insurgency, and Civil War," *American Political Science Review* 97:1 (March 2003), 75–90.

Finnemore, Martha, *The Purpose of Intervention* (Ithaca: Cornell University Press, 2003).

Frank, David John, "Social Bases of Environmental Treaty Ratification, 1900–1990," *Sociological Inquiry* 69:4 (October 1999), 523–550.

Gabel, Matthew, "Public Support for European Integration: An Empirical Test of Five Theories," *Journal of Politics* 60:2 (May 1998), 333–354.

Gartzke, Erik and Kristian Skrede Gleditsch, "Identity and Conflict: Ties that Bind and Differences that Divide," *European Journal of International Relations* 12:1 (March 2006), 53–87.

Goertz, Gary and Paul Diehl, "The Initiation and Termination of Enduring Rivalries: The Impact of Political Shocks," *American Journal of Political Science* 39:1 (1995), 30–52.

Goldstein, Judith, Douglas Rivers, and Michael Tomz, "Institutions in International Relations: Understanding the Effects of the GATT and the WTO on World Trade," *International Organization* 61:1 (January 2007), 37–67.

Hartz, Louis, *Liberal Tradition in America* (New York: Harcourt, Brace and World, 1955).

Hayes, Jarrod, *Constructing National Security* (New York: Cambridge University Press, 2013).

Hemmer, Christopher and Peter Katzenstein, "Why is There No NATO in Asia? Collective Identity, Regionalism, and the Origins of Multilateralism," *International Organization* 56:3 (Summer 2002), 575–607.

Henderson, Errol A., "Ethnic Conflict, the Similarity of States, and the Onset of War, 1820–1989," *Journal of Conflict Resolution* 41:5 (October 1997), 649–668.

Herman, Robert G., "Identity, Norms, and National Security: The Soviet Foreign Policy Revolution and the End of the Cold War," in Peter J. Katzenstein, ed., *The Culture of National Security* (New York: Columbia University Press, 1996), 271–316.

Hopf, Ted, *Social Construction of International Politics* (Ithaca: Cornell University Press, 2002).

Hopf, Ted, "Making the Future Inevitable," *European Journal of International Relations* 8:3 (September 2002a), 404–436.

Hopf, Ted, "The Limits of Interpreting Evidence," in Richard Ned Lebow and Mark Lichbach, eds., *Theory and Evidence in Comparative Politics and International Relations* (New York: Palgrave, 2007), 55–84.

Hopf, Ted, "Identity Relations and the Sino-Soviet Split," in Rawi Abelal, Yoshiko Herrera, Iain Johnston, and Rose McDermott, eds., *Measuring Identity* (Cambridge and New York: Cambridge University Press, 2009), 279–315.

Hopf, Ted, "The Logic of Habit in International Relations," *European Journal of International Relations* 16:4 (December 2010), 539–561.

Hopf, Ted, *Reconstructing the Cold War* (New York: Oxford University Press, 2012).

Jackson, Patrick Thaddeus, *Civilizing the Enemy* (Ann Arbor: University of Michigan Press, 2009).

Katzenstein, Peter, *Cultural Norms and National Security* (Ithaca: Cornell University Press 1996).

Keck, Margaret and Kathryn Sikkink, *Activists beyond Borders* (Ithaca: Cornell University Press, 1998).

Keohane, Robert, *After Hegemony* (Princeton: Princeton University Press, 1985).

Kindleberger, Charles, *The World in Depression, 1929–1939* (Berkeley: University of California Press, 1973).

Krasner, Stephen, "State Power and the Structure of World Trade," *World Politics* 28:3 (April 1976), 317–347.

Laitin, David, *Identity in Formation* (Ithaca: Cornell University Press, 1998).
Larsen, Knud S., David H. Groberg, Krum Krumov, Ludmilla Andrejeva, Nadia Kashlekeva, Zlatka Russinova, Gyorgy Csepeli, and Reidar Ommundsen, "Ideology and Identity: A National Outlook," *Journal of Peace Research* 32:2 (May 1995), 165–179.
Lebow, Richard Ned, *Politics and Ethics of Identity* (Cambridge: Cambridge University Press, 2012).
Luthi, Lorenz, *The Sino-Soviet Split* (Princeton: Princeton University Press, 2008).
March, James and John Olsen, "The Institutional Dynamics of International Political Orders," *International Organization* 52:4 (1998), 943–969.
Neumann, Iver, *Russia and the Idea of Europe* (New York: Routledge, 1996).
Neumann, Iver and Jennifer Welsh, "The Other in European Self-Definition," *Review of International Studies* 17:4 (October 1991), 327–348.
Oren, Ido, "The Subjectivity of the 'Democratic' Peace," *International Security* 20:2 (Fall 1995), 147–184.
Packenham, Robert, *Liberal America and the Third World* (Princeton: Princeton University Press, 1973).
Popper, Karl, *Logic of Scientific Discovery* (New York: Routledge, 1959).
Price, Richard, *The Chemical Weapons Taboo* (Ithaca: Cornell University Press, 1997).
Risse, Thomas, *A Community of Europeans?* (Ithaca: Cornell University Press, 2010).
Ross, Andrew, "Coming in from the Cold: Constructivism and Emotions," *European Journal of International Relations* 12:2 (June 2006), 197–222.
Rothman, Jay and Marie L. Olson, "From Interests to Identities: Towards a New Emphasis in Interactive Conflict Resolution," *Journal of Peace Research* 38:3 (May 2001), 289–305.
Rummel, Rudolph, "Is Collective Violence Correlated with Social Pluralism?" *Journal of Peace Research* 34:2 (May 1997), 163–175.
Sambanis, Nicholas, "Do Ethnic and Nonethnic Civil Wars Have the Same Causes? A Theoretical and Empirical Enquiry (Part 1)," *Journal of Conflict Resolution* 45:3 (June 2001), 259–282.
Sartori, Giovanni, "Concept Misformation in Comparative Politics," *American Political Science Review* 64:4 (December 1970), 1033–1053.
Schaffer, Frederic, *Democracy in Translation* (Ithaca: Cornell University Press, 1998).
Schatz, Edward, "Ethnographic Immersion and the Study of Politics," in Edward Schatz, ed. *Political Ethnography* (Chicago: University of Chicago Press, 2009), 1–22.
Shafer, D. Michael, *Deadly Paradigms* (Princeton: Princeton University Press, 1988).
Snidal, Duncan, "The Limits of Hegemonic Stability Theory," *International Organization* 39:4 (Autumn 1985), 579–614.
Subotic, Jelena, "Europe Is a State of Mind: Identity and Europeanization in the Balkans." *International Studies Quarterly* 55:2 (2011), 309–333.
Tannenwald, Nina, *The Nuclear Taboo* (New York: Cambridge University Press, 2007).
TRIP Survey, accessed June 2014, http://www.wm.edu/offices/itpir/_documents/trip/trip_around_the_world_2011.pdf.
Tsygankov, Andrei, *Pathways after Empire* (Lanham, MD: Rowman Littlefield, 2001).
Von Stein, Jana, "The Engines of Compliance," in Jeffrey Dunoff and Mark Pollack, eds., *Synthesizing Insights from International Law and International Relations* (Cambridge: Cambridge University Press, 2012), 477–501.
Vucetic, Srdjan, *The Anglosphere: A Genealogy of a Racialized Identity in International Relations* (Stanford: Stanford University Press, 2011).
Walt, Stephen, *Origins of Alliances* (Ithaca: Cornell University Press, 1985).
Waltz, Kenneth, *Theory of International Politics* (Reading, MA: Addison-Wesley, 1979).
Wedeen, Lisa, "Conceptualizing Culture: Possibilities for Political Science," *American Political Science Review* 96:4, 2002, 713–728.
Wedeen, Lisa, "Reflections on Ethnographic Work in Political Science," *Annual Review of Political Science* 13:2 (2010), 255–272.
Wendt, Alexander, *Social Theory of International Politics* (Cambridge: Cambridge University Press, 1999).
Zarakol, Ayse, *After Defeat* (Cambridge: Cambridge University Press, 2011).

2

Recovering Discourses of National Identity

BENTLEY B. ALLAN

Introduction

An intersubjective database must bridge the gap between interpretive and quantitative methods. The chasm is wide in part because interpretivism developed out of a critique of the positivist assumptions that underlie quantitative methods.[1] Indeed, some interpretivists would disavow the whole project of building a body of comparable data that could be turned into a quantitative data set. Some quantitative scholars would disavow the project of resting statistical variables on subjective interpretations of reality. One source of conflict is differing beliefs about measurement reliability and validity. A measure is reliable to the degree that the "measuring procedure yields the same results on repeated trials."[2] A measure is valid to the extent that "it measures what it purports to measure."[3] The demands of quantitative measurement all too often reduce identity and other social concepts to inadequate proxies. In short, quantitative methods trade validity for reliability. Interpretivists, in contrast, prize validity.

Despite these differences, in this chapter I argue that the inductive demands of interpretivist methods can be combined with a reliable, replicable method for studying national identity in a variety of countries. That is, analysts can carefully and inductively recover the central identity categories in national discourses, interpretively relate them to one another, and present their findings in a comparable fashion. The results are reliable, not necessarily in the standard sense of resting on individually reproducible measurements, but in the sense of producing reproducible results at the level of discursive interpretation.

Our method is designed to recover the competing discourses of national identity in a given country by performing discourse analysis guided by simple coding rules on a standardized sample of texts. Our coding rules produce raw counts of all the categories linked to national identity. These raw counts can then be translated into simple quantitative indicators and tables that can support a variety of quantitative variables.

This chapter proceeds from theorization and conceptualization to operationalization and measurement.[4] We theorize national identity as intersubjective beliefs about the national self in relation to others, conceptualize it as embedded in a society's shared stock of knowledge, operationalize it as a set of texts, and measure it as the salience and valence of identity categories.

I. Theories of Identity

For the purposes of this project, we define national identity as a constellation of categories that define the nation or what it means to be a member of a nation.[5] National identities are constituted by societal discourses that are shaped by and constrain individuals who draw on shared knowledge to form their personal identities. Personal identities define "what I am and how I am recognized" in relation to other people.[6] An individual may see herself as a student, worker, aunt, soldier, Shawnee, American, and so on, combining several personal and group identities.[7] Social psychology since Tajfel argues that when individuals are placed in groups, arbitrarily or otherwise, their identities shift from the personal to the group level.[8] The individual tends to see herself in terms of the social categories associated with the group rather than the personal characteristics of her relation to other individuals. Much of subsequent social psychology has demonstrated the power and persistence of in-group identity. For example, in intergroup settings, individuals are more likely to engage in self-assimilation, in-group favoritism, out-group discrimination, and social competition for resources.[9]

Our aim to recover discourses of national identity does not mean that we posit "a coherent, unified, fixed identity."[10] Tajfel and Turner's work does exhibit a tendency toward reifying identity. They contend that intergroup behavior was distinguished by the fact that individuals act with little variability. Moreover, they posit "objective" conflicts over power, wealth, and territory.[11] The more recent social psychological literature criticizes these tenets, but maintains the enduring value of their approach. For some critics, however, any attempt to stabilize national identities with empirical methods reifies them. The study of identity then becomes less an analytical or empirical claim than a political act that justifies and legitimates chauvinism and power politics. It exhibits the very drive to "diminish difference" it should be critiquing.[12]

In contrast, scholars like Sarup theorize identity as "fabricated, constructed, in process" and thus "fragmented, full of contradictions and ambiguities."[13] For

Connolly, identity depends on defining others as different, which introduces a fundamental element of dialogic instability. So identity is a "slippery, insecure experience, dependent on its ability to define difference and vulnerable to the tendency of entities it would so define to counter, resist, overturn, or subvert definitions applied to them."[14]

Variants of both positions can be found in interpretivist theories and epistemologies. For interpretivists, individuals are always embedded in a web of meanings that brings coherence to their world. Theoretically, interpretivists presuppose that intersubjective beliefs and meanings have effects on action.[15] But interpretivists differ about the degree to which these meanings are stable enough to be reliably recovered by social scientific methods. For Taylor, the human sciences should be oriented to grasping the meanings that agents have.[16] But Rorty argues there is no stable self distinct from an agent's constant reweaving of beliefs and actions in her environment.[17] Gusterson's ethnographic research finds that "interviewees did not much manifest an unchanging essence . . . they drew on the complex repertoires of their speech community to perform themselves in response to particular lines of questioning."[18]

In the end, there is not much to divide more recent social psychological accounts of identity and the view espoused by Gusterson. Recent findings show that personal identity is created from socially constructed categories and biographical experiences into a narrative or conceptual constellation that exhibits varying degrees of continuity and stability.[19] There are some theoretical reasons to believe that personal identities are quite stable, but this debate is of secondary concern since we are not aiming to apprehend individual identity.[20] Moreover, for the purposes of this project, we deploy an inductive empirical method that remains open as to whether societal identities are stable or unstable. We propose to recover discourses of national identity—the set of categories that individuals use to understand the nation and themselves as members of a country. With interpretivists, we believe that these categories draw relational meaning from their position in a web of shared beliefs. Thus, interpretation of the categories by trained discourse analysts is necessary to produce valid data. But for the purposes of social scientific analysis, we are willing to freeze identities to some degree. In short, our work is inspired by and comes out of the interpretivist tradition, but we may violate some of its tenets in order to build a bridge to other approaches.

Berger and Luckmann's intersubjective account of identity combines features from a variety of approaches and so helps articulate our interdisciplinary understanding of identity. They begin from the assumption that individuals perceive the world through categories they inherit from the social stock of knowledge.[21] In positing this, Berger and Luckmann participate in the European social theoretic tradition of theorizing the intersubjective or shared background knowledge that makes social order possible.[22] These categories provide the schemes that structure face-to-face interactions.[23] But they also allow meaning to travel beyond face-to-face situations via language.

For Berger and Luckmann, an individual's actions are strongly shaped by the rules and habits they internalize during primary socialization. Primary socialization is the period from birth to young adulthood in which individuals form the dominant categories and typifications that structure their reality.[24] Secondary socialization in adult life alters these categories, but not fundamentally.[25]

The categories individuals inherit in primary socialization strongly shape their habitual behavior. Habits narrow the range of choice and provide a stable basis for intentional actions.[26] Institutions are shared habits that "control human conduct by setting up predefined patterns of conduct, which channel it in one direction rather than another."[27] Institutions and habits are only challenged when something goes awry, forcing individuals to rethink the schemes and roles deployed. But institutionalization is never complete, and social order is filled with enclaves, sub-universes, and segmentations that add diversity to the multiplication of individual life perspectives.[28] Nonetheless, social order is maintained by the reproduction and legitimation of the social stock of knowledge that is widely shared and understood.

Thus, the decisions and feelings of individuals are shaped by the stocks of social knowledge they receive and reproduce in everyday life. Even diplomats and presidents have everyday lives and their perceptions and beliefs are structured by the dominant categories that circulate in society. On this view, it makes sense to study the intersubjective background that structures international politics in the societies in which leaders live and work.[29] Moreover, the desires and categories of the masses matter a lot in international politics. The decisions of presidents and diplomats must be intelligible and acceptable to the masses.[30] So political elites are doubly constrained by the intersubjective stock of knowledge of everyday life. First, their own categories and perceptions are constituted by societal discourses. Second, the categories and perceptions of the publics that hold them to account are constituted by societal discourses.

Since individual identities are drawn from a common set of identity categories in a society, we must study identity via the dominant stocks of knowledge that circulate in a country. In scaling up to the level of discourses of national identity, we begin from the assumption that national units are ideationally integrated and that decision-makers in international politics act from the socially constructed stock of knowledge in the societies that raised them. The underlying claim here is that since the reproduction of categories happens mostly within the borders of national units, it makes sense to talk about there being a national set of categories. But "national" here should not recall the old terms of

"national character" and other thinly veiled racialisms. Of course, racial categories were once central to national identity. But this empirical fact should not
dissuade us from continuing to track the terms in which citizens understand
their nations. Our reports show that today national identities are defined less in
terms of race than in terms of modernity, political institutions and values, and
the state's place in the world. Nonetheless, the nation remains a salient con-
tainer of group identities in global politics.

None of this means that there is one single "national identity" in a country;
rather, there is a topography of identity categories that are combined and assembled into multiple "discursive formations." Some discourses become hegemonic
and thus give the appearance of a single national identity, but discourses are
always contested. The stability of discourses depends on the degree of contestation over the core categories of identity in a given country. If many powerful
institutions back a common discourse of national identity that is shared by the
elites and masses, it is likely that the identity of a country will remain stable for
some time. If agreement on central categories is thin and highly contested, we
expect the core discourses of identity to shift from year to year. But as with individual identities, the stability of discourses of national identity is an empirical
question. But importantly, methods of recovering national identity inductive so
they can apprehend the ongoing changes in national identity discourses.

Our assumption that there is such a thing as a discourse of national identity
is subject to two important scope conditions. First, the importance of *national*
identity is socially constructed and specific to the historical era of interest to us
(the 19th and 20th centuries). Nationalism was a transnational project, purpo-
sively constructed and contested all over the world.[31] In the end, the national
project was extremely successful and so it has major theoretical and empirical
relevance. However, it would be a mistake to assume national identification is
universal. Our method and our project are thus subject to significant historical
scope conditions: we do not expect that identity-based theories would have as
large effects prior to or perhaps after the period 1810–2010, in which mass publics took up the cause of nationalism and internalized its categories.

Second, the relevance of shared stocks of knowledge is bounded by the
assumption laid out above that societies are ideationally integrated. In Berger
and Luckmann's terms, this means that people and institutions share similar
ideas about what reality consists of, how it works, and how everything is embedded in the overarching symbolic universe.[32] However, this assumption may not
hold going forward. As Sarup suggests, "now that people spend a lot of their
time doing many things in different places, there is a decline in unified identities."[33] Identities proliferate with the decline of unions, ethnic politics, and
so on. In some countries, socialization practices may vary from place to place
so much that to speak of common categories is pointless. We are open to this

possibility. Indeed, our method could show that this is the case. If a discourse analysis reveals that few national categories recur or that categories do not appear in both mass and elite texts, then our analyst may conclude there is no coherent discourse of national identity. This would raise many questions: is the basis of foreign policy in this country completely subjective, that is, beholden to one individual's idiosyncratic socialization and perception? Does foreign policy change from one leader to the next? Or, is there a hegemonic discourse that has nothing to do with identity that heavily constrains leaders? From this perspective, our theory of identity does not reify national identity. Moreover, the inductive empirical method we have chosen allows us to subject our own assumptions to empirical tests.

The Making Identity Count Framework

For the purposes of this method, we theorize national identity as discursive categories that define the nation or what it means to be a member of the nation. We measure it with simple questions posed to a sample of texts: how do French people understand themselves as French? What does it mean to be French? What is France?

We conceptualize the central identities of a country as *discursive formations*: clusters of concepts, values, metaphors, and rules that hang together to order perceptions of the national self. We also refer to these simply as "discourses." The social stock of knowledge of any country may reveal many competing and overlapping discourses of identity. Moreover, some discourses are more legitimate, more widely reproduced, and thus more dominant than others. In general, the predominant discourse of national identity is propagated by the state, in the public speeches of political elites, on the editorial pages of major national newspapers, and in the state-authorized textbooks used in public schools.

Discursive formations are comprised of *identity categories*: the classifications attached to the nation and members of the nation. In the reports assembled here, people and countries categorize themselves in political, economic, historical, moral, cultural, and many other ways. In France, the dominant discursive formation is the "republican cluster" that draws on the categories secular, democratic, liberal, fraternal, and equal. In Brazil, the discursive formation "limited democracy" is infused with meaning from classifications of Brazil as corrupt, authoritarian, exclusionary, and a young democracy.

Identity categories must be differentiated from themes or tropes in the social stock of knowledge. Themes such as the virtues of hard work, invocations of the good life, or personal complaints about injustices are not properly speaking identity categories. We make this differentiation so that only the themes and tropes related to national identity are included in our codings. Themes can be coded as identity categories only when hailed to or explicitly connected to identity statements such as the "French people are . . ." or "the nation embodies . . ." and so on. At this point, previously coded themes can be recoded as identities. For example, letters to the editor may continually reveal that individual German citizens see themselves as "responsible." This is an important theme, but it only manifests itself as an identity category when movies, novels, op-eds, and speeches suggest that "Germans are responsible." The category responsible may then be revealed as part of a larger discursive formation: Germany takes responsibility for its past and its economic health.

In sum, the core identities of a country are constellations of identity categories that hang together in discursive formations, according to which clusters of concepts and categories are regularly invoked as defining a group. Every society has multiple identities or discursive formations that recur in discourse. The relationship between these identities can be thought of as a "topography" or relational map. This relational map reveals the social stock of knowledge that constrains thought and action in a society. Political actors are everyday people who see themselves within the categories given to them by the social stock of knowledge. Thus, political action unfolds within a discursive space structured by identity categories and their relationships to one another.

These concepts can be arrayed in a ladder of abstraction (Figure 2.1): Since the goal of the method is to reliably code identity categories without losing meaning, analysts should move up the ladder of abstraction only if they feel comfortable doing so. The creation of well-defined discursive formations is to proceed purely inductively, when the texts suggest these moves on their own. So, as we explain in more detail below, analysts were given options about how to make the move from categories to discourses. In a first stage, we asked analysts to prepare a topographical table that clusters the identity categories into groups of categories that are related to one another. We then asked them to think about whether the topographical table leads them to see a clustering of concepts that hang together in a discursive formation.

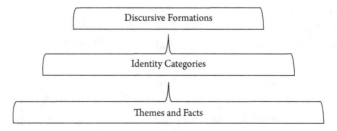

Figure 2.1 The Making Identity Count Framework

II. Approaches to the Study of Identity

Our intersubjective theory of identity has implications for the empirical study of identity. Since identity exists in the intersubjective stock of knowledge available to individuals, it must be studied as such. That is, identity must be recovered from ideas institutionalized in social orders. How can intersubjective background knowledge be recovered?

Empirical studies of identity in International Relations (IR) have deployed a variety of methods to analyze identity. Approaches vary according to the way identity categories and units of analysis are theorized or operationalized (see Table 2.1). First, empirical studies of identity may draw their data from objective, subjective, or intersubjective sources. Purportedly objective measurements rely on visible markers or demographic data. Subjective measurements rely on self-reporting by individuals. Intersubjective approaches recover identity categories from texts and other sources of shared meaning. Second, categories of identity may be pretheorized: analysts choose which identity categories to look for before data collection begins. Or, categories can be inductively recovered: analysts create the list of relevant identities and markers in the process of data collection. Each approach has advantages and disadvantages. Pretheorizing categories produces more reliable results that can be compared easily across cases. While they sacrifice some reliability, inductive strategies are more valid because they are more likely to produce a picture of identity that the persons under study would understand and agree with.[34] But inductive strategies risk producing unique and contextualized categories that are not comparable across cases. In aiming to build quantitative databases, scholars want to ensure that categories will be comparable, and so they sacrifice measurement validity.

One way to reliably measure identity is to use linguistic or ethnic proxies from demographic data. Demographic analysis of identity relies on statistics collected by states, international organizations, and nongovernmental organizations. For example, Fearon and Laitin operationalize ethnic identity as population data translated into an "ethnolinguistic fractionalization index" that is based on "the

Table 2.1 **Approaches to the Empirical Study of Identity**

	Objective Units of Analysis	Subjective Units of Analysis	Intersubjective Units of Analysis
Pretheorized Categories	Demographic Analysis	List Surveys	Content Analysis
Inductive Categories	—	Open-Ended Surveys	Ethnography and Discourse Analysis

population share of the largest ethnic group."[35] From the perspective of the social scientist, this data is "objective" in the sense that regardless of who accesses it, it will be the same. But, this objectivity is an illusion because state statistics are socially constructed and rooted in pretheorized ideas about which ethnic groups will be counted. But the larger problem is that measures based on demographic data are invalid because they lack any sense of what the intersubjective content of identity might be, which is crucial to determining its causal effect on political outcomes. In addition, an ethnolinguistic fractionalization index does not consider the *intensity* or *scale* of the cultural identities. As Wedeen points out, "developing a dataset based on an intensity scale accounting for people's experiences of identification would produce a more precise and generalizable explanation of how the lived conditions of ethnic identity-formation might determine conflict when they do."[36]

Subjective, psychological approaches achieve better validity than objective approaches, but still do violence to identity. Closed list surveys, for example, ask members of a nation to categorize themselves or rank potential identity markers. This produces more reliable results, but risks priming subjects and confirming the salience or intensity of pretheorized categories. Open list surveys can sidestep this problem if they ask people *if* and *how* they identify as members of the nation. This would sacrifice reliability in exchange for increased validity. But even this open subjective method has problems. This captures only what an individual thinks of their identity or national identity. If identity is intersubjective then it cannot be controlled by individuals and their responses are more likely to reflect their idiosyncratic feelings rather than the intersubjective categories that constrain their thoughts. Moreover, survey responses to a direct question will invariably yield answers, but we would have no way of telling the significance of national identity in political discourse as a whole, or how identity is conceptualized when no one is paying attention.

The best subjective operationalization in the extant literature uses "a measure of cultural difference or distance based on questions from the World Values Survey" in various trade studies.[37] This is much better than demographic data, but is problematic in two ways. First, the World Values Survey standardizes the questions across all cultures. Taking cultural diversity seriously, it is unlikely that these questions track the same underlying intersubjective reality in all countries. Ethnographic and discursive studies have repeatedly shown that the same concepts can have different meanings in various cultural contexts. Schaffer's interpretivist research shows that even though the word "democracy" is used all over the world, it is infused with local meanings in each context.[38] For example, in Senegal he finds that "demokrasi" means a fair distribution of goods, not procedural liberalism. It is unlikely that a single set of survey questions will track the same meanings across cultures. The results will not be valid or comparable.

Second, surveys like this put the cart before the horse: they pretheorize which identities and meanings will be significant. That is, all the studies outlined above tacitly assume that the salient intra- and inter-state identities are ethnic, linguistic, religious, or colonial. From an interpretive perspective, there is no theoretically compelling reason to assume that these identities will be more important than identities rooted in class, political institutions, gender, modernity, race, or geography.

Intersubjective approaches study identities from their traces in the common stock of knowledge. Content analysis is the quantitative study of texts by computers trained to count words or networks of concepts. Content analysis studies identity by coding texts according to a set list of categories. Content analysis can be performed either by computers or by human coders. Computerized content analysis is lauded as highly reliable and scientific.[39] This method would access the "overheard conversation" via its sedimentation in texts, provided the texts were sampled appropriately. However, there are a variety of weaknesses with it. First, because content analysis relies on dictionaries created by the analysts, it must pretheorize the words and concept networks that are central to national identity in a given country. Content analysis cannot proceed inductively. Second, content analysis cannot capture the subtlety of meaning in a text. As we shall see below, we cannot hope to train computers to make the kinds of judgments necessary to recover dominant and challenger discourses of national identity.

Ethnography can induce identity categories from close observation of the practices of everyday life.[40] Ethnography aims to uncover taken-for-granted common sense as well as how people express their beliefs when no one is listening or asking. Hence the advantage of ethnography over pretheorized approaches and surveys: it uncovers how people understand themselves only if it comes up in the course of everyday life. Surveys, even open-ended surveys, prompt people to think about national identity, but maybe they never do. Perhaps national identity itself is not salient, but if they are asked they may respond as if it matters a great deal. In this case, the analyst interacts with and alters the subjective basis of the data.

However, ethnography is difficult to do on a large scale, impossible historically, and suffers from threats to reliability and external validity. Ethnographers can only study a small number of people and it is difficult to generalize from small groups to national discourses. That said, we do recognize ethnography as valuable in itself and also as a potential validity check on discourse analysis.

Discourse analysis offers an intersubjective method for recovering national identity that can be made reliable enough to produce a body of comparable reports across time for the same country and across countries as well. Discourse analysis is the interpretive study of texts to uncover the intersubjective background that forms the basis of social order. There are many varieties of discourse analysis, but they are united by this central aim. In linguistic variants, discourse analysis aims to reconstruct the syntactical and semantic rules that govern how sentences are structured and linked together.[41] Foucauldian discourse analysis seeks to uncover the historically constructed rules that make statements possible. Fairclough's Critical Discourse Analysis seeks to combine linguistic analysis with an account of the social, economic, and institutional origins of discursive production to reveal hidden ideological elements.[42] In IR, Milliken, for example, argues that forms of predicate analysis can reveal the implicit hierarchies coded into social order.[43] Howarth defines discourse analysis broadly as "the process of analyzing signifying practices . . . as 'texts' or 'writings' that enable subjects to experience the world of objects, words and practices."[44] These definitions leave what counts as a "text" open, so as to include visual images in books and movies.

Discourse analysis uncovers the social stock of knowledge that individuals use to create meanings and beliefs from its traces in texts. For us, discourse analysis best approximates the ethnographic ideal of recovering data from "overheard conversations" that have not been corrupted by pretheorization or interaction with the analysts.[45] Identities are best uncovered with an interpretive approach that does not pretheorize what the relevant identity relations are in a given society. Fearon argues that the ideal for uncovering identity relations within a society should be to find an approach that identifies "those groups that would be listed most often if randomly chosen individuals in the country in question were asked 'what are the main ethnic (or racial or ascriptive) groups in this country?' "[46] We believe that a discursive method is the most feasible way to approximate such an analysis. But our method goes two steps further: it does not prime individuals by asking for ethnic or racial identities and it does not ask individuals directly, but waits to see what they say when no one is looking. So long as the analyst does not impose order and coherence on the meanings in the texts too soon, discourse analysis allows the salient identities to emerge in context. It does not pretheorize and thereby constrain identity categories and it does not rely on time machines or surveys. Indeed, using survey analysis usually gives respondents a list of identities from which to choose, thus substituting the researcher's hunches for the subjects' local knowledge. What we propose is a recovery of salient identities inductively through a sample of texts which could then be used, if one were so inclined, to specify survey instruments or focus group protocols. Abdelal, Herrerra, Johnston, and McDermott have recently endorsed a "methodological eclectism" in the study of identity. For them, identity definition, conceptualization, and measurement should be integrated and coherent, but they suggest that content analysis, surveys, discourse analysis, and experiments are all equally valid.[47] While we also believe that there is something to be learned from each approach, there is a necessary temporal order to the use of these methods: ethnography and discourse analysis first, and then and only then, surveys, experiments, and perhaps focus groups.

Discourse analysis involves the close examination of relevant texts to uncover the underlying identity relations that shape perceptions of the self. We train our analysts to look for the identities embedded in the common stock of knowledge on two levels. First, we instruct analysts to record the themes and categories connected to the idea of "what does it mean to be American?" or "what is America?" Second, we ask the analysts to look beneath this long list of themes and categories to see how they are connected and linked together in constellations we call discursive formations. There is a third level, of course, associated with linguistic or Foucauldian discourse analysis: recovery of the deeply embedded set of ontological and logical rules that make thought and meaning possible. It is not necessary to recover this level for our purposes and it would be difficult to train a large number of people in the methods necessary to reach this level. But by restricting ourselves to the explicitly stated surface-level categories and their concepts, we do not reduce discourse analysis to a human version of content analysis. Interpretation of the texts is still necessary to avoid pretheorization, to reveal the unexpected connections between categories, and to convey the rich meaning these concepts have. So while our analysts produce and present "raw counts" of identity categories, they also demonstrate what these categories mean and how they fit into a larger "topography" of identity within a country.

Often interpretivist methods like discourse analysis are portrayed as anti-scientific or unscientific.[48] However, our method strives to make discourse analysis more reliable, replicable, and falsifiable by introducing transparent principles of text sampling, quantitative counting procedures, and standardized presentation of evidence. The goal of achieving reliability may seem to violate the interpretivist tenet that there is no outside from which we can achieve "objective" knowledge of the world. If reliability is about measuring "reality" free from error, then it contradicts the position that there is "there is no outside, detached standpoint from which we gather and present brute data."[49] Of course, in striving for reliability we will not be able to achieve a privileged objective position or final recounting of identities. But to achieve reliability one need not posit that a measure captures the world of meaning as it is or as subjects experience it.

Indeed, as interpretivists argue, the very act of interpretation does violence to meaning because it brings the analyst's unique mental state, language abilities, biographical history, and access to intersubjective background knowledge to bear on the text. Perhaps each time the analyst returns to a text she brings a different mental state, a different stock of knowledge, a different set of ideas in short-term memory, and so on. Each time, the reading will be different, of course. But it will not be so different as to render any meaning in the text unintelligible to other analysts or unrecognizable to other interpretations. Meanings can be imperfectly recovered from texts, but it will not be precisely the meanings those texts had for the citizens of the country. Those meanings are irretrievable. But we can recover the categories they were thinking in and, by setting those categories in relation to one another, some sense of the meanings they must have attached to those categories.

Thus, our claim to validity does not rest on a claim to capture the world as it is from a detached standpoint, but on the claim that analysts can reliably capture similar categories within which identities were formed and constructed. This is still an attempt to reconstruct intersubjective realities as accurately as possible with transparent operationalizations and measurements that recover the central categories from a group of texts that serve as a proxy for the manifold representations of national identity that circulate in society. We choose our texts from a wide range of genres in the expectation of generating as representative a sample of discourses as possible. Nonetheless, we recognize that our analysts do violence to the webs of meaning in a country by reducing it to a small number of texts, that our coding questions exclude certain forms of meaning that may be relevant, and that the subjectivity of the analyst will remain inscribed in the results. These are problematic from the perspective of a fully inductive interpretivist method. But, we believe the payoffs of the project as a whole justify these acts of simplifying, exclusionary violence. Moreover, we are convinced that we retain the core tenet of interpretivism: the commitment to the inductive, interpretive analysis of shared webs of meaning that individuals draw on to create meaning and form their identities.[50]

III. Operationalizing and Measuring Discourses of National Identity

I have outlined our intersubjective theory of identity and conceptualized discourses of national identity as discursive formations embedded in the social stock of knowledge. I have argued that discourse analysis is the best available method to inductively recover these identities. Two vital methodological tasks remain: operationalizing discourses of national identity as a sample of texts and specifying the measurement rules that guide discourse analysis.

Text Selection

We operationalize discourses of national identity as a variety of widely circulated texts. The theoretical warrant for this is that the categories which people use to make sense of both themselves and the world are drawn from intersubjectively shared stocks of knowledge. On our theory, evidence of discourse can be found in "[e]verything that is said or written in a given state of society, everything that is printed or talked about and represented today through electronic media."[51] Along these lines, Sarup argues that identity can be seen as "a multi-dimensional space in which a variety of writings blend and clash. These writings consist of many quotations from the innumerable centres of culture, ideological state apparatus and practices: parents, family, schools, the workplace, the media, the political parties, the state."[52] Our goal is to sample texts from these centers of power, so as recover the central categories that circulate in discourse. The expectation is that identities can be found in the jokes told, movies viewed, and newspapers read in everyday life. This common stock of knowledge constrains political identities and political decision-making. Leaders are constrained by the necessity that they make sense of the world with categories and values drawn from their everyday lives. So the study of political identity must begin within states, even if those identities are also shaped by interactions with other societies and international politics.[53]

While these principles support sampling widely and deeply, to make the large scale of this project tractable, we operationalize discourses of national identity as a smaller sample of texts that can be analyzed in about one hundred hours. There are potential problems with such a small sample. One or two outlier texts may distort the findings if they present many instances of a single category. We guard against this possibility in a number of ways. First, we give analysts autonomy to tell us, interpretively, what meanings they think matter. Though they must present raw counts up front, they have an opportunity to bring in or leave out categories from the topographical table that follows. For example, in the French discourse, "decline" had low counts, but was deemed interpretively significant as it expressed a common implicit theme that united other categories (France as cultural leader, former colonial power). Second, the topographical table differentiates the text by genre, so if a category only appeared in one text, it wouldn't seem relevant across genres and thus would not be coded as a central category. In Germany, at first environmentalism seemed overrepresented in the counts due to its prominence in one of the films. However, environmentalism appeared elsewhere in the sample and thus the analysts felt they could get a better sense of how important it really was.

There are two general principles for document selection. First, sample documents that are widely read and thus can be expected to reflect the available stock of social knowledge from which identities are assembled. We do not want documents that explicitly or normatively discuss the central identity categories of the country. Rather, we want to overhear discussions about what it means to be Brazilian in the context of everyday life. Second, sample documents that reflect both the elite political discourses around political institutions and the discourses that structure mass common sense.

To achieve each of these goals, for the year 2010 we asked analysts to sample texts from five genres:

Leadership Speeches: Choose two leadership speeches by the head of government or ruling party on significant occasions. These might be the national holiday address or a budgetary speech.

Newspapers: Choose two newspapers with the highest national circulation. From these, for the 15th of each month, read all opinion-editorials and letters to the editor.

History Textbooks: Choose two widely read high school history textbooks on your country's national history. Start with the 20th century as your time of origin.

Novels: Choose the top two bestselling novels in the country, by country's authors, in an official language.

Movies: Choose the top two most-attended movies in the country, by country's directors/producers, in an official language.

As you will see, in each report, analysts present the results of their analysis according to the prevalence of a given identity category in each genre. In doing so, each analyst must place these genres in order along a continuum from elite to mass based on the particular situation in their country. A text is more reflective of "elite" discourse if it is produced and consumed by political and social elites that dominate powerful institutions of a society. A text is more reflective of "mass" discourse if it is produced for and consumed by a large, multi-class, multiethnic, etc., collection of people in the country. Leadership speeches are usually produced by elites for consumption by both elite and mass sources, and so they also give us a window into widely shared ideas. However, they are produced by the political elite and so provide a key reflection of elite political discourse. From newspapers we sample both op-ed pieces and letters to the editor. The idea is that the op-ed pages capture views produced by and for members of elite political circles, while the letters capture views produced by the masses. We have asked analysts to code these separately and watch for differences. In some countries, history textbooks are more likely to reflect elite or official discourses because their production is tightly controlled by the state. In others, they will reflect the shared, uncontested, taken-for-granted history of a country taught to every child. Analysts had to make choices about what textbooks best captured and place them in the continuum accordingly, based on how states regulate textbook production and adoption in each country. By specifying bestselling novels, we aim to capture novels produced for and consumed by many people, thus revealing widely shared stocks of knowledge. Of course literary novels are produced by and for elites, but we are hoping to filter them out with the bestselling criterion. Movies are also consumed by the masses and so the blockbusters will reveal themes and identity categories that resonate with them. Of course, directors and executive producers are often members of the elite, but we assume that they want to reach as many people as possible with their stories, and so they are more likely to use identity references that resonate with the masses. Since norms and practices surrounding the collection of bestseller lists and box-office receipts, etc., vary widely from country to country, analysts have had to modify the criteria in context. Their explanations and justifications appear at the beginning of the reports that follow.

This operationalization makes sense for great power states in the year 2010, but as the project is expanded to other country years, the basic sampling strategy will have to be adapted. In the 19th century, there may not be history textbooks to sample. Similarly, movies are only a relevant text in the 20th century. There will also be problems going forward. Newspapers may no longer be relevant and web-based media will need to be incorporated. However, we believe the principles used to select texts are flexible enough to be adapted while still producing comparable results.

Analyst Selection and Training

Our analysts were selected from three pools:

i) undergraduates trained by the editors at a two-week workshop in July 2013;
ii) undergraduates trained in qualitative methods and discourse analysis in coursework by the editors;
iii) graduate students and junior faculty trained in qualitative methods and discourse analysis in graduate coursework.

The two-week workshop combined seminars and workshops to clarify coding rules and compare findings. Days 1–3 were conducted in seminar format. The analysts read and discussed classics in interpretivist theory, introductions to discourse analysis methods, and exemplary studies of national identity.[54] These readings introduced the analysts to a variety of approaches to discourse analysis: linguistic and metaphorical discourse analysis; social discourse analysis; ethnographic approaches to identity; the semiotic analysis of artifacts; and attending to absences.[55] But introductions to these various approaches were presented as different ways at getting to our core question: how is national identity understood in societal discourses? That is, how do French people understand themselves as French, or what it means to be French?

Days 4–8 were daily workshops designed to make coding decisions more reliable. Each day a new genre was covered: speeches, newspapers, textbooks, novels, and movies. On these days, every analyst would give a 20-minute presentation on their coding choices. They were instructed to present examples of both easy and difficult coding decisions. The instructors would intervene to help clarify ambiguous cases and point out places where the analyst stretched or overreached. A frequent intervention was that the coder had identified a theme but had not yet produced enough evidence to claim this was an identity category. Instructors also pointed out categories in sections of text presented by the analysts that had not been coded.

The workshop was designed to increase reliability, reduce overreading, and guide analysts to be as inductive as possible. There was no common list of categories given to the analysts (unlike in the Party Manifesto Project and other qualitative coding projects).[56] However, we expected analysts to come to both the workshop and their analysis with certain expectations about what they would find. We encouraged the analysts to forget these priors. Moreover, we tried not to prime them by telling them which categories we expected them to find. Throughout days 1–3, the authors were careful not to prime the analysts to look for specific categories. Wherever possible we made illustrations using a single example: modernity. We assumed some version of modernity would be present in each discourse, but that it would mean different things everywhere, so it would be an acceptable category to prime the analysts with. Exemplary studies of course did include some categories that we expect would prime the analysts. On days 9 and 10, after most of the coding was done, analysts finally presented their tentative findings to one another.

While pools ii) and iii) did not receive this detailed training, they did benefit from extensive discussion of coding rules with the editors. In this manner, many of the same clarifications and interventions were made in the production of those reports.

Coding Rules

We asked analysts to write down all the possible identity categories invoked in their sample. This can entail from 50 to 100 discrete categories. They were to proceed inductively, using categories in the texts rather than their own pretheorized notions and classifications. We gave them one simple question: What does it mean to be China or be Chinese?

Answers to this question were to be coded in three ways:

1. Valence: distinguish between positive, negative, neutral, and ambiguous identities with valence symbols (+, –, /, or ~). Note whether the identity is considered a good or a bad feature of being China or Chinese.
2. Aspirational or Aversive: Is the identity you have found one that China aspires to become, or one it is trying to avoid becoming?

3. Significant Others: These are the countries, historical periods, ideas, etc., with which China compares itself. These can be historical, contemporary, or prospective. They can be positive or negative. They can be aspirational or aversive.

For example:

> "To our compatriots overseas, I want to convey my determination to that which the Republic holds to, with regards to their promises of equality and dignity that was not sufficiently held in to in the past."

This sample from the French report was coded as: EQUALITY+, DIGNITY+, HISTORICAL OTHER–. The term "Republic" here stands in for France (indeed, Republican categories are part of the dominant French discourse) and hails equality and dignity as key components of what it means to be French. The analyst has also highlighted the possibility that this could be linked to representations of the past as regrettable, marking present France as distinct from that past other.

Computerized, quantitative content analysis is unable to capture the difference between themes and identities or make the judgments and interpretations necessary to move up the ladder from categories to discursive formations. However, in the spirit of quantitative content analysis, our method offers checks against the subjective biases of individual coders. The counting procedure forces analysts to defend their interpretive impressions with evidence. So our method is both transparent and quantitative: analysts must count coding decisions and justify their judgments about significant identity categories with counts of coding decisions.

From Categories to Discourses

Coding produces a long list of categories with raw counts of how many times each category was invoked. Analysts are next asked to perform a series of exercises to help them represent the dominant discourses in a country. First, they produce a raw count table (Table 2.2) of the top twenty or so categories by frequency, combining positive, negative, neutral, and ambiguous codings. Then analysts are asked to produce a "topographical" table that clusters categories or compares discourses. In the topographical table, raw counts are translated into percentages normalized by genre, and then converted into valence symbols (+, –, /, or ~). So the topographical table represents frequency and valence as well as salience and content.

These tables are arranged from left to right, from texts that reflect the elite views to those that reflect mass views. This allows the analysts and readers to see which categories feature in all texts. If a category is distributed from elite to

Table 2.2 **United Kingdom Consolidated Identity Categories [Excerpt]**

Categories	Speeches	Newspapers (Op-eds)	Newspapers (Letters)	Textbooks	Movies	Novel
Anti-Britain						
Contrarian		−	−	−	++	/
Modern Britain						
Democratic	++	++	++	++		+
Four-national	///	//	~	/		/
Declining	− −	−	~	−	− −	− −
Modern	++	+	+	+	++	++
Orderly	++++	++	+++	++	//	+
Secular		+	++	+		+
Socially progressive	++	++	+++	+	++++	++++

mass, then we conclude that it is a consensual category and thus a candidate for membership in the predominant discourse.

Analysts are then asked to construct the predominant discourse of national identity and its challenger/s. This is the most theoretical move in which analysts are asked to think about the consensual and contested aspects of the national identity, the difference between mass and elite representations, and so on. Each of the following chapters follows the same outline, moving from raw counts to discourses.

The reports that follow proceed according to the same format. In section I, the analysts explain how they adapt our text selection principles to their specific country. In section II, each analyst presents the raw counts of their findings: a list of the top twenty or so identity categories coded. They then briefly explain what these categories mean and, where space allows, provide quotes and evidence to support the interpretations.[57] In section III, analysts present their "topographies" of national identity discourse. Here, they present the predominant discourses of identity and their challengers. Finally, analysts draw conclusions and relate their findings to the themes of democratic, neoliberal hegemony.[58]

IV. Evaluating National Identity

Our method increases validity by allowing analysts to inductively recover identity categories from their basis in important and widely circulated texts. We think we can achieve this without reducing reliability so far as to render the analyses irreducibly subjective. A potential problem with our method is that we do not provide a consistent set of coding categories to the analysts. Rather, we offer something like a coding framework: theory, definitions, and inductive injunction to catalogue all the categories which are connected to what it means to be Brazil or Brazilian. Analysts are not employed as high-functioning, easily programmable computers. They are active interpreters that have to make choices about which identity categories matter and how to assemble these categories into dominant discursive formations. But since the goal is to produce a set of codings and interpretations that could be translated into statistical tables, our inductive method may come at the cost of being unable to achieve the reliability necessary to support statistical data sets. It is unlikely that our method can achieve the mainstream standard of intercoder reliability. However, on conceptions of reliability relevant to the project, we achieve reasonable reliability, thus vindicating the method.

The first potential evaluation of reliability would happen at the level of individual coding decisions. Do analysts code the same sentences as containing the same identity category? This is the standard definition of intercoder reliability in large data-generating projects. This standard is the reason why computer-based content analysis is appealing: given the same dictionary and rules, any computer will code the same sentence the same way every time. Intercoder reliability is easier to achieve when a dictionary or standard list of coding categories exist. The Manifesto Project, for example, includes a "category scheme" that provides an exhaustive list of the coding decisions an analyst might make.[59] In this way, they narrow the range of possible meanings a text can have in order to achieve reliability. We are not willing to do this because we believe that the results obtained would be invalid and so achieving reliability would be pointless. If we really want to know what Chinese discourses of national identity looked like in 1970, we cannot presume that the inductively recovered list from India 1950 or France 1990 will have relevance. Of course, if we were to provide a list, our analyst might find plenty of confirming evidence, but this might be coding squares into round holes and may leave out a whole host of triangles.

The typical definition of reliability is a high standard and our analyst selection and training is meant to help us achieve as much reliability as possible. However, for the purposes of this project it is not necessary to achieve intercoder reliability on this level. A more appropriate standard for our purposes is whether the findings at the level of discursive formations are the same. That is, do two analysts working on the same set of texts draw the same conclusions about the most important identity categories and their position in dominant discourses of national identity? On this standard, the results below offer tentative support for our approach.

As an experiment, we commissioned two reports on India, one to be performed on Hindi texts and one to be performed on English texts. Both reports, though they were conducted on separate sets of texts (except the movies, which overlapped), find that the number one identity category is "democracy." What does this mean? It means that even though the two India analysts could not possibly have made the same discrete coding decisions, they converged on the same result at the level of identifying the main category through which India is understood.

This undermines the intuitive idea that reliability is solely about reproducible measurements. Rather, reliability in social science is about equifinal methods that produce the same results albeit from different paths. Great discourse analysis may often fail discrete reliability tests, but can nonetheless pass equifinality reliability tests. This is suggestive, but of course more experiments like this should be done. We hope to be able to commission independent reports on country years we already have reports for to test their replicability. These might fail equifinality tests in some cases, in which case, we will have to rethink our methods. But failing equifinality tests would not necessarily mean that our results were useless. More likely they mean that each analyst has captured a subset of the relevant categories and meanings. The task then would be to have the analysts engage in a dialogue, to see if they could come to agreement on the dominant categories and discursive formations. This would introduce a juristic or dialogic concept of reliability that fits better with considered views in the philosophy of science.[60] Since Popper, theories are not to be tested against reality but against other theories.[61] Similarly, measurements should not be thought of as capturing some segment of reality, but as performing consistently with other measures designed to get at similar phenomena. Thus, we support the validation of our measurements with multiple methods, although according to the correct order laid out above: surveys and other measurements should be informed by the results of inductive discourse analysis and ethnography.

Conclusion

In this chapter, I have laid out our conceptualization of identity as categories embedded in intersubjective stocks of knowledge, or discourses. I argued that the most valid way to operationalize discourses of national identity was as samples of texts drawn from both elite and mass sources. I outlined how we train and instruct analysts to measure identity as the categories attached to the idea of the nation. In sum, our approach to recovering national identity has three main elements: a theory of intersubjective identity, theoretically informed principles of text selection, and simple, reliable rules to guide discourse analysis. These elements combine to produce a relational, topographical presentation of national identity discourses. Although the reports may not achieve reliability at the level of individual coding decisions, they can achieve equifinal reliability. In either case, more research will be needed to replicate and test the findings presented herein.

Notes

1. Rabinow and Sullivan 1987.
2. Carmines and Zeller 1979, p. 11.
3. Carmines and Zeller 1979, p. 12. Adcock and Collier identify 37 different adjectives for validity (2001, p. 530). Some of these apply to causal inference (e.g., external v. internal validity) and some to descriptive inference (content, criterion, construct). Here, we are interested primarily in descriptive or measurement face validity. Adjectives modifying validity tend to refer to strategies of validation (Carmines and Zeller 1979, pp. 17–25). We envision a variety of potential forms of validation (to establish variants of criterion, substantive, or construct validity). First, our ideal is that national citizens themselves would be able to, upon reflection, agree with the results our analysis, via either surveys or focus groups. Second, replication by further discourse analysis would find similar results. Finally, as Hopf 2002 demonstrates, theoretical predictions based on the findings, such as expectations of alliance formation, can be empirically verified.
4. Following, roughly, the framework in Adcock and Collier 2001.
5. On definitions of identity, see Abdelal et al. 2009, p. 19.
6. Connolly 1991, p. 64.
7. Brewer and Brown 1998, p. 559.
8. Tajfel and Turner 1979; Brewer and Brown 1998; Huddy 2003.
9. Hewstone and Cairns 2001, pp. 324–325; Brewer and Brown 1998, pp. 565–568. For applications to international relations, see Mercer 1995; Larson and Shevchenko 2003.
10. Sarup 1996, p. 14.
11. Hewstone and Cairns 2001, pp. 324–325. On identity change and competition change, see Mercer 1995, pp. 251–252.
12. Connolly 1991, p. xv.
13. Sarup 1996, p. 14.
14. Connolly 1991, p. 64.
15. Rabinow and Sullivan 1987, p. 15; Yanow and Schwartz-Shea 2006, p. xii. This seems uncontroversial, but Dunn, for example, argues that "[r]epresentations do not cause policies" (2008, p. 84).
16. Taylor 1987; Taylor 1991.
17. Rorty 1991, p. 60.
18. Gusterson 2008, p. 105.
19. E.g., Klimstra 2010; Becker 2012.
20. Mitzen 2006.
21. Berger and Luckmann 1966, p. 23. Cf. Hopf 2002, pp. 4–6.
22. Cf. Durkheim's collective representations, Husserl's (and later Habermas') lifeworld, Gramsci's commonsense, Foucault's episteme, Bourdieu's doxa and habitus, Kahneman and Tversky's heuristics, and so on.
23. Berger and Luckmann 1966, pp. 33–40.
24. Berger and Luckmann 1966, pp. 129–131.
25. Berger and Luckmann 1966, p. 148.
26. Berger and Luckmann 1966, p. 53. This and other pieces of Berger and Luckmann's theory have been supported by subsequent social psychological research. See Brewer and Brown 1998, p. 562.
27. Berger and Luckmann 1966, p. 55.
28. Berger and Luckmann 1966, pp. 80–87.
29. Hopf 2002.
30. Hopf 2002, p. 37; Hayes 2013, p. 28.
31. Anderson 1991; Hanchard 2003.
32. Berger and Luckmann 1966, pp. 81–97.
33. Sarup 1996, p. 48.
34. This would be a form of criterion validity, if conducted via focus groups or surveys, but there are other forms of validation. See fn. 3.
35. Fearon and Laitin 2003, p. 82. See also, Cederman and Girardin 2007; Gartzke and Gleditsch 2006.

36. Wedeen 2003, p. 725.
37. LeBlang 2010, p. 589.
38. Schaffer 1998.
39. Neuendorf 2002.
40. Adams 2009.
41. Howarth 2000, p. 6.
42. Fairclough 1995.
43. Milliken 1999.
44. Howarth 2000, p. 10.
45. Hopf 2007, p. 60.
46. Fearon 2003, p. 195. This captures the intuition behind our ideal form of criterion validation.
47. Abdelal et al. 2009, p. 9. See the multimethod approach of Brady and Kaplan 2009 in the same volume.
48. Rabinow and Sullivan 1987; Neuendorf 2002.
49. Rabinow and Sullivan 1987, p. 7.
50. Geertz 1973.
51. Angenot 2000, p. 200. Cf. Howarth 2000, p. 10; Sarup 1996, p. 25.
52. Sarup 1996, p. 25.
53. Weldes 1999; Hopf 2002, 2012; Telhami and Barnett 2002; Hayes 2013.
54. The central theoretical texts were Berger and Luckmann 1966; Rabinow and Sullivan 1987; Hopf 2002.
55. The central methods texts were Milliken 1999, Angenot 2004, Adams 2009, Savage 1994, Cowan 1991. In the interest of full disclosure, these readings primed students to look for certain identity categories:

   • Milliken 1999 is a review article, but a prominent example suggests that the United States represented itself as a leader while representing Japan as an emotional, subordinate nonagent. It highlights colonial and racial relations among states.
   • Angenot 2004 lays out a plan for a study of France in 1889 and mentions political identities like Anarchism, ethnic identities such as anti-Semitism, as well as thematizing bawdy and sexual elements of discourse.
   • Hopf 2002 mentions class, modernity, region, urban-rural divide, and ethnicity as central to the "New Soviet Man." The Soviet Past is mentioned as an ambiguous Historical Other, as well as liberalism, democracy, etc.
   • Cowan 1991 discusses gender in a Macedonian village.
   • Savage 1994 uses an analysis of monuments to disclose discourses of race in post–Civil War America.

56. Werner, Lacewell, and Volkens 2011.
57. A key part of the project will be an online database of the sources for each of the texts. Although copyright laws will prohibit posting the texts themselves in some cases, analysts will produce detailed instructions for finding and accessing the texts.
58. More information on the method and presentation of the evidence can be found in the codebook, attached to this volume as an appendix.
59. Werner, Lacewell, and Volkens 2011.
60. Kratochwil 2007.
61. Popper 1959.

References

Abdelal, Rawi, Yoshiko Herrera, Alastair Iain Johnston, and Rose McDermott, eds., *Measuring Identity: A Guide for Social Scientists* (Cambridge: Cambridge University Press, 2009).
Adams, Laura L., "Techniques for Measuring Identity in Ethnographic Research," in Abdelal, Rawi, Yoshiko Herrera, Alastair Iain Johnston, and Rose McDermott, eds., *Measuring Identity: A Guide for Social Scientists* (Cambridge: Cambridge University Press, 2009).
Adcock, Robert and David Collier, "Measurement Validity: A Shared Standard for Qualitative and Quantitative Research," *American Political Science Review* 95:3 (2001), 529–546.

Anderson, Benedict, *Imagined Communities* (New York: Verso, 1991).

Angenot, Marc, "Social Discourse Analysis: Outlines of a Research Project," *Yale Journal of Criticism* 17:2 (2004), 199–215.

Becker, Maja, Vivian L. Vignoles, Elinor Owe, Rupert Brown, Peter Easterbrook, et al., "Culture and the Distinctiveness Motive: Constructing Identity in Individualistic and Collectivistic Contexts," *Journal of Personality and Social Psychology* 102:4 (2012), 833–855.

Brady, Henry E. and Cynthia S. Kaplan, "Conceptualizing and Measuring Ethnic Identity," in Rawi Abdelal, Yoshiko Herrera, Alastair Iain Johnston, and Rose McDermott, eds., *Measuring Identity: A Guide for Social Scientists* (Cambridge: Cambridge University Press, 2009).

Brewer, Marilynn B. and Rupert J. Brown, "Intergroup Relations," in Susan T. Fiske, Daniel Gilbert, and Gerdner Lindzey, eds., *Handbook of Social Psychology*, 4th Edition (Hoboken, NJ: Wiley & Sons, 1998).

Bohman, James F., David R. Hiley, and Richard Shusterman, "Introduction: The Interpretive Turn," in David R. Hiley, James F. Bohman, and Richard Shusterman, eds., *The Interpretive Turn: Philosophy, Science, Culture* (Ithaca: Cornell University Press, 1991).

Carmines, Edward G. and Richard Zeller, *Reliability and Validity Assessment* (London: Sage University Press, 1979).

Cederman, Lars-Erik and Luc Girardin, "Beyond Fractionalization: Mapping Ethnicity onto Nationalist Insurgencies," *American Political Science Review* 101:1 (2007), 173–185.

Connolly, William, *Identity/Difference* (Minneapolis: University of Minnesota Press, 1991).

Cowan, Jane K., "Going Out for Coffee?," in Peter Loizos and Evthymios Papataxiarchis, eds., *Contested Identities: Gender and Kinship in Modern Greece* (Princeton: Princeton University Press, 1991).

Dunn, Kevin C., "Historical Representations," in Audie Klotz and Deepa Prakash, eds., *Qualitative Methods in IR: A Pluralist Guide* (New York: Palgrave MacMillan, 2008).

Fairclough, Norman, *Critical Discourse Analysis: The Critical Study of Language* (New York: Longman, 1995).

Fearon James D., "Ethnic and Cultural Diversity by Country," *Journal of Economic Growth* 8 (2003), 195–222.

Fearon, James D. and David D. Laitin, "Ethnicity, Insurgency and Civil War," *American Political Science Review* 97:1 (2003), 75–90.

Gartzke, Erik and Kristian Skrede Gleditsch, "Identity and Conflict: Ties that Bind and Differences that Divide," *Journal of International Relations* 12:1 (2006), 53–87.

Geertz, Clifford, *The Interpretation of Cultures* (New York: Basic Books, 1973).

Gusterson, Hugh, "Ethnographic Research," in Audie Klotz and Deepa Prakash, eds., *Qualitative Methods in IR: A Pluralist Guide* (New York: Palgrave MacMillan, 2008).

Hanchard, Michael, "Acts of Misrecognition: Transnational Black Politics, Anti-imperialism and the Ethnocentrisms of Pierre Bourdieu and Loïc Wacquant," *Theory, Culture & Society* 20:4 (2003), 5–29.

Hayes, Jarrod, *Constructing National Security* (Cambridge: Cambridge University Press, 2013).

Hewstone, Miles and Ed Cairns, "Social Psychology and Intergroup Conflict," in Daniel Chirot and Martin E. P. Seligman, eds., *Ethnopolitical Warfare* (Washington, DC: American Psychological Association, 2001).

Hopf, Ted, *The Social Construction of International Politics* (Ithaca: Cornell University Press, 2002).

Hopf, Ted, "The Limits of Interpreting Evidence," in Richard Ned Lebow and Mark Lichbach, eds., *Theory and Evidence in Comparative Politics and International Relations* (New York: Palgrave MacMillan, 2007).

Hopf, Ted, *Reconstructing the Cold War* (Oxford: Oxford University Press, 2012).

Huddy, Leonie, "Group Identity and Political Cohesion," in David O. Sears, Leonie Huddy, and Robert Jervis, eds., *Oxford Handbook of Political Psychology* (Oxford: Oxford University Press, 2003).

Klimstra, Theo A., Koen Luyckx, William A. Hale, Tom Frijns, Pol A. C. can Lier, and Wim H. J. Meeus, "Short-Term Fluctuations in Identity: Introducing a Micro-Level Approach to Identity Formation," *Journal of Personality and Social Psychology* 99:1 (2010), 191–202.

Kratochwil, Friedrich, "Evidence, Inference, and Truth as Problems of Theory Building in the Social Sciences," in Richard Ned Lebow and Mark Lichbach, eds., *Theory and Evidence in Comparative Politics and International Relations* (New York: Palgrave MacMillan, 2007).

Larson, Deborah Welch and Alexei Shevchenko, "Shortcut to Greatness: The New Thinking and the Revolution in Soviet Foreign Policy," *International Organization* 57:1 (2003), 77–109.

LeBlang, David, "Familiarity Breeds Investment: Diaspora Networks and International Investment," *American Political Science Review* 104:3 (2010), 584–600.

Mercer, Jonathan, "Anarchy and Identity," *International Organization* 49:2 (1995), 229–252.

Milliken, Jennifer, "The Study of Discourse in International Relations: A Critique of Research and Methods," *European Journal of International Relations* 5:2 (1999), 225–254.

Mitzen, Jennifer, "Ontological Security in World Politics: State Identity and the Security Dilemma," *European Journal of International Relations* 12:3 (2006), 341–370.

Neuendorf, Kimberley, *The Content Analysis Guidebook* (London: Sage, 2002).

Popper, Karl, *The Logic of Discovery* (London: Routledge, 1959).

Rabinow, Paul and William M. Sullivan, eds., *Interpretive Social Science. A Second Look* (Berkeley: University of California Press, 1987).

Rorty, Richard, "Inquiry as Recontextualization: An Anti-Dualist Account," in David R. Hiley, James F. Bohman, and Richard Shusterman, eds., *The Interpretive Turn: Philosophy, Science, Culture* (Ithaca: Cornell University Press, 1991).

Sahlins, Peter, *Boundaries: The Making of France and Spain in the Pyrenees* (Berkeley: University of California Press, 1989).

Sarup, Madan, *Identity, Culture and the Postmodern World* (Edinburgh: Edinburgh University Press, 1996).

Savage, Kirk, "The Politics of Memory: Black Emancipation and the Civil War Monument," in John Gillis, ed., *Commemorations: The Politics of National Identity* (Princeton: Princeton University Press, 1994).

Schaffer, Frederic C., *Democracy in Translation: Understanding Politics in an Unfamiliar Culture* (Ithaca: Cornell University Press, 1998).

Tajfel, H. and J. C. Turner, "An Integrative theory of Intergroup Conflict," in W. G. Austin and S. Worchel, eds., *The Social Psychology of Intergroup Relations* (Monterrey, CA: Brooks/Cole, 1979).

Taylor, Charles, "Interpretation and the Sciences of Man," in Paul Rabinow and William M. Sullivan, eds., *Interpretive Social Sciences: A Second Look* (Berkeley: University of California Press, 1987).

Taylor, Charles, "The Dialogical Self," in David R. Hiley, James F. Bohman, and Richard Shusterman, eds., *The Interpretive Turn: Philosophy, Science, Culture* (Ithaca: Cornell University Press, 1991).

Telhami, Shibley and Michael Barnett, *Identity and Foreign Policy in the Middle East* (Ithaca: Cornell University Press, 2002).

Weldes, Jutta, *Constructing National Interests* (Minneapolis: Minnesota University Press, 1999).

Werner, Annika, Onawa Lacewell, and Andrea Volkens, *Manifesto Project Coding Instructions*, 4th Edition, 2011. Available at: https://manifesto-project.wzb.eu/down/papers/handbook_v4.pdf.

PART TWO

NATIONAL IDENTITY REPORTS

3

"The Rascals' Paradise"

Brazilian National Identity in 2010

MARINA DUQUE

The dominant identity discourses in Brazil portray the country as a limited democracy: the rascals' paradise, riddled with corruption and opportunism, that is nonetheless a fledging democracy. While democratic ideals are defended widely, corruption, incompetent government, and inequality damage Brazil's democratic status. The texts express a desire to develop into a peaceful, global leader, but these are aspirational identities the country has not yet achieved. The national identity discourse in Brazilian provides mixed support for Western democratic neoliberal hegemony. On the one hand, the limited commitment to democracy supports Western hegemony. On the other, the rejection of neoliberalism creates support for a statist alternative to Western economic order.

I. Text Selection

The sample includes elite and mass texts selected for their wide reach.[1] The category of presidential speeches that draw large audiences would traditionally include the speech delivered on the national holiday, but President Lula da Silva did not speak then. Therefore, I selected two other speeches: the Presidential Message to Congress[2] and the first speech by President-Elect Dilma Rousseff.[3] I selected two high school textbooks covering Brazilian history in the 20th century: *General History and History of Brazil*[4] and *History of Brazil in the Context of Western History*.[5] Both were among the textbooks most frequently adopted by private schools in Belo Horizonte, one of Brazil's largest cities.[6]

I selected the two highest-circulating newspapers that publish editorials: *Folha de S. Paulo* (*FSP*) and *O Globo* (*OG*)—which are considered to be respectively left- and right-leaning, and had average circulations of 294,498 and

262,435 in 2010.[7] The sample includes all the op-eds and letters to the editor published on the 15th of every month, in a total of 46 editorials and 350 letters. I also selected the novels *The Battle of the Apocalypse*[8] and *Elite Squad 2*,[9] which spent the greatest number of weeks on the bestsellers list published by the magazine *Veja* in 2010.[10] Few Brazilian novels feature on the list, where translations of American bestsellers such as *The Shack* predominate. Finally, I selected the first- and fourth-highest-grossing movies in 2010: *Elite Squad 2*[11] and *Our Home*,[12] with respectively 11 million and 4 million viewers.[13] *Elite Squad 2* was especially successful in the box office: it broke a 34-year attendance record for national movies. Only three Brazilian movies feature on the list of the twenty most-attended movies, which is otherwise comprised of American movies.

II. Brazilian Identities in 2010

I used interpretive discourse analysis to recover identities from the sample.[14] I first read the texts to catalogue identity categories, and then identified categories that dealt with related aspects. It was possible to see that the categories addressed one of the following aspects: domestic politics, government, socio-economic aspects, economic position in the world, and political role in the world. Finally, I aggregated categories dealing with each aspect into a cluster. From this process emerged five identity clusters that represent Brazilian identities in 2010: limited democracy, incompetent government, divided society, developing country, and peaceful leader. Table 3.1 shows the raw counts for each category. In this section, I present the categories that form each cluster, and examine how they inform each other.

A Limited Democracy

Democracy is a core part of Brazilian identity. The categories that directly or indirectly describe Brazilian democracy make 53% of all counts. Although there are nuances in the way democracy is portrayed, as a group the categories suggest the identity of a limited democracy. There are six categories that explicitly describe Brazilian democracy. According to the first category, an **authoritarian government** constrains democracy. This discourse is present most frequently in textbooks, which consider historical periods when the Executive increased its share of power and/or limited individual liberties. But the newspapers also reveal concerns about government authoritarianism in contemporary politics. Newspapers discuss President's Lula persistent campaigning for the Workers' Party presidential candidate: "[the president] says whatever he pleases, whenever

Table 3.1 **Identity Category Raw Counts**

Category	Total	Sp	Txt	Ns (Op-ed)	Ns (Lett)	Mov	Nov
Corrupt/non-liable/opportunistic (−)	72		15	11	39	4	3
Incompetent/irresponsible/weak government (−)	29			7	15	2	5
Revolt/coup d'état/regime change	22		22				
Socially unequal (−)	22	3	12		2	3	2
Authoritarian government (−)	21		12	5	3		1
Influenced by Europe/United States (8−, 7/, 6+)	21		21				
Lower classes exploited by the elite (−)	19		17				2
Exploited by economic elites (−)	16		16				
Repressive politics (−)	16		16				
Manipulated voters/ populist or paternalistic leaders (−)	15		12		3		
Exclusionary politics (−)	12		7			3	2
Participation of the military in politics (9/, 1−)	10		10				
International leader (+)	9	6	3				
State intervention in the economy (4+, 4−)	8		8				
Corrupt society	7				2	2	3
Agricultural exporter (−)	6		6				
Competent government (aspirational, +)	6	4	2				
Becoming modern (+)	5		4	1			
In good economic conditions (vs. North) (+)	5	3	2				
Neutral (West vs. East) (+)	5						5
Total	**321**	**16**	**185**	**24**	**64**	**14**	**18**

Note: The letters at the top of each column indicate the sources, from left to right: Category, Total, Speeches, Textbooks, Newspaper(Op-ed), Newspaper(Letters), Movies and Novels. Aspirational categories are described as such between parentheses; all others are perceived as current identity categories.

he pleases, wherever he pleases, as if he were beyond reproach. The fact that he mocked the judges after receiving five fines for disrespecting electoral law demonstrates his disdain for the Judiciary" (*FSP* op-ed, August 2010). Editorials argue that, in the process leading to the adoption of the Human Rights National Plan, the Executive not only overstepped its powers but also ignored civil society inputs. For example: "the authoritarian nature of the project is evident in the way it was imposed on society" (*OG*, May 2010).

The second category suggests that Brazil possesses only a low level of democracy, as **voters are manipulated and leaders are populist or paternalistic**. This category is highly concentrated in textbooks that describe populist or paternalist practices adopted by previous presidents. Moreover, it is present in letters to *O Globo* that see the government as intentionally maintaining low levels of education. For example: "The more ignorant the people, the bigger the odds that the powerful will manipulate it. In a country with no education and culture, democracy is the same as despotism" (*OG*, September 2010).

The third category involves another constraint on democracy: **exclusionary politics**. It is found in textbooks that describe how large portions of the population did not have a right to vote or had no political influence due to the concentration of power in the hands of economic and military elites. References to political exclusion also appear in *Elite Squad 2*. The movie describes the poor as being subject to police violence and a merciless application of the law, which does not touch the rich. The *Elite Squad 2* novel posits that the state is absent from the slums in Rio: "[Journalists] were mistaken to believe that the slum belonged to the nation and was regulated by the Federal Constitution and the democratic rule of law."[15]

The fourth and fifth categories—**young/fragile democracy** and **advanced democracy**—have a more optimistic tone, stressing achieved or desired advances in democracy. This discourse is concentrated in speeches and textbooks, and therefore has a statist character. An example is found in Rousseff's speech: "My election demonstrates the advance of democracy in Brazil: for the first time, a woman will be president . . . Equality in opportunities for men and women is an essential democratic principle." Finally, a couple of texts mention the incipient nature of democracy in Brazil. Among these, only the letter to the editor has a negative connotation: "our democracy still has much to improve" (*FSP*, August 2010).

The remaining categories in the cluster deal with political aspects related to democracy: corruption, the use of violence, the participation of the military in politics, and state intervention in the economy. Each of them emphasizes problems and therefore reinforces the identity of limited democracy.

Corruption is by far the most salient identity discourse in Brazil. The three categories dealing with it make 21% of all counts, which is the highest count across all categories. References to corruption are absent from speeches and concentrated at the "mass" end of the spectrum. At the "elite" end, textbooks describe practices such as clientelism and electoral fraud, which were common at the beginning of the 20th century; political campaigns based at least in part on claims to fight corruption; or the corruption scandal involving President Collor in the 1990s. However, it is in letters to the editor that references to corruption and opportunism abound: "corruption is endemic in Brazil, and it involves all levels and powers of the government" (*OG*, February 2010); "is our vote merely a ticket to power?" (*FSP*, May 2010). In *Elite Squad 2*, corruption is especially salient in parts that discuss incestuous relationships among drug traffickers, the police, and politicians.[16]

Most discourses see corruption as a problem that afflicts only the political class, rather than the entire country. A few texts at the "mass" end of the spectrum see the whole society as corrupt or responsible for what happens in politics: "Brazil, the rascals' paradise. You turn a blind eye to what I do, and I turn a blind eye to what you do. And everything works itself out."[17] Yet, the vast majority paints the picture of the Brazilian politician who has corruption basically written in their genes: "every politician is equally bad, and the only thing that changes is the [party] label" (*OG*, June 2010). Connected with this perception is the notion that Brazil is not a serious country: "In more decent parts of the world, only the prisoners are subject to body [cavity] searches; those visiting them in prison only have to go through detection machines."[18]

Another group of identity categories deals with the use of violence. Although Brazilian history is marked by violently repressed revolts, coups d'état, and unconstitutional regime changes, these events do not reflect on national identity. The first two categories—**revolt/coup d'état/regime change** and **repressive politics**—show up in textbooks but are completely absent from the other texts. The use of violence appears only in *Elite Squad 2*, which characterizes Brazil as a country **at war with organized crime.**[19]

The last two categories in the cluster refer to the participation of the military in politics and the intervention of the state in the economy, which were frequent in the 20th century. Taken together, these categories indicate a limited commitment to liberal democracy. The **participation of the military in politics** assumes a negative valence only 10% of the time, when it refers to the military dictatorship. Most references have a neutral valence, indicating the involvement of the military in politics is not rejected in essence—which contradicts democratic principles. Similarly, there seems to be a limited commitment to neoliberal principles. To textbooks, the state was the only actor that could bear the burden of investment necessary for development. Import substitution policies are not inefficient in and of themselves; they just stopped working at a certain point.

State intervention in the economy thus assumes a negative or positive valence in equal proportions.

An Incompetent Government

In this cluster, mass and elite, statist texts are neatly divided: while newspapers and popular culture see the government as incompetent, irresponsible or weak, speeches and textbooks emphasize government competence and responsibility. Claims to **competence and responsibility** are especially salient in Rousseff's speech. They are directed at domestic audiences: "We will focus on improving the quality of public spending, on tax reform, and on the improvement of public services," and also at foreign investors: "Brazil is a generous nation that gives back twice as much as what is invested in it . . . We will take care of our economy responsibly." In textbooks, claims to effectively represent the people come from past presidential candidates.

However, such claims do not seem to gain traction. Editorials point to **incompetence and irresponsibility**: "we witness a squandering of human lives and a spectacle of [government] incompetence and cynicism every rain season" (*FSP*, April 2010); "the management of public funds seemed to be entering the realm of irresponsibility" (*FSP*, May 2010). A similar discourse is present in letters to the editor, especially in *O Globo*: "The Judiciary is clearly incompetent . . . the Executive, be it at the municipal, state, or federal levels, neglects the population" (*OG*, April 2010).

The image of incompetence is perhaps best illustrated in the narrator's frustrated reaction in *Elite Squad 2* when a federal police agent's cell phone does not work during an operation: "Brazil!"[20] In both novel and movie, the government seems ill equipped to combat crime: "It is pointless to arrest criminals, because the system produces new ones to replace them"[21]; "There is always the problem of witness intimidation [by criminals]. Were this a serious country, we would not rely so much on witnesses [to investigate crimes]."[22] Even *The Battle of the Apocalypse*, which is less politically engaged, describes organized crime as a parallel power.[23]

A Divided Society

The third cluster describes a society divided along economic lines. In this cluster, discourses are concentrated at the "elite" end of the spectrum, and appear less frequently in mass texts. The cluster comprises two discourses that emphasize divisions: social inequality, and the exploitation of the lower classes by the elite. The social inequality discourse is present in three categories: (i) **social inequality** itself is the only category in the cluster to be mentioned in most genres; (ii) **social equality as an aspiration** appears in speeches and textbooks; and (iii) **improving conditions for the poor** shows up in speeches, as an affirmation or aspiration: "The opportunities for a better present and future are being shared."[24]

The **exploitation of the lower classes by the elite** is a recurring image especially in textbooks, which emphasize the lack of legal protection to workers, and even compare industry workers to slaves. This script also appears in *Elite Squad 2*, which describes police officers as earning little and sacrificing their safety, while politicians take credit for their work.[25] Connected to this notion are claims that **work is not valued/respected**—found in letters, and also a textbook according to which part of slavery's legacy is that work is seen as an activity suited only to inferior beings.[26]

In contrast to texts that emphasize economic division, speeches mention **national unity** as a fact or an aspiration: "The entire Brazilian society mobilized itself to face the [financial] crisis"[27]; "now is the time to be united; united for education, united for development, united for the country."[28]

A Developing Country

In the categories that describe Brazil's economic position in the world, three aspects are combined to form the identity of a developing country. First, there is a perception that developed countries have exploited Brazil. According to textbooks, Brazil is connected to the world economy via the exportation of primary goods, which is a type of economic **exploitation**. Beginning with colonization, Brazil became trapped in a cycle of exploitation: it provides wealthy countries with cheap goods, while not receiving technology transfers or being more closely integrated into the world market. Both national and international elites stand to gain in this situation, while the country itself remains poor. In this view, development is equated with industrialization and urbanization, which would put Brazil on a par with the wealthy countries.

Second, Brazil is described as **poor** alongside African and Latin American countries,[29] while an aspiration for economic growth is present both in Lula's speech and in an editorial (*FSP*, February 2010). Finally, Brazil is perceived as having abilities that are usually associated with the poor, such as spiritual virtue and physical prowess. In *The Battle of the Apocalypse*, Rio is described as a place where "the spiritual world was clean,"[30] while war took over the globe. Furthermore, the depiction of Brazil as a "soccer nation" appears in three letters to the editor. This image is rejected by two of the letters: "Despite what our diplomacy thinks, Brazil will not be respected internationally because of its soccer, carnival or natural beauty; our country will be respected for its economy, culture, welfare, honesty, for its people's labor, for its technological development and scientific achievements" (OG, April 2010). However, a third letter takes pride of the depiction: "The national team's jersey is a patrimony of the Brazilian people, which has reached inestimable value and is loved by people from the four corners of the world" (OG, April 2010).

A Peaceful Leader

The categories describing Brazil's role in international politics reveal a couple of aspects. First, the significant others in the discourses are mostly Western developed countries—rather than the country's neighbors, which are strikingly absent. In all texts, Brazil is described as South/Latin American only twice.[31] Textbooks do not address relations with South/Latin America in the history of Brazil. Moreover, most of world history revolves around Europe, Russia, the United States, and to a lesser extent China; only one of the textbooks has a short world history section that deals with Latin America.

Significant others appear most frequently in textbooks, which mention political and cultural **influences received from Europe and the United States**. European influence assumes a negative valence in a minority of cases, for example in the assertion that the Brazilian modernist movement denounced submission to European cultural trends.[32] Textbooks posit that anarchism gained prominence in Brazil with the arrival of European immigrants,[33] who played a key role in industrialization.[34] The adoption of labor laws was part of a "global trend" in Europe,[35] as was the creation of communist and fascist parties,[36] and the ideological polarization in the 1930s.[37] Moreover, the 1937 Constitution was modeled after Italian and Polish constitutions."[38] World War I spurred industrial development[39] and led to the decline of anarchism,[40] while World War II made a democratic transition "inevitable."[41]

In contrast, American influence assumes a positive or neutral valence only a couple of times, when textbooks compare Brazilian democracy with the "American model,"[42] or describe alignment with the United States as a central part of domestic politics debates.[43] Most references have a negative valence: Brazil adhered to American-based consumerism,[44] and was "flooded with non-durable products (. . .) from the United States"[45]; the military dictatorship resulted from American efforts to avoid revolutions such as the one in Cuba[46]; Brazil unfortunately adopted the American doctrine of national security in the 1970s,[47] as well as neoliberalism, the "Anglo-American model," in the 1990s.[48]

Second, although there is some variation in terms of how Brazil's status is perceived, the role of leader shows up frequently. Statist texts emphasize Brazilian leadership. President Lula represents Brazil as a leader that invests in regional integration, provides support to Haiti, and actively participates in multilateral forums to fight economic protectionism and promote sustainable development. The country is also a regional **leader**: "We earned the right to be the first South American nation to host the Olympic Games."[49] A similar discourse appears in one of the textbooks, which depicts Brazilian diplomacy as increasingly active.[50] References to leadership are less frequent in Rousseff's speech, but still present as she promises to lead efforts to regulate the international financial market. Moreover, statist texts describe Brazil as practically immune to the financial crisis, in contrast to developed countries: "While unemployment and economic stagnation took their toll in the North, we kept creating employment, investing in infrastructure and industry."[51]

The depiction of the country as a **great power** finds echoes in two letters in *O Globo*. While one letter describes Brazil as a continent (*OG*, May 2010), another calls for a bigger involvement in Haiti: "If Brazil wants to occupy a leadership position in the UN, it has to act like a great nation. We should send our aircraft carrier to Haiti (. . .). The United States is already doing that. We should not be stingy. We have the money" (*OG*, January 2010). Yet, not all discourses grant Brazil the status of a traditional great power. The notion of "great-power myth" appears in a textbook to describe official propaganda during the military dictatorship.[52] *The Battle of the Apocalypse* tells a story about a world war in which Brazil remains neutral and plays only the role of receiving refugees.[53]

Although views regarding Brazil's leadership role differ somewhat across texts, there is consensus that Brazil's engagement with other countries is **cooperative**. Across texts, Brazil's actions involve promoting regional integration, participating in multilateral forums, providing aid, or receiving refugees. In combination with the other categories in the cluster, this discourse suggests the identity of a peaceful leader.

III. The Topography of Brazilian Identity in 2010

There seems to be a widespread view that corruption is endemic in Brazil. Corruption is by far the most salient, consensual identity category. It is mentioned in all genres except speeches, and its average percentage across genres—which is an overall measure of category salience—is the highest of any category, at 23%. Corruption is very present in history and contemporary politics, and is often treated as a problem that is typically Brazilian, rather than existing in other countries and resulting from specific institutional arrangements: "it is about time we give the opportunity to another president to show that Brazil can be fixed . . . fighting corruption and bad politicians is the public's duty" (letter in *OG*, June 2010).

References to corruption reflect popular discontent, which marked the political scene in 2010.[54] Discontent is also expressed in the very popularity achieved by *Elite Squad 2*, as both novel and movie deal with the problems of organized crime, violence, and corruption in Rio de Janeiro. However, references to corruption should not be interpreted as a mea culpa on the part of Brazilians. Most discourses see corruption as a problem that afflicts only the political class, rather than the entire society. The country itself is usually not seen as corrupt, but rather its politicians are (Table 3.2).

In general, there is a clear division between statist and non-statist discourses, with the former emphasizing positive representations of Brazil, while the latter overwhelmingly contain negative representations. Most of the salient categories in speeches have a positive valence, but textbooks are usually the only other genre where these categories are mentioned. Textbooks are the genre that overlaps with speeches the most, especially for categories that have a positive valence—e.g., **advances in democracy** and **good economic conditions**. Textbooks also overlap with the other genres, except for discourses criticizing the current government. In contrast, the most salient categories both in newspapers and popular culture are generally critical of the government. Therefore, while textbooks are statist, the other genres are not.

Overall, there are four main areas of elite-mass contention. First, although there is consensus about the constrained nature of Brazilian democracy, the sources of constraint differ across elite and mass texts. Statist discourses seem to attribute limitations to Brazil's relative lack of historical experience as a democracy, and therefore portray advances as a matter of time. In contrast, newspapers and popular culture attribute problems to an insufficient commitment to democratic principles on the part of elites, which is more resilient to change.

After **corruption**, the second most salient category overall is **incompetent government**, with an average percentage of 13%. Mass and statist texts are clearly divided in their descriptions of the government. Although speeches and textbooks emphasize government competence and responsibility, newspapers and popular culture see the government as incompetent, irresponsible, or weak. The next most salient category overall is **social inequality** (7%), in which a similar pattern appears. The frequency distribution of the social inequality discourse along the mass-elite spectrum indicates that although there is consensus that Brazil is an unequal country, the public does not necessarily recognize the situation as improving. Moreover, the national unity discourse from speeches is the least frequent in this cluster, and does not appear in any other genre.

Finally, there is elite-mass contention in the representations of Brazil's position in the world. Statist discourses emphasize Brazilian leadership; in fact, the most salient category in speeches is **leader**, with an average percentage of 15%. However, this representation does resonate much with the public. In *The Battle of the Apocalypse*, the war between West and East starts with American expansionism, and intensifies as the United States forms an alliance with Europe and Taiwan, which is opposed by China and North Korea. Brazil is described as poor, and its neutrality suggests that it is not on a par with Taiwan, China, or North Korea. Moreover, in all clusters Brazil's role in relation to its significant other—Western developed countries—is usually a passive one, as the receiver of influences or the exploited periphery.

Notwithstanding the contrast between statist and non-statist texts, there are also some areas of elite-mass consensus. There is agreement about the constrained nature of Brazilian democracy, which appears across all genres. Similarly, there seems to be a consensus that Brazil is an unequal country: **social inequality** is the third most salient category overall (7%), and appears in most genres. And while class divisions are acknowledged explicitly and rejected, race and gender divisions are generally not questioned. Race and gender inequalities are practically absent from discourse,[55] although fictional characters and their creators are disproportionately white males.

Moreover, in all of the identity clusters, whenever the significant other is another country, it is usually a European country or the United States. There is a saying according to which Brazil is always looking toward the North Atlantic, with its back turned to South America—and that seems to apply to the texts examined here. Finally, there is consensus that Brazil's engagement with other countries is cooperative. This discourse suggests a peaceful identity, especially if analyzed in combination with other categories. The general absence of references to violence indicates that Brazilians see themselves (or their leaders) as corrupt but not violent; the image that comes to mind is indeed of rascal, or a malicious yet likable con artist. Likewise, Brazil's alleged spiritual virtue reinforces the quality of peacefulness.

Conclusion

In an interpretive discourse analysis of a range of widely read texts—including speeches, history textbooks, newspaper editorials and letters to the editor, movies, and novels—five clusters of Brazilian identity in 2010 emerged. The first cluster describes Brazil as a limited democracy, due to government authoritarianism, the manipulation of voters, political exclusion, corruption, state use of violence, the participation of the military in politics, and state intervention in the economy. The second cluster portrays an incompetent government, while the third cluster describes a society divided along economic lines. The fourth

Table 3.2 **Brazilian Identity Topography**

Category	Sp	Txt	Ns (Op-ed)	Ns (Lett)	Mov	Nov
Limited Democracy						
Authoritarian government		– –	– – – – –	–		–
Manipulated voters/populist or paternalistic leaders		– –		–		
Exclusionary politics		–			– – – – –	– –
An improving democracy	+ +	+				
Young/fragile democracy	+	+		–		
Advanced democracy (aspirational)	+ + +					
Corrupt/non-liable/opportunistic		– – –	– – – – –	– – – – –	– – – – –	– – –
Corrupt society				–	– – – –	– – –
Not a serious/decent country						– –
Revolt/coup d'état/regime change		////				
Repressive politics		– – –				
At war with organized crime					/////	/
Participation of the military in politics		+ +				
State intervention in the economy		~				
Incompetent Government						
Incompetent/irresponsible/weak			– – – – –	– – – – –	– – – –	– – – – –
Competent (aspirational)	+ + +	+				
Responsible (fiscal/economic terms)	+ + +					
Divided Society						
Socially unequal	– – –	– –		–	– – – – –	– –
Lower classes exploited by the elite		– – –				– –

(*Continued*)

Table 3.2 **(Continued)**

Category	Sp	Txt	Ns (Op-ed)	Ns (Lett)	Mov	Nov
Socially equal (aspirational)	+ +	+				
Improving conditions for the poor	+ + +					
Improving conditions for the poor (aspirational)	+ + +					
Work is not valued/respected		–		–		
United nation (aspirational)	+ +					
Developing						
Exploited by economic elites		– – –				
Agricultural exporter		–				
Becoming modern		+	+			
Poor						//
Maintaining economic growth (aspirational)	+		+			
Clean spiritually (despite being poor)						+
A soccer nation				~		
Peaceful Leader						
Influenced by Europe/United States		– – / +				
Leader	+ + + + +	+				
Neutral (West vs. East)						/////
In good economic conditions (vs. North)	+ + +	+				
South/Latin American	/					/

Note: The letters at the top of each column indicate the sources, from left to right: Category, Total, Speeches, Textbooks, Newspaper(Op-ed), Newspaper(Letters), Movies and Novels. Aspirational categories are described as such between parentheses; all others are perceived as current identity categories.

cluster depicts a developing country—which is poor, connects to the world economy via the exportation of primary goods, and has spiritual virtue and physical prowess. The fifth cluster suggests the identity of a peaceful leader. Despite some variation in terms of how Brazil's status is perceived, the role of leader appears frequently, and there is a consensus that Brazil will use peaceful means to perform its role. Overall, **corruption** is the most salient category; the predominant identity discourse thus describes a rascals' paradise.

The implications of Brazilian identity for the persistence of Western hegemony are mixed. On the one hand, discourses about domestic politics suggest the identity of a limited democracy. According to the texts, the Executive oversteps its powers and limits individual liberties, while citizens lack the tools for an informed vote and a share of the population is excluded from the political process. Moreover, neutral or positive evaluations of the participation of the military in politics and the intervention of the state in the economy indicate a limited commitment to liberal democracy. The abundant references to corruption suggest that the democratic system of checks and balances does not work properly, while the use of force by the government signals a limited ability to solve problems using the regular political process.

In addition, there is resistance to neoliberalism coming from the perception that, as a developing country, Brazil is at a disadvantage in the world economy. More specifically, the texts suggest a limited faith in the market to solve problems, as well as a mostly positive view of state intervention in the economy. Other key features of neoliberalism—such as a positive attitude toward liberal policies and reforms, individualism, and the attribution of a positive value to competitiveness—are absent from discourse. Although criticism of the government is frequent, it does not originate from neoliberal views. None of the texts call for a reduction in the government's responsibilities in favor of the market. Instead, they represent an expectation that the government will improve its performance in the tasks under its responsibility.

However, there are no counterhegemonic discourses on the horizon. The predominant discourses represent a strong aspiration for advances in democracy, while references to alternative political regimes are absent. Democracy is taken for granted, and neoliberalism is not rejected altogether. Moreover, Brazil sees itself as Western, or at least aspires to be part of the West. The significant others in the discourses are mostly Western developed countries. The overall positive valence of references to Europe indicates that Brazil is proud of its European heritage, although views of the United States tend to be negative. The findings thus bolster democratic neoliberalism, even if slightly adapting it.

Notes

1. All texts are originally in Portuguese; citations were translated by the author. A more detailed explanation of the criteria used to select texts is presented in Chapter Two.
2. L. I. Lula da Silva, "Mensagem ao Congresso Nacional, 2010: 4ª Sessão Legislativa Ordinária da 53ª Legislatura" (Speech, Brasília, February 2, 2010), http://www2.planalto.gov.br/acompanhe-o-planalto/mensagem-ao-congresso/mensagem-ao-congresso-nacional-2010.
3. Dilma Rousseff, "Dilma Rousseff: Primeiro Pronunciamento" (Speech, Brasília, October 31, 2010), http://www.brasil.gov.br/governo/2010/11/dilma-rousseff-primeiro-pronunciamento.
4. Claudio Vicentino and Gianpaolo Dorigo, *História Geral e do Brasil* (São Paulo: Scipione, 2010).
5. Luiz Koshiba and Denise Manzi Frayze Pereira, *História do Brasil no Contexto da História Ocidental* (São Paulo: Atual, 2003).
6. I could not have access to lists of textbooks adopted by public schools.
7. Associação Nacional de Jornais, "Os Maiores Jornais do Brasil de Circulação Paga, Ano 2010," accessed May 21, 2014, http://www.anj.org.br/maiores-jornais-do-brasil.
8. Eduardo Spohr, *A Batalha do Apocalipse: Da Queda dos Anjos ao Crepúsculo do Mundo* (Campinas: Verus Editora, 2010).
9. Luiz Eduardo Soares et al., *Elite da Tropa 2* (Rio de Janeiro: Nova Fronteira, 2010).
10. I used this method because there is not a reliable annual list of best-selling books in Brazil.
11. José Padilha, *Tropa de Elite 2: O Inimigo Agora é Outro* (Rio de Janeiro: Zazen Produções, 2010).
12. Wagner de Assis, *Nosso Lar* (São Paulo: Fox Filmes, 2010).
13. Agência Nacional do Cinema, *Informe de Acompanhamento de Mercado, 2010*, accessed December 30, 2013, http://www.ancine.gov.br/media/SAM/Informes/2010/Informe_Anual_2010.pdf.
14. The method is described in more detail in Chapter Two.
15. Soares et al., *Elite da Tropa 2*, 180.
16. Ibid., 11, 12, 17.
17. Ibid., 127.
18. Ibid., 202.
19. Ibid., 261.
20. Ibid., 65–66.
21. Padilha, *Tropa de Elite 2: O Inimigo Agora é Outro*.
22. Ibid., 99.
23. Spohr, *A Batalha do Apocalipse: Da Queda dos Anjos ao Crepúsculo do Mundo*, 432.
24. Rousseff, "Dilma Rousseff: Primeiro Pronunciamento."
25. Soares et al., *Elite da Tropa 2*, 11, 13.
26. Koshiba and Pereira, *História do Brasil no Contexto da História Ocidental*, 428.
27. da Silva, "Mensagem ao Congresso Nacional, 2010: 4ª Sessão Legislativa Ordinária da 53ª Legislatura."
28. Rousseff, "Dilma Rousseff: Primeiro Pronunciamento."
29. Spohr, *A Batalha do Apocalipse: Da Queda dos Anjos ao Crepúsculo do Mundo*, 42.
30. Ibid., 40.
31. da Silva, "Mensagem ao Congresso Nacional, 2010: 4ª Sessão Legislativa Ordinária da 53ª Legislatura"; Spohr, *A Batalha do Apocalipse: Da Queda dos Anjos ao Crepúsculo do Mundo*, 42.
32. Vicentino and Dorigo, *História Geral e do Brasil*, 606.
33. Vicentino and Dorigo, *História Geral e do Brasil*, 563; Koshiba and Pereira, *História do Brasil no Contexto da História Ocidental*, 343.
34. Koshiba and Pereira, *História do Brasil no Contexto da História Ocidental*, 403.
35. Ibid., 348.
36. Ibid., 446.
37. Vicentino and Dorigo, *História Geral e do Brasil*, 630.
38. Ibid., 634.
39. Ibid., 600.
40. Koshiba and Pereira, *História do Brasil no Contexto da História Ocidental*, 347.

41. Vicentino and Dorigo, *História Geral e do Brasil*, 639; Koshiba and Pereira, *História do Brasil no Contexto da História Ocidental*, 460.
42. Ibid., 555.
43. Koshiba and Pereira, *História do Brasil no Contexto da História Ocidental*, 469, 494.
44. Vicentino and Dorigo, *História Geral e do Brasil*, 671.
45. Ibid., 675.
46. Ibid., 734–735; Koshiba and Pereira, *História do Brasil no Contexto da História Ocidental*, 473.
47. Koshiba and Pereira, *História do Brasil no Contexto da História Ocidental*, 515.
48. Ibid., 522.
49. da Silva, "Mensagem Ao Congresso Nacional, 2010: 4ª Sessão Legislativa Ordinária Da 53ª Legislatura."
50. Vicentino and Dorigo, *História Geral e do Brasil*, 807–808.
51. da Silva, "Mensagem ao Congresso Nacional, 2010: 4ª Sessão Legislativa Ordinária da 53ª Legislatura."
52. Vicentino and Dorigo, *História Geral e do Brasil*, 743.
53. Spohr, *A Batalha do Apocalipse: Da Queda dos Anjos ao Crepúsculo do Mundo*, 42, 128, 194, 343, 355.
54. While manifestations followed corruption scandals, the clown-turned-candidate Tiririca, with the campaign slogan "It can't get any worse," was the most voted state representative nationally with 1.3 million votes.
55. There is one mention of sexism in Soares et al., *Elite da Tropa 2*, 208; and one mention of racism in Vicentino and Dorigo, *História Geral e do Brasil*, 563–564.

Sources

Speeches

Lula da Silva, L. I., "Mensagem ao Congresso Nacional, 2010: 4ª Sessão Legislativa Ordinária da 53ª Legislatura" (Brasilia, February 2, 2010), http://www2.planalto.gov.br/acompanhe-o-planalto/mensagem-ao-congresso/mensagem-ao-congresso-nacional-2010.
Rousseff, Dilma, "Dilma Rousseff: Primeiro Pronunciamento" (Brasília, October 31, 2010), http://www.brasil.gov.br/governo/2010/11/dilma-rousseff-primeiro-pronunciamento.

Textbooks

Koshiba, Luiz and Denise Manzi Frayze Pereira, *História do Brasil no Contexto da História Ocidental* (São Paulo: Atual, 2003).
Vicentino, Claudio and Gianpaolo Dorigo, *História Geral e do Brasil* (São Paulo: Scipione, 2010).

Newspapers

Folha de S. Paulo
O Globo

Movies

de Assis, Wagner, *Nosso Lar* (São Paulo: Fox Filmes, 2010).
Padilha, José, *Tropa de Elite 2: O Inimigo Agora é Outro* (Rio de Janeiro: Zazen Produções, 2010).

Novels

Soares, Luiz Eduardo, et al., *Elite da Tropa 2* (Rio de Janeiro: Nova Fronteira, 2010).
Spohr, Eduardo, *A Batalha do Apocalipse: Da Queda dos Anjos ao Crepúsculo do Mundo* (Campinas: Verus, 2010).

4

"Development" as a Means to an Unknown End

Chinese National Identity in 2010

LIANG CE AND RACHEL ZENG RUI

Introduction

The predominant discourse of Chinese national identity in 2010 is "developing." This identity, which supports the ideology of neoliberal capitalism, emphasizes economic openness and cooperation. A counter-discourse, here called "egalitarianism," appears frequently in the mass discourse. It criticizes the widening divisions between classes, genders, and regions as a result of the implementation of neoliberal economic policies. Both discourses reflect that the Chinese strongly believe in the importance of making progress. After completing the discourse analysis for Chinese national identity in 2010, we argue that the mass texts are generally forward-looking but are less optimistic than the elite ones regarding development.

I. Text Selection

Our archive includes political speeches, newspapers, high school history textbooks, movies, and novels (see Sources). We have selected three speeches made by Premier Wen Jiabao on three nationally significant occasions—the National Day Celebration, the National Congress on Education, and the Shanghai Expo. The two editions of high school history textbooks that we have chosen are published by People's Education Press and the Yuelu Press. These two editions are the most widely used in China.

For newspapers, we examined *People's Daily* and *Southern Metropolis Daily*, the two newspapers that have the highest readership in China (see Sources). However, it is worth noting that state-controlled news media may distort actual public opinion. Nonetheless, the *Southern Metropolis Daily* is believed to be the most outspoken and pro-liberal voices among all forms of Chinese media. Of all the articles published, we have chosen to analyze opinion articles (op-eds) and letters to the editor. In doing so, we assume the op-eds reflect the views of the elites whereas the letters are more likely to reflect the views of the masses. In addition, the *People's Daily* does not publish op-eds and letters every day. Opinion articles are published only after significant events such as the National People's Congress (NPC) and Chinese People's Political Consultative Conference (CPPCC). A Commentary Column, which is a supplement to the op-eds in *People's Daily*, is also published only on alternate weekdays.[1] Therefore, we have selected both the op-eds and articles from the comment section for the analysis.

For movies, we have selected *Let the Bullets Fly* and *Aftershock*. They are the most-viewed ones in 2010 according to a report on China's film market by China Film Distribution and Exhibition Association. To obtain a reference on the popularity of novels, we used Douban and Amazon China, which are two popular Chinese websites for sharing book reviews.

II. Chinese National Identities in 2010

In this section we will introduce the Chinese national identities in 2010. We obtained these identities by following the coding rules, inductively recovering the identities from the sampled texts. The following paragraphs will explain the identities listed in Table 4.1 in detail.[2]

Progress

Progress refers to the emergence of a "new" China. Compared to ancient China, and China prior to "economic reform" and "opening up," a "new" China signifies a break away from old political and economic views. For instance, the term "New Look" is one of the most frequently used phrases to describe China today in the elite discourse. Phrases describing how China "has made new progress," "has achieved new results," and "has been brought to a new level"[3] often appear to summarize and reiterate various achievements in areas such as legislation and education.[4]

The manifestation of a "new" China is evident in the structure of the history textbooks used by high school students. Both history textbooks begin with the

Table 4.1 **Identity Category Raw Counts**

Category	Total	Speeches	Newspapers (Op-eds)	Newspapers (Letters)	Textbooks	Novels	Movies
Developing	143	22	32	13	52	15	9
Progressing	113	20	23	19	33	11	7
Catching up	108	26	11	10	52	6	3
Pragmatic	86	21	13	16	20	7	9
Insecure	55	0	3	13	2	26	11
Persevering	44	12	2	1	20	0	9
Hardworking	44	8	1	10	13	9	3
Corrupt	38	0	1	2	7	12	16
Materialistic	38	0	8	1	7	13	9
Socialist with Chinese characteristics	34	9	7	0	7	4	7
Socially divided	33	5	2	4	2	11	9
The West	32	1	5	4	14	3	5
Marketizing	30	12	2	3	9	1	3
Mutually courteous	29	0	7	0	0	16	6
Bureaucratic	25	0	0	5	6	11	3
Individualistic	24	0	0	4	0	7	13
Patriotic	16	4	0	1	8	0	3
The Chinese dream	16	9	1	0	5	1	0
United States (government)	12	0	2	1	9	0	0
Japan (aggressors)	11	0	0	0	9	0	2
United States (culture)	11	0	2	3	0	4	2
Japan (economic model)	10	0	0	1	5	0	4
Total	**952**	**149**	**122**	**111**	**280**	**157**	**133**

chapter titled "splendid and glorious,"[5] which talks about China's achievements in ancient times. However, the subsequent chapters talk about Chinese sufferings as a result of Western imperialist domination, before concluding with a final chapter titled "An Entirely Independent, Unified, and New China."[6] From textbook chronology and organization, we can identify significant changes in Chinese national identities.[7] Such changes were largely perceived to be positive, especially by the elites. In the mass discourse, however, the absence of opinion toward **Progress** implies a sense of uncertainty or ambiguity.[8]

Catching Up

China is widely recognized by its people as a developing country. This identity appears often in the history textbooks. In particular, it means to increase economic output and to improve the standard of living for the population, to that of developed countries. To draw some examples from the texts: "[Our goal is] . . . to catch up with the UK in two years, and the US in three years." "China had been humiliated by western imperialism for almost a century. The establishment of the new PRC marked a new beginning in the history . . . [China] began to catch up with the developed West."[9]

In history textbooks, **Catching Up** is often, if not always, associated with **Progress**. However, in the speeches and newspapers of 2010, this identity appears much less frequently. More importantly, **Catching Up with the West** (in the history textbooks) has been replaced by a discourse of **Catching Up with Ourselves** in speeches and newspapers. For instance, in a speech made by Premier Wen, he mentioned that "[China has made] remarkable progress in the past five years . . . we have achieved tremendous successes . . ." The comparisons are made between China in the past and China today. This change of meanings across different historical contexts shows that elites have become more cautious about drawing explicit comparisons between themselves and the West. It could also be understood as a strategy that the Chinese government adopted to highlight the achievement under the CCP.

Pragmatism

Pragmatism is an emerging category in China. It means to deal with things sensibly and realistically. Chinese proverbs such as "*shishi qiushi* (seek truth from facts)" and "*cong shiji chufa* (from a practical standpoint)" are reiterated in each context examined.

For the masses, it is pragmatic to support a winning cadre rather than a promising policy. This is because in China, electoral victory enables access to resources and can use them to benefit the people. For example, a scene in the movie *Let the Bullets Fly* shows that ordinary people who were oppressed by the local gentry are not willing to support the cadre who was aiming to free them from tax burden.

Materialism

Materialism is mostly viewed as a negative trait in the elite discourse. In political speeches, it is clear that the Chinese government opposes materialism. One newspaper article from *People's Daily* criticizes people's obsession with material benefits. "Materialism is flourishing in China today, and it is eroding our traditional moral values . . ."[10] Materialism is bad because it is perceived to have undermined traditional societal values.

However, in the mass discourse, materialism is positive. It is reflected as a byproduct of the rapid economic expansion in China. Sometimes, material interest appears to be the most important, if not decisive, working principle. One example of how materialism is viewed positively can be inferred from a commentary on *Southern Metropolis Daily*: "I was motivated by those fellow villagers' passion for voting, who had left the village to earn a life in city . . . [their] passion for voting came from self-interests . . . [they] found out that the result of village committee election put [each of their] interests at stake—e.g. the distribution of road project payment, the lessee of the collective land, the dividends of collective enterprise."[11]

Marketization

In the elite discourse, marketization is viewed positively, because "as an essential part of the economic reform, marketization has brought remarkable economic growth [in China]."[12] In contrast, the response of the masses toward marketization is mixed with favor and disgust. This can be seen from their responses to marketization. On the one hand, marketization is "the focus of future reform."[13] On the other hand, market failures have been criticized as simply "talk with money."[14] In addition, it is admitted by the masses that marketization has brought negative externalities to China, especially in areas with heavy industry. One newspaper article titled "The Red-Bean Soup River" sarcastically criticizes the environmental pollution that is happening very often in China: ". . . the river that flows through the town has been heavily polluted by waste-water from a newly established factory. Now the river looks like red bean soup!"[15]

Corruption

Corruption is a negative trait across the five genres. The idea of corruption appears most frequently in movies and novels. Bureaucratic and political corruption is heavily criticized in these texts. In China, corruption is negatively perceived as "pursuing self-interest at the expense of the public goods." In the novel *Lala's Promotion,* the manager of the company is depicted as a corrupt figure because he "made use of his authority as a top manager to pursue material benefits for himself . . . [The manager] . . . stole the welfare funds and used the money on travelling to Europe." Despite widespread criticism, corruption remains a pervasive political and social phenomenon in China. It exists across all societal levels. Corruption has become a social norm in that although people hate it, they are forced to be corrupt because they have to play according to the "rules of the game."

Bureaucracy-Oriented Consciousness

Bureaucracy-oriented consciousness (*guanbenwei*) is a concept developed from the Confucian tradition. Today, this identity continues to be relevant in China. The notion means working as a civil servant is an honor. In the current Chinese political system, civil servants have lifelong employment. In China, it is referred to as the "iron bowl." Thus, many young Chinese today are competing to become civil servants not only because it is an honor, but for a more practical reason. In *Let the Bullets Fly* and *Under the Hawthorn Tree,* bureaucracy-oriented consciousness is explicitly represented by the characters' physical and mental struggles for top-ranked positions in the government and in business, respectively.

Socialism with Chinese Characteristics

This identity is the official ideology of the Chinese Communist Party after 1978. This ideology supports the creation of a socialist market economy dominated by the public sector since China is at the primary stage of socialism. Under the category of **Socialism with Chinese Characteristics**, there are sub-categories such as "spiritual civilization," "harmonious society," "moderately affluent society," and "people orientated" which appeared constantly in the official discourses.

Patriotic

Patriotism is understood as a key nationalist identity in the elite discourse. It describes a person's emotional and cultural attachment to the nation. In history textbooks, the "patriotic spirits of the brave Chinese people" are manifested in the battles fighting against the Japanese invaders during WWII. Apart from that, Patriotism is also identified as a communist identity is often expressed in a fixed permutation such as "love the nation and love the party." Hence it implies that the concepts of the "nation" and the "party" are interchangeable.

This identity also resonates well with the masses. The movie *Aftershock* celebrates patriotism in a subtle manner. The female protagonist Fang Deng is an orphan whose parents died in the 1976 Tang Shan Earthquake. Fang migrated to America when she grew up. However, when Fang Deng saw the disastrous 2008 Wen Chuan earthquake on TV, her patriotism led her to immediately return to China as a volunteer to save the victims. Fang's new American identity did not destroy her affection for China. Through the depiction of Fang's decision, the movie is sending a message to the audience that to be Chinese means to demonstrate love and commitment to China no matter where you go.

The Chinese Dream (Great Rejuvenation of the Chinese Nation)

While the **Chinese Dream** is not clearly defined, it has nonetheless become a popular slogan used by the government to project its vision. In the speeches, the elite politicians make claims such as "we must make persistent efforts . . . and strive to achieve the Chinese Dream of great rejuvenation of the Chinese nation." What it means here is far from clear. However, it suggests that all Chinese have one dream, the dream of bringing the past glories back. Development is the means to achieve the end (the Chinese dream). This identity is made by the elite to support the dominant national identity **Developing**.

Social Divide

In the elite discourse, the rural-urban division is recognized as the most acute type of social division. However in the mass discourse, social division is defined by class instead of region.

In speeches and newspaper articles, **Social Divide** does not appear as often as in the mass discourse. However, the developmental gap between the urban and the rural areas seems to be growing. To be rural is seen as "primitive," "backward," "poor," and "closed." In the history textbooks, the texts discussed the changes in Chinese material life and custom in the 20th century. Rural areas were identified as "places remaining stubbornly faithful to tradition." Therefore, the Chinese elites identify traditional customs or practice as the root cause of rural backwardness. However, the elites are confident that the problems caused by the rural-urban divide are not impossible to be resolved. This is because the younger generations of the rural population are thought to be better educated and more liberal minded. To give an example, "[The younger generations] are better educated than the older generation. They are much more aware of their legal rights and have a stronger sense of law. They are also more motivated to express their own views."[16]

However in the mass discourse, it is clear that the division between the privileged and the commoners is viewed as more prominent and hence, there is a greater concern for the masses. In the novel *Under the Hawthorn Tree,* the protagonist Jingqiu was sent to a village near her hometown to help write textbooks before her graduation. The hostess liked her so much that she wanted Jingqiu to marry her son. The hostess narrated her personal experience of how her family was persecuted during the era of land reforms, leaving her little choice but to marry the son of the village head. It turned out that her marriage to a privileged person had protected her. Her marriage had given her a better life.

The wealthy and the privileged in China are those who hold bureaucratic positions. Another example to illustrate this social divide is extracted from the newspaper: "The civil servants are the citizens of the first class; those who work in state enterprises are the second class citizens; and those who work in private enterprises are the third class citizens ... [State enterprises] can be further divided into those that receive financial funding from government, and those that are self-sustaining.[17]

Insecure

This identity appears frequently in the mass discourse. People are insecure because they are afraid the state does not protect their rights. Some fundamental problems in China's current social security system are the lack of money to fund pensioners and the poorly enforced law on migrant workers' rights. An interesting point to note is that, in the elite discourse, this identity appears only in history textbooks, and is absent from speeches and editorials. It suggests that the elites regard a "new" China under the leadership of the CCP as having a good capacity to protect its people.

However, this identity resonates well among the masses. For example, the notion of *"rennai* (bear with it)" emerges frequently in the mass discourse. The Chinese strongly believe in the principle of endurance and they often deliberately hold back from giving any active response or taking public action.[18] A sense of powerlessness is embedded in the popular culture. To give an example from one letter to the editor: "Although [the] ordinary folks have so many gripes about the inflation that [people's] tolerance has already reached the limit, [people] have to face the reality that the prices will keep rising. . .. What else can the low-income groups do except to tolerate again and again?"[19] From these quotes, we are able to infer that the Chinese do not suffer from false consciousness. They kept silent because they can do nothing about it. Ordinary Chinese take the "bear-with-it" attitude to overcome the insecurity that they are confronted with daily.

Persevering/Working Hard

Persevering and **Working Hard** are two traditional virtues in China. They are perceived to be the key to success at both the individual and national levels. This can be seen in the novels and movies. Du Lala, the main character from *A Story of Lala's Promotion*, set herself the goal to be a regional manager when she joined the company, and worked diligently toward the goal with energy and commitment. She did not receive the promotion or reward she was entitled to after her completion of a large project. Nonetheless, she continued to make steady efforts and dedicated herself to her career in the company. Similarly, Jingqiu in the book *Under the Hawthorn Tree* also displayed conscientiousness and perseverance to remain in the city despite bureaucratic obstructions.

In the speeches and the textbooks, hardworking is framed as a positive national identity. "Hardworking enables China to thrive" is a recurring theme in the elite discourse. In Chinese, the proverb *jianding buyi* (determined to complete the task) is a synonym for the idiom *jianchi buxie*, which means perseverance.[20] "We must unswervingly push forward . . ."[21] and "We must firmly seize . . ."[22] are some of the phrases that are frequently used in the political speeches.

Reciprocal Courtesy

Reciprocal courtesy or "courtesy demands reciprocity" (*lishang wanglai*) literally means that well-mannered people return favors and kindness. Reciprocity is considered necessary for building friendship. In today's context, reciprocal courtesy is not just a traditional Chinese virtue but also loaded with political and social implications. "Courtesy demands reciprocity" sets the basic rules for all forms of interpersonal interaction. To the Chinese masses, reciprocal courtesy is an art that an ambitious person must acquire. However, the practice of reciprocal courtesy has led to financial problems for many Chinese. One newspaper article reports that: ". . . the Enshi Tujia and Miao Autonomous Prefecture in Southwest Hubei Province are two of the most underdeveloped areas. The per capita net income of farmers there is less than 3000 yuan (c. $500). In recent years, the societal trend of 'courtesy' (*renqing*)[23] has become increasingly prominent. As a result, farmers are economically over-burdened."[24]

Individualism

Individualism emerges only in the mass discourse. In these texts, individual desires are highly respected. To quote from the newspaper: "Individuals should be responsible to their own fate . . . personal struggles are meaningful."[25] Similarly, *A Story of Lala's Promotion* reflects an individual's desire to break away from state control. Individualism is highly celebrated in that novel. *Han Han's* novel *1988: I Want to Talk to the World* is probably the best description of Chinese desire for individualism.[26] Thus, individualism is not merely an emerging ideology, but is also a weapon of the masses against state control.

The United States

In the elite discourses, the United States is referred more specifically as the US government. The United States is presented as a hegemonic power in a negative light. Conversely, fewer political implications are attached to this identity in the mass discourses. In fact, among all the developed countries around the world, the United States was the only one that had been constantly identified across all the texts, and most of the time, with positive evaluation.

Japan the Aggressor

The negative conception of Japan as an aggressor appears only in textbooks. For the Chinese today in general, Japan continues to be associated with this notion and images. The "Japanese devils"[27] remain deeply embedded in people's memories. The history textbooks use adjectives such as "brutal," "beyond ordinary evil," and "inhumane" to characterize the crimes the Japanese military had committed in China during WWII.

Japan the Economic Model

Japan as a post-WWII economic model for the Asian countries is well recognized by the Chinese. A chapter in the history textbooks describes the post-WWII economic development in Japan as the "economic miracle." In 1978, during Deng Xiao Ping's visit to Japan, he commented that "speed is development" after he took the bullet train *Shinkansen*.[28] Similarly, the novel *A Story of Lala's Promotion* portrays the Japanese enterprises as productive, diligent, and united. However, the institutional memories of the war crimes committed by the Japanese military remained salient and strong for the Chinese. Hence, Japan as an aggressor becomes a dominant identity whereas Japan as an economic model is less pronounced.

The West

The West refers to people's general understanding of a wide range of characters associated with the Western countries. In the elites' discourse, the West is used as a body of comparison. The Chinese masses have a more nuanced interpretation of this identity. For example, Western fashion is regarded by many young Chinese as being trendy and having good taste. Possession of imported Western technologies or working in a Western enterprise is equated with money and high social status.

III. Chinese Identity Topography

Table 4.2 is a topographic table of the aggregated identities. The identities recovered from each text are aggregated within a particular genre and their relative frequencies noted. In this process, the dominant identities present in each genre are revealed, but at the same time, the more sporadic and isolated identities are dropped. The identities presented across five genres are consolidated, where twenty-one identities remained. The identities are clustered into five categories, which are as follows: **Developing, Economic Identities, Political Identities, Social-Cultural Identities,** and **Significant External Other.**

Developing

Progressing and **Catching Up** are grouped as **Developing**. The term **Developing** best captures the essence of China's predominant identity for both the elites and the masses. Developing reflects a state of mind the majority of Chinese possess, and it can be interpreted as a state of moving forward. Departure from poverty, backwardness, and the past preoccupies the mind of the Chinese. In short, this category of identities can be seen as the essential Self to the Chinese that it directs the way Chinese people live, think, and judge.

Within this category, there are nuanced differences between each identity. For example, Progressing means something more visible and concrete to the Chinese masses than Catching Up. Catching Up, unlike Progressing, contains a set of meanings that are less concrete. Progressing means to improve by itself, but Catching Up gives a sense of comparison. Interestingly, however, catching up with whom or with what is not clear in the texts. Progressing in general

Table 4.2 **Chinese Identity Topography**

	Speeches	Textbooks	Newspapers (Editorials)	Newspapers (Op-eds)	Novels	Movies
Developing (Essential Self)						
Progressing	+++++	+++++	+++	\\	+\	+
Catching up	++	++++	+	+	\	\
Economic identities						
Pragmatic	+++	++	\\	\\	+	+\
Materialistic		−	−		~	− −
Marketizing	+	++	+	+\	\	~
Political identities						
Corrupt		−	−	−	− −	− −
Bureaucratic		\		−	−	\−
Socialist with Chinese Characteristics	+	++	++		−	\
Patriotic	++	++				+
The Chinese dream	+	+	+		\	
Social-Cultural identities						
Socially divided	\	−	−	− −	− −	− − −
Insecure		−	−	− −	− \	\\
Persevering	++	+++	+			++
Mutually courteous			~		\ −	−
Individualistic				~	−	− −
Hardworking	+	+		++	+	+
Significant external other						
United States	−		\	\	+	\
Japan (aggressor)	− −					−
Japan (economic model)	\				+	
The West		\\	~	~	+	

implies economic development, reforms, and foreign investment. To the elites, those identities are clearly positive. However, to the masses, interpretation of Progressing is mixed. This is because economic reforms and foreign investments have produced environmental pollution and other negative externalities which are deemed as undesirable to the masses. In the movie *Let the Bullets Fly*, for instance, the "steam train," which is a symbol of progress, has been portrayed as a mockery of blind faith in Western modernity. Since the positive perception of this identity in movies outweighs the negative perception as a whole, the one symbol I put in the table of topography is a positive sign. However, it is important to note that there are negative instances of this identity in the mass discourse.

Economic Identities

Materialistic, **Pragmatic**, and **Marketizing** are grouped into this category. The economic identities characterize economic activities and people's attitude toward economic development. With China's market becoming increasingly capitalistic, people are starting to associate economic growth with materialism and pragmatism.

Political Identities

Corrupt, **Bureaucratic**, **Socialist with Chinese Characteristics**, **Patriotic**, and **The Chinese Dream** are grouped as the Political Identities. There is a clear mass-elite division in terms of political identification. Socialism with Chinese Characteristics, Patriotic, and The Chinese Dream are closely associated with the Chinese Communist Party (CCP) and are found almost exclusively in the elite identity discourse. They appeared as a positive recurring theme, or formula in the elite texts, especially in the speeches. On the contrary, Corruption and Bureaucracy-Oriented Consciousness represent the average Chinese perception of the political elites as well as the political culture in the society.

Sociocultural Identities

This category consists of quite a few important identities—**Socially Divided**, **Insecure**, **Persevering**, **Mutually Courteous**, **Individualistic**, and **Hardworking**. These identities are important because they reflect the everyday social reality—how Chinese people see China and themselves. In this category, there are also clear discrepancies between the elites' identities and the masses' common sense. The discrepancies show that the elites are trying to represent China in a way with which the masses clearly disagree.

Significant External Other

This category includes the "Others" that China deems as the most crucial to its international relations. Three of these categories are represented as countries—the United States represents one category, and Japan (as an aggressor and as an economic model) represents two categories. Apart from that, the concept of **The West** is a discursive formation of a Western population, Western ideas, and Western countries; a symbol of **Other** that is distinctively different from the Chinese **Self**. It is important to note that there are two "Japans," both appearing as Significant Others in the history textbooks: Japan as an aggressor and Japan as an economic model.

The Predominant Identity Discourse

The predominant Chinese national identity of 2010 is **Developing**. This is an agreement between the elites and masses. It is a predominant identity because it has the highest frequency of occurrence among the texts we have selected. It is important because it also influences Chinese perception on other issues. The precise content of this identity varies across different texts. In the mass texts, **Developing** is largely interpreted as progressing toward a more modernized economy. In the elite texts, however, **Developing** implies a very broad yet ambivalent vision of what China hopes to become.

As mentioned above, **Developing** is a consolidated identity. It implies that China is changing constantly in almost all arenas. Under this category there are two sub-identities: **Progress** and **Catching Up**. The Chinese elites perceive progress and catching up as positive national identities. However, the elites did not specify what they meant by "progress" and "catching up"; nor did they clarify why progress and catching up are necessary. There are unanswered questions such as "What exactly is progress?" and "With whom are we catching up?" We believe that the Chinese government has not articulated a concrete vision for China's future development. Hence, there is room for the masses to interpret and act according to their own understandings of what it means to be **Developing**. It is an open-ended question. This ambiguity could be possibly explained by the ambiguous nature of the language used in the political speeches. Another explanation could be that the Chinese government is still in search of a developmental path.

However, the mass interpretation of development is different from the elites' interpretation. As mentioned above, the mass texts render the meaning of **Developing** through daily experiences. To the masses, **Developing** specifically means the improvement of living standard. Development at the expense of the environment is thus viewed as an undesirable outcome. In some letters to the editor that we have read, people have expressed anxiety about worsening environmental pollution, deforestation, and other negative outcomes that result from unsustainable economic policies. Therefore the central identity feature of China today is the promotion of **Developing** by the elites and a troubled, ambiguous acceptance by the masses.

The mass texts also question the neoliberal capitalist system because not every individual has benefited equally from neoliberal economic policies that have transformed China from a command economy to a free market economy. The newly introduced capitalist economic model emphasizes openness and free market competition, often at the expense of social equality. Hence, the biggest elite-mass disagreement lies in the acknowledgment of the contingency of social division. Drawing reference from the topographic table, it is clear that the masses hold a much stronger negative view toward social division. People's dissatisfaction with social divisiveness may develop into a viable counter-discourse. Here, we label it as **Egalitarianism**. This counter-discourse challenges neoliberal economic policies because the implementation of those policies has eroded social equality. For example, people with more political and social connections have greater access to resources while the less privileged groups remained poor and disconnected. It is thus not surprising that people who have not benefited or benefited less from China's economic liberalization were less satisfied. However, we believe that **Egalitarianism** has yet to emerge as a meaningful challenger to the predominant identity, **Developing**, because the masses generally agree that economic development directed by the government is necessary to improve the standard of living. So the mass texts, despite demonstrating concern with widening social divisions, are supportive of economic and social development.

There are other obvious differences between elite and mass discourses in other identity categories. The most obvious ones are in terms of the **Political Identities** and the **Sociocultural Identities**. The ruling party (CCP) has constructed a set of political identities to facilitate governance. These unique political identities, or what we call the "CCP formula," has constantly appeared in speeches and history textbooks. Most of the time, these identities do not resonate among the masses. The CCP formula seldom appears in the mass texts, which could mean that the masses cannot be bothered with CCP propaganda or simply see it as absurd. In particular, the masses saw internal contradictions within these discourses. In particular, holding on to socialism contradicts with elites' espousal of marketization and capitalism. This is because the same communist ideology that advocates social equality conflicts with the capitalist ideology of profit-making and market competition. More importantly, the one-party system is believed by the masses to be responsible for rampant corruption, bureaucratic inefficiencies, and social division.

In the Chinese national discourse of 2010, **The West** is a significant external Other. The term **The West** appears rather frequently in the elite discourse, especially in the history textbooks. The elite discourse consistently compares China with the West to highlight the backwardness of pre-Communist China. The history textbooks had treated the "West" as a model for China to catch up with and emulate in order to justify the nationalist objective of self-strengthening. China had been humiliated by the Western imperialist powers for more than a century. Hence, the Chinese masses have mostly internalized the mentality of being "left behind by the West."

However, in the elite discourse today, the portrayal of **The West** has changed from "a model to emulate" to "a point of reference for economic development and social progression." In the elite discourse, this identity has mixed meanings. In both political speeches as well as in the newspapers, Chinese economic achievements in 2010 are often compared with the economic achievements made by Western countries such as the United States and the United Kingdom in the same year. On the other hand, the "West" is sometimes presented as a negative and undesirable identity. One newspaper article titled "To Recover from Economic Recession, Western Countries Should Rethink Consumerism" and published in *People's Daily* suggests that the economic and social problems in those countries are caused not only by the government's misguiding policies, but also by the influence of the culture. Hedonism and consumerism are two major problems perceived in Western culture. This reiterates that the Chinese elites are anti-materialist, because materialism undermines the sustainability of economic development. Inferring from those texts, the Chinese elites in many ways are using **The West** as political rhetoric to criticize the downsides of the developmental trajectory in the Western countries.

Conclusion

The Chinese national identity discourse reveals a complex and ambivalent relationship to Western neoliberal democratic hegemony. On one hand, elite discourse demonstrates strong support for some aspects of neoliberalism. Economically, the Chinese elites have acknowledged the positive effects brought by marketization, free trade, and market forces in bolstering economic growth. On the other hand, the elite discourse continues to emphasize the importance for China to remain "socialist" and resist democracy. State intervention remains crucial for China's grand economic projects. To a large extent, "Socialism with Chinese characteristics" legitimizes state intervention and state ownership.

Furthermore, the socialist component in the political identities clearly contradicts liberal democracy.

In the mass texts, democracy appeared only occasionally in the newspapers. In the newspaper article, democracy appeared as "aspirational," "law," and "checks and balances." Since each of them has only one or two counts in total, we did not include this identity in our topographic table. However, despite of the low counts, we think it is still important to take note of how Chinese understand democracy and relate themselves to it. Here is an example of how democracy is presented in the selected text. The article titled *Spiritual Crisis Brings Cultural Disciplines* says: "Absolute power is doomed to corrupt . . . Democracy should not be copied from other countries, but to be democratic the state power has to be checked and balanced. This is a universal rule. To avoid absolute power, we should limit the power of the executive body."[29] This newspaper article suggests that China's one-party system tends to undermine the rule of law and checks and balances, which are constitutive of liberal democracy. Hence, the identity "democracy" is largely aspirational in China, if it appears at all.

Furthermore, the "West" appears often as an undifferentiated, monolithic identity in the elite discourse. This is because **The West** is treated as a point of reference by the Chinese elites to highlight both Chinese achievements and the downsides of Western ideas such as materialism.

Notes

1. See an introduction for the column on People's Daily's official website: http://opinion.people.com.cn/GB/35560/3457110.html (accessed April 27, 2013).
2. Table 4.1 combines two sets of coding that we obtained separately.
3. Editorials, "Jiakuai Cong Jiaoyu Daguo Xiang Jiaoyu Qiangguo Maijin" (From Ancient Civilization to Advanced Civilization), *People's Daily*, July 15, 2010.
4. Ibid. "A big developing country with 1.3 billion population has realized the century-old dream of basically universalizing the compulsory nine-year education . . . realized the transformation from a country with large population to a country with huge human resources."
5. People's Education Press Textbook Research Centre, *History* (Beijing: People's Education Press, 2010).
6. Ibid.
7. Cao Dawei and Zhao Sheyu, *History* (Changsha: Yuelu Press, 2010).
8. It is possible that open criticism of "New China" was too sensitive to be free from censorship.
9. Cao Dawei and Zhao Sheyu, *History*.
10. Qiufeng, "Diyu Wuzhi Zhuyi, Chongzhen Jiaoshi Lunli" (Resist Ignorance and Revive Education Ethics), *People's Daily*, September 9, 2010.
11. Shinian Kanchai, "Toupiao Reqing He Minzhu Suyang Yuanyu Liyi Kaoliang" (Passion of Voting and Economic Consideration of Democracy), *Southern Metropolis Daily*, March 15, 2010.
12. People's Education Press Textbook Research Centre, *History*.
13. Ma Hongman, "Qidai Jianshui Jiangfu de Gongjianzhan" (A Tough Fight toward Tax Reduction), *Southern Metropolis Daily*, September 15, 2010.

14. A Wu, "Nali Shi Maicai, Gengxiangshi Dubo" (Gambling Instead of Buying Vegetables), *Southern Metropolis Daily*, September 15, 2010.

15. Wu Wei, "Hongdou Tang" (The Red-Bean Soup River), *Southern Metropolis Daily*, April 6, 2010.

16. Shinian Kanchai, "Toupiao Reqing He Minzhu Suyang Yuanyu Liyi Kaoliang" (Passion of Voting and Economic Consideration of Democracy), *Southern Metropolis Daily*, March 15, 2010.

17. Cao Lei, "Tuixiujin Zhengce Ying Jinkuai Chongxin Xipai" (Reallocation of Pension), *Southern Metropolis Daily*, March 15, 2010.

18. "As a consumer in China, you need to simply trust everything and tolerate everything. Since you've chosen to buy it, don't regret it and swallow the bitterness. . . . his life is a life against counterfeits, not that the ordinary can imitate. . . . as long as you can afford it, don't bother. To complain, to negotiate, to field a lawsuit, to make a claim, the road to protect and defend rights is never plain. Opportunity cost will be too great. It's just not a big deal. 'Who told you to be so unfortunately born in China?'" You Youfang, "Yi Er San Yi Wu, Yao Da Xiaosongshu" (One Two Three One Five, Beat the Little Squirrel), *Southern Metropolis Daily*, March 15, 2010.

19. Wei Junxing, "Baixing Ruhe Renshou Genggao De Wujia Shangzhanglv?" (How Do the Masses Tolerate the Rising Prices?), *Southern Metropolis Daily*, March 15, 2010.

20. Xue Xiaoping, *Chinese Idiom Dictionary* (Xian: Shanxi People's Education Press, 2009).

21. Wen Jiabao, "The Speech by Premier Wen at the Celebrating Reception of the 61th Anniversary of the People's Republic of China," (Beijing, September 30, 2010), http://news.xinhuanet.com/2010-09/30/c_12624413.htm (accessed April 27, 2013).

22. Ibid.

23. *Renqing*, referring to a moral obligation to maintain personal relationship, is a concept closely related to *Guanxi*, which describes the dynamic in a personalized network of influence.

24. Song Wen, "Renqingfeng Gua Qiong Le Shanliren" (The More Popular the Culture of *Renqing*, the Poorer the Villagers), *People's Daily*, June 18, 2010.

25. Mu Mao, "Gongshi Polie, Shehui Caihui Bei Silie" (A Broken Consensus Leads to a Torn Society), *Southern Metropolis Daily*, April 15, 2010.

26. ". . . I thought I was a seed, being brought up and down by the seasonal wind. But I finally realize that I am not a seed. I am a plant with roots. As for what kind of plant I am, I cannot see myself. I have to ask other plants. As for why I keep changing places, because I thought I was rooted in the land; indeed I was rooted in the quicksand. Years after years, I have been drifted by the quicksand I rooted in. He did not swamp me. He just reminds me now and then, you don't have another choice, or you will be blown away by the wind. My life then shuffled. My heady times have passed. I was drifted to east and then west. I was even worse than when I was a seed.

> A week ago, I told the quicksand, let the wind blow me away.
> The quicksand said, you would die immediately with no roots.
> I said, I have saved enough water. I can sustain for a while.
> The quicksand said, but the wind would keep you in the air. You will be dehydrated.
> I said, I still can have rain.
> The quicksand said, rain will pour down to the land and form a pond. When it's in the air, it's merely a decoration.
> I said, then I will fall into the pond.
> The quicksand said, then you are drowned.
> I said, let me try.
> The quicksand said, I drift you to the dune and you'll find out that many plants like you are relying on us.
> I said, drift me higher. Let me have a look at all the plants in the world; to see whether we are all living in the same way.
> The quicksand said, how dare you resist me! I will swamp you.
> I said, let the wind blow me away.

I resolutely struggle upward, not that hard indeed. I left the quicksand and take a look down. Fuck. I was not a plant. I am an animal. That son of bitch cheated me for more than 20 years! As an animal with feet, I can finally decide my own direction. I look back at the quicksand; he said, go, don't tell other plants that they are animals." Han Han, *1988: I Want to Talk to the World* (Beijing: International Culture Press Ltd., 2010), pp. 21–22.

27. Cao Dawei and Zhao Sheyu, *History*.
28. Ibid.
29. "Du Weiming: Jingshen Weiji Dailai Wenhua Zijue" (Du Weiming: Spiritual Crisis Brings Cultural Disciplines), *Southern Metropolis Daily*, September 19, 2010.

Sources

Speeches

Jiabao, Wen, "Premier Wen's Keynote Speech at 2010 Shanghai Expo Summit Forum" (温家宝总理在2010年上海世博会高峰论坛上的讲话) (Shanghai, July 22, 2010). Retrieved on July 22, 2013 from http://www.gov.cn/ldhd/2010-10/31/content_1734483 .htm.

Jiaobao, Wen, "The Speech by Premier Wen at the Celebrating Reception of the 61th Anniversary of the People's Republic of China" (国务院总理温家宝在庆祝中华人民共和国成立六十一周年招待会上的讲话) (Beijing, September 30, 2010). Retrieved on April 27, 2013 from http://news.xinhuanet.com/2010-09/30/c 12624413.htm.

Jiaobao, Wen, "Strong Power Must Firstly Strengthen Its Education" (强国必强教) (Beijing, April 27, 2010). Retrieved on April 27, 2013 from http://www.china.com.cn/policy/txt/ 2010-09/01/content_20837265.htm.

Newspapers

According to the data released by World Association of Newspapers (WAN-IFRA), the top-paid papers in China ranked by circulation are as follows:

Title	Publisher	Circulation (million)
1. *Cankao (Reference) News*	Xinhua News	3.136
2. *People's Daily*	People's Daily News	2.381
3. *Southern Metropolis Daily*	South Media Group	1.91

Source: people.com, http://media.people.com.cn/n/2012/1023/c40628–19354980. html (accessed April 27, 2013).

Textbooks

Dawei, Cao and Zhao Sheyu, eds., *History I* (Changsha: Yuelu Press, 2010).

People's Education Press Textbook Research Centre, *History* (Beijing: People's Education Press, 2010).

Novels

Title	Issue Date	Author	Readers Counted by Douban.com	Rank by Amazon.cn	Remarks
1988: 我想和这个世界谈谈 (*1988: I Want To Talk to the World*)	Sept. 10, 2010	韩寒 Han Han	111,168	1	
杜拉拉升职记 (*A Story of Lala's Promotion*)	Sept. 7, 2010	李可 Li Ke	100,220	6	Both the film and TV drama based on the novel were released in 2010
山楂树之恋 (*Under the Hawthorn Tree*)	Sept. 7, 2010	艾米 Ai Mi	46,038	7	The film based on the novel was released in 2010

Movies

Release Date	Name	Screening Sessions	Audiences (million)	Box Office (million yuan)	Rank
July 22, 2010	*Aftershock*	372,840	18.17	673.32	1
Dec. 16, 2010	*Let the Bullets Fly*	210,190	12.72	659.28	2

Source: China Film Distribution and Exhibition Association, *The Report of China Film Market*.

5

Whither La France?

French National Identity in 2010

BENJAMIN CHAN JIAN MING AND REBECCA OH

Introduction

France's predominant discourse of national identity is Republican and its two challenger discourses are social democratic and declinist. Republican France is free, egalitarian, just, secular, democratic, constitutional, cultured, and civilized. The Republican discourse is primarily an elite discourse. With the affirmation of Republican value categories and the absence of mass derogation, there is some weak evidence of an elite-mass consensus. This discourse identifies with Western hegemony and positions France as civilized and culturally superior, relative to other non-Western states.

The social democratic discourse reflects a mass French negative attitude toward work and is critical of liberal economic policies and liberalizing reforms. Urban life and work are negatively contrasted to rural France and leisure. A second challenger is the declinist discourse, which suggests France is old and past its economic and political prime. According to this discourse, France is insecure and threatened by significant external others such as Brazil, Russia, India, China, and South Africa (BRICS). Instead of striving to be competitive and relevant, the declinist discourse is one that is resigned and pessimistic about France's future and retreats to a glorious past that romanticizes rural France. We posit that the challenger social democratic or declinist discourses, if empowered by the state, would alter, but not replace, the predominant discourse of Republican France. Republican values would still remain, but they would be reinterpreted according to the empowered mass challenger discourses. If these mass challenger discourses are empowered, France's position at the core of Western hegemony could be weakened.

I. Text Selection

The texts sampled for the discourse analysis were selected according to the sizes of their audiences. The political speeches, newspaper op-eds and letters to the editor, high school history textbooks, best-selling novels, and best-attended movies reflect both elite and mass discourses of French national identity. Political speeches and high school history textbooks reflect a largely elite discourse of national identity on the one end of the elite-mass continuum, while letters to the editor, novels, and movies reflect the mass discourse on the other end. Two political speeches by President Nicolas Sarkozy were sampled: the first was a New Year's Day address and the second was a speech made on Bastille Day (French National Day). The newspapers selected were *Le Figaro* and *Le Monde*, the top two of France's most widely circulated daily national newspapers. *Le Figaro* is a right-leaning newspaper, while *Le Monde* leans left. The editorial and letters-to-the-editor sections from the 15th of each month were sampled; in the case of an absent newspaper circulation on the 15th, those of the 16th would then be selected. Two of the most common high school history textbooks published by Hachette Technique and Nathan Technique were selected. Two best-selling local novels were selected, *Les Écureuils de Central Park sont tristes le Lundi* (*The Central Park Squirrels Are Sad on Mondays*) by Katherine Pancol and *La Carte et le Territoire* (*The Map and the Territory*) by Michel Houellebecq. The list of the best-selling novels was sourced from the website of *L'Express*, a French weekly newsmagazine. Two movies with the best box-office showing in 2010 were selected, according to information retrieved from Cinefeed France, which keeps a systematic annual record of box offices in France. The movies are *Camping 2* and *Les Petits Mouchoirs* (*Little White Lies*).

II. Identity Categories

Republican

Republican refers to an indivisible set of values that constitute the secular, democratic French Republic (Table 5.1). These fundamental values are reflected in the French motto Liberty, Equality, and Fraternity (*Liberté, Egalité, Fraternité*). France is commonly referred to as "la République" or the Republic, which heralds to its historical break with a monarchical past and the abolition of aristocratic privileges. A quote from one of the history textbooks explicitly links the identity category of Republican with secularism: "Throughout the 20th century, the French progressively accepted secularism. The French identity is founded on this Republican value even today" (Fugler et al. 2010). Another quote from one of the newspapers associates Republican values with democracy and diversity: "that was why I was raised in the admiration of France, its Republican values, of its democracy that respects diversity without harming the unitary whole" (*Le Figaro*).

Modern

Modern as an identity category refers more to the idea of "contemporary" than "modernity." Isolation and loneliness have been employed in the speeches to describe the "modern society of France," and provide a foil for fraternity, another republican value, as an aspirational ideal, as quoted from one of the speeches: "with isolation and loneliness so prevalent in our modern society, I wish that 2010 would be the year where we will give a beautiful sense to the word fraternity that is inscribed in our republican motto" (Sarkozy, Vœux 2010 de Nicolas Sarkozy—Président de la République 2009).

Secular

Secular refers to the separation between the church and state as well as a clear division between the public and private spheres, which is a distinctive feature of the republican discourse of French national identity. This is exemplified in this quote where "the founders of the 3rd Republic wanted a secular society, this is to say freed from the influence of religion. The struggles of the opposition between republicans and Catholics dominate the political life from 1880 to 1914" (Fugler et al. 2010). Hence, the negative historical other is clearly the Catholic Church that the Republican discourse explicitly rejects. This point is further supported by another quote from one of the history textbooks that describes the relationship between the Republicans and the Catholics: "when the Republicans permanently came to power in 1880, they fought against the influence of the Catholic Church, notably in the school. By the separation of church and state, the Republic implements secularism that guarantees the free practice of all religions" (Fugler et al. 2010).

Civilized

The identity category of civilized refers to the French perception that France belongs to a stage of social, moral, and cultural development that is high and superior in some respects to other societies. "Olga was one of these Russians who had learnt to admire a certain image of France: gallantry, gastronomy, literature and so on—and were henceforth regularly disappointed to find out that her real country

Table 5.1 **Identity Category Raw Counts**

Category	Total	Speeches	Newspapers (Op-eds)	Newspapers (Letters)	Textbooks	Movies	Novels
Social conflict (rebellious, resistance)	54	0	11	1	40	2	0
Catholic/Christian	19	0	4	0	10	0	5
Secular	19	0	8	1	10	0	1
Britain/Anglo-Saxon	16	0	0	0	0	1	15
Pension/aging/welfare state	15	0	8	0	6	1	0
America	11	0	0	0	0	3	8
Anti-work	10	0	3	0	4	2	1
BRICS*	10	0	3	2	0	0	5
Egalitarian	10	1	9	0	0	0	0
Republican	10	1	7	2	0	0	0
Colonial master (historical)	9	3	6	0	0	0	0
Anticapitalist	8	0	1	0	0	0	7
Meritocratic/elitist	8	0	5	0	0	0	3
Africa as a friend of France	7	6	1	0	0	0	0
Civilized	7	0	7	0	0	0	0
Cultural center	7	1	3	0	0	0	3
European	7	1	5	0	0	0	1
Western	7	0	5	0	0	0	2
Freedom/liberty	6	1	3	0	2	0	0
Rule of law	6	0	5	0	0	0	1
Justice	6	1	3	0	0	0	2
Old literary	6	0	3	3	0	0	0
Rural, pastoral	6	0	0	0	0	2	4
Democratic	5	0	5	0	0	0	0
Neurotic, overworked urban	5	0	0	0	0	2	3
Patriarchal	5	0	1	0	4	0	0
France as German (external other)	4	0	1	3	0	0	0
Decline	3	0	3	0	0	0	0

(*Continued*)

Table 5.1 **(Continued)**

Category	Total	Speeches	Newspapers (Op-eds)	Newspapers (Letters)	Textbooks	Movies	Novels
Modern	3	1	1	0	0	0	1
Postmodern	3	0	2	0	0	0	1
Respects diversity	3	0	3	0	0	0	0
Universal/humanist	3	0	3	0	0	0	0
Total	**298**	**16**	**118**	**12**	**76**	**13**	**63**

* BRICS stands for the emerging economic powers Brazil, Russia, India, China, and South Africa.

corresponded so poorly to their expectations" (Houellebecq 2010). "Civilized" further connotes the significance of France as a cultural center, with literature, ideas, gastronomy, and other cultural heritage that other societies would benefit from having more of. According to Sarkozy "An unprecedented plan of investment allows us to accomplish the digital revolution, granting high speed (internet) to all, digitizing our books so that our language, our culture can continue to spread" (Sarkozy, Vœux 2010 de Nicolas Sarkozy—Président de la République 2009).

Old

Old refers to a France that is aging, past its prime, and threatened by a process of deculturation. "The debate on national identity reveals the indifference of numerous high officials towards the process of deculturation that is affecting this old literary country" (*Le Figaro*, January 15, 2010). Another quote evidenced this point, highlighting also the nostalgia that often accompanies France's identification of itself as old: "But it is wrong to classify Jean-Louis Curtis as a reactionary; he is just a good and slightly sad author, convinced that society cannot really change in one way or another. [. . .] In you also I feel this sort of nostalgia, but this time it is a nostalgia of the modern world, of the time when France was an industrial country, am I right?" (Houellebecq 2010).

Capitalist

The neoliberal capitalist France found in the newspapers and novels was consistently criticized. Capitalism, based on a free market that emphasizes profit-making and the role of private enterprises, is clearly perceived to be vulgar and threatening to the French: "In a more general manner we lived in a period that was ideologically strange, where everyone in Western Europe seemed to be convinced that capitalism is bad, and even sentenced it to a premature death"

(Houellebecq 2010). Capitalism also besmirches the honor of work: "before capitalism, scientific research and technical progress, people worked hard, really hard, without being motivated by profit, but by something else which is vaguer to the modern man: the love of God, in the case of monks, or more simply the honor of his function" (Houellebecq 2010).

Attitude toward Work

There is a consensus across almost all the genres, except elite speeches, on the negative French attitude toward work. In the first film, *Camping 2*, the main character, Jean Pierre, was driven by his work to become so neurotic that it affected his relationship and was made to take a break or timeout in rural France at a camping ground near the beach. A quote from one of the newspapers highlights the negative French attitude toward work: "as evidenced by our 35 hours (work week) as much as our surrealist debates on these pensions that we want to receive but not finance, we entered in a civilization of the decline of work" (*Le Figaro*, April 15). The historical idea of work for the French is tied to the experience of labor exploitation during its period of industrialization. Work has been traditionally associated with the loss of liberty, as quoted from the textbooks: "in a century and a half (150 years), the laborers work in factories that are increasingly bigger. They gradually lose a large part of their autonomy in the exercise of their trade" (Aujas et al. 2010). A quote from one of the novels highlights the place of work as central in the shared identity of a "Western man": "What defines a man? What's the question you first ask a man, when you want to find out about him? In some societies, you first ask him if he's married, if he has children; in our society, we first ask what his profession is. It's his place in the productive process and not his status as reproducer that above all defines Western man" (Houellebecq 2010).

Pastoral Rural, Neurotic Urban

This identity category refers to the affective divide observed between the idyllic pastoral rural and an overworked and neurotic urban. Urban France is portrayed to be a stressful work center, while rural France is depicted as bucolic and harmonious. This identity category surfaces particularly in the novels and the movies. In both of the films, there are central characters who are driven to neurosis by their urban lives, Jean Pierre in *Camping 2* and Max in *Little White Lies*, the latter being so uptight and neurotic that he went into fits of rage over the weasels in the country house, smashing his entire bedroom wall with an axe and had uncontrollable outbursts at his godson, who was playing hide-and-seek. Rural France is portrayed to be bucolic and harmonious while "in Paris the atmosphere is saturated with information. Whether you like it or not, you see the headlines in the kiosks, you hear conversations in the supermarket queues. When he went to the Creuse for his grandmother's funeral, he'd realized that the atmospheric density of information diminished considerably the further you got away from the capital; and that, more generally, human affairs lost their importance, and gradually everything disappeared except plants" (Houellebecq 2010).

Social Conflict (Rebellious, Resistance)

Resistance/confrontational is an identity category that enjoys a consensus across the genres of texts. As understood from the history textbooks, engaging in a form of resistance and holding demonstrations are characteristic French modes of existence and political expression. From the French Revolution, where the people rebelled against the monarchy, to the industrialized period, where they fought for their labor rights and organized themselves through unions, to the fight to liberate France from a negative "unfree" historical other, the Vichy Regime, resistance/confrontation as an identity category has been an integral part of French identity. The history textbooks are replete with examples of French struggling for their rights to be recognized as humans with dignity: "The victory of 3000 workers affirms that the solidarity of millions of workers that labor/struggle in France will be right in all the resistances." In addition, "to obtain better conditions of work 12 000 spontaneous strikes broke out in May–June 1936." These strikes are described to be "the times of a moral awakening and the expression of a reconquered dignity" (Aujas et al. 2010).

Meritocratic

Meritocratic as an identity category refers to France as a country that rewards ability and talent rather than nobility or wealth. There is a clear affiliation to the other identity categories clustered as Republican. This affiliation can be inferred from the following quotes: "but it is not the social composition that worries the leaders of these establishments: they say they fear a lowering of the rigor of competitive exams in the name of a positive discrimination that dares not say its name" (*Le Figaro*, January 15, 2010); "fundamentally, the Republican meritocracy will only be pursued by secularizing a Christian ideal" (*Le Figaro*, April 15, 2010).

Europe

Europe as an identity category of France refers to France identifying itself with a supranational entity that is based on a shared history and common socioeconomic challenges. As Sarkozy observed, with reference to a common significant other, Africa, "We others, French and Europeans, know henceforth that it is with Africa, the whole of Africa that we must find common solutions to common challenges" (Sarkozy 2010). As expressed in *Le Figaro*, "It is time that Europe recognizes that she is no longer the beacon of humanity. The future— our future—can be summarized in two key words: adaptation and innovation" (*Le Figaro*, February 15, 2010). To be French is to be European.

Social Welfare State

The rejection of the neoliberal capitalist model and a generally negative portrayal of work in the texts analyzed do not naturally lead to an affirmation of the French social welfare state. The social welfare state is considered a positive identity category in the movies and in the textbooks but is viewed negatively in the newspapers. A pension reform introduced as part of an overall effort by the French government to reduce its budget deficit and to ensure the economic sustainability of its model of social democracy has met with strong societal resistance. A quote from one of the newspapers—"the socialist leaders consider the question of pensions as a true national cause that has implications on the future and the social cohesion of the country" (*Le Figaro*, February 15, 2010)—reveals the tension between the social justice afforded by the social welfare state and the economic sustainability of the model.

Africa

Africa is overrepresented in the speeches because one of the two speeches selected was a French National Day address to the political representatives from the former French colonies. Controlling for that, Africa still remains a significant external other because of its colonial links with France. Africa is a colonial burden on France's conscience, a rising economic partner, and a looming demographic threat. A quote from one of the newspapers stresses the strong sense of French historical responsibility that was shown toward Africa: ". . . its historical responsibility in the sorrows it has caused the Algerian people, the unjustified occupation, the unjust colonial system and the unrelenting repressions that characterized the 132 years of its presence across the Mediterranean Sea . . ." (*Le Monde*). Sarkozy further underlines Africa as a significant other for the French: "50 years ago, General De Gaulle ended the movement which he had initiated sixteen years before at Brazzaville. He opened the way to emancipation, the way of independence to your countries and to your people" (Sarkozy 2010).

Germany

Germany is an important external other for France. While their shared and common interests are acknowledged, it is a relationship that is marked by differences. A quote from one of the newspapers evidenced this point: "So that the European economy could be piloted in a more closely coordinated manner, a French-German compromise must be present" (*Le Monde*). Another example from one of the newspapers highlights the significance of the French-German relationship for Europe: "There must be a compromise because the termination of the Airbus 400M would have terrible consequences by creating a social and industrial shock such that a political tsunami would engulf Europe and would break the French-German couple" (*Le Figaro*).

BRICS

BRICS is recovered as a collective significant external other from the newspapers and the novels. As quoted from one of the newspapers, "More fundamentally, the emergence of a new nonaligned movement is able this time to seriously contest the supremacy of the Occident" (*Le Figaro*); such a group of emerging countries is a competitive external other that is perceived to threaten France's position and influence in the world, on one level, and on another level, to challenge Western dominance and supremacy. Although these powers are recognized by France for their economic potential, they are perceived to be culturally inferior. A quote from the novel *The Map and the Territory* highlights how the nouveau riche of these countries are seen as uncultured: "A Chinese family, a few meters from them, were stuffing themselves with waffles and sausages. Sausages at breakfast had been introduced at the Vault-de-Lugny chateau to satisfy the tastes of a traditional Anglo-Saxon clientele, attached to a protein-rich and fattening breakfast; they were debated during a brief but decisive company meeting; the uncertain and badly formulated tastes of the new Chinese clientele, which were apparently inclined towards sausages, caused them to preserve this choice of food. Other hotels came to the same conclusion, and it was thus that the Martenot sausages, which had been present in the region since 1927, escaped [an otherwise uncertain fate]" (Houellebecq 2010).

Catholic

Catholic France is a clear historical other that is rejected by the predominant discourse of French national identity. Catholicism is seen to have a profound influence on Western culture and tradition, but that influence has waned considerably and is regarded as "a millennial-old spiritual tradition that nobody really understood anymore" (Houellebecq 2010). Catholic France is associated with a patriarchal, "unfree" France, where the Church and monarchy exercise great political control. Further, one of the history textbooks associated Vichy France with Catholicism, describing how "Catholicism was valorized as well as peasants and artisans" during that period (Fugler et al. 2010).

Colonial

Colonial refers to the period of French history where France had a number of colonies. Colonial France is a historical other that is rejected. In the speeches, the colonial period was referred to as unjust. Sarkozy made this point: "Some criticized my proposition to reunite you here today, and to attend tomorrow the parade of 14 July. They believed that it signaled the expression of a colonial nostalgia, or the temptation of France to take ownership of the celebration of your independences. That is an absolute misinterpretation—it is mistaken to think that I could be inspired by such a sentiment of nostalgia towards a period for which I had, more than once, underscored the injustice and errors" (Sarkozy 2010). A quote from one of the French history textbooks suggested that this period of history was a sensitive one: "The construction of the big mosque of Paris was a way to pay tribute to the colonial troops of North Africa who fought in France during the First World War. However, not everyone agreed with this initiative" (Aujas et al. 2010).

Patriarchal

Patriarchy is a third historical other that is rejected by the predominant discourse of national identity. The successful struggle for equal political rights for women after World War II has led to a France with greater gender equality. Together with Catholic and "unfree," patriarchy is associated with Vichy France as a negative other. A quote from one of the history textbooks referring to Vichy France suggests this: "The Vichy Regime suppressed the basic liberties and re-established censorship. It launched the National Revolution and adopted a new motto in conformity with its ideology: Work, Family, and Fatherland. Returning to traditional values, women were made to stay at home, Catholicism was valorized as well as peasants and artisans. Unions were dissolved." Another quote from this textbook emphasized this point. "The history of women in France since the start of the 20th century, known as the 'Belle Époque,' was that of a long quest for emancipation to get out of the state in which laws and customs had placed them . . ." (Fugler et al. 2010).

America

This identity category refers to America as an ambiguous French significant other. American culture is viewed as "cool." This can be seen in a number of instances in the movies such as in *Camping 2*, where the character Jacky Pic has a conversation with his wife expressing the superiority of American goods. Although American culture is much admired, opinions toward its ethics in the economy and political leadership do not reflect the same tone. A quote from one of the novels suggests perceived irresponsible American economic leadership. In *Central Park Squirrels Are Sad on Mondays*, one of the main characters exclaimed such sentiments by saying, "They promise a lot and give nothing. We can never count on them . . ." (Pancol 2010). Another quote supports this point when the same character stated that "many factories were closed due to a lack of orders or due to unpaid American debts" and where "they closed and did not pay what they owed . . ." (Pancol 2010).

Anglo-Saxon

The Anglo-Saxon identity category as a significant other to the French national identity appears most frequently in mass sources. Anglo-Saxon as a significant other draws admiration but is also one that is potentially threatening. For instance, in the novel *Central Park Squirrels Are Sad on Mondays*, the French main character, Hortense, had mixed sentiments toward the Anglo-Saxon culture, as she often feels handicapped by her inability to speak perfect English, which caused her to be scorned by her English-speaking counterparts. As a French girl living in London, she illustrates this tension well, oscillating between self-pity ("Me, Hortense Cortes, plebeian, unknown, poor and French, I don't stand a chance"), self-denial (Hortense introduced herself, trying to hide her French accent), and outright dislike for the Anglo-Saxon other, where she proclaimed once in a chapter that "I'm going home, I have endured enough of this. I hate the British Isles, I hate scones, I hate the English, I hate England, I hate Turner, the corgis and the fucking queen, I hate the status of Hortense" (Pancol 2010).

III. The French National Identity Topography

We have grouped the identity categories in five main clusters. They are Republican values, being cultured and civilized, socioeconomic values, historical others, and external others. Republican values are the core identity categories or abstract ideals. They were mainly recovered from the sources capturing elite discourses. The cluster of being cultured and civilized describes how the French people and culture are perceived. In contrast, the socioeconomic values cluster of identity categories pertains to the country's economy and society. The external others cluster contains identity categories of actors that France compares itself against and relates to. Lastly, the historical others cluster groups the identity categories that belong to a French national identity discourse that preceded the present discourse.

Republican Discourse

The Republican discourse is the predominant French national identity discourse in 2010. Elements of this discourse include values such as liberty, egalitarianism, justice, and other identity categories such as secular, democratic, constitutional, cultured, and civilized. This discourse is primarily an elite discourse, with the associated identity and value categories surfacing most frequently in the political speeches and history textbooks. Republican identity and value categories are conspicuously absent in the movies and novels. Without any evidence of mass derogation of this Republican discourse, and with the affirmation of these values and elements of this identity discourse, the Republican discourse can be said to have some weak elite-mass discursive fit (Table 5.2).

The Republican discourse of French national identity also implies the rejection of historical others such as Catholic France that have been associated with French monarchy and aristocracy. Secularism, which involves relegating the role of religion to the private sphere and out of public life, features prominently in the Republican discourse. Egalitarianism does away with any distinctions apart from that of ability which serves as a cornerstone of French meritocracy. The Republican discourse of French national identity further positions the French as civilized and culturally superior relative to other non-Western states. Pretensions of universal republican ideals aside, there is also a sense that immigrants and foreigners threaten the French literary and cultural heritage. This discourse of French national identity regards francophones, Europeans, and the Anglo-Saxon world as sharing a greater cultural affinity than the Oriental other. Evidence from mass sources such as novels and movies further suggests that American culture is attractive.

Social Democratic Challenger Discourse

The social democratic discourse is a mass discourse of national identity that challenges the predominantly elite-driven Republican discourse. To be French is to engage in some form of social confrontation or resistance typically framed around civil-political or socioeconomic rights. Strikes and political demonstrations are a set of practices helping to define what it means to be French. These practices of pursuing one's rights or seeking concessions are affirmed both in elite and mass texts. For instance, the high school textbooks framed the history of France as one of social struggle, with different social groups fighting for their rights to a particular way of life.

Negative representations of work and capitalism are important elements of this social democratic discourse. The neoliberal capitalist economic model is perceived by the French in negative terms, as coded in the novels. This discourse challenges the neoliberals' faith in the market to solve problems, and is critical of liberal economic policies and reforms. This is connected to a negative portrayal of work across all genres except in the elite speeches. Work is associated with the exploitative labor of an industrializing France of the past and is hence undesirable. Proper work, for the French, is a meaningful activity that provides dignity to an individual. However, the work that is demanded in a capitalist world does not enhance an individual's well-being. There is mass consensus that urban life and work lead to neuroses and are detrimental to an individual's development. Rural France, on the other hand, is an idyllic and pleasant place where one can escape from the bustling work life. Rural and pastoral France as an aspirational other does not appear to be present in elite sources. Hence, a mass social democratic discourse that goes against an elite Republican discourse can be observed.

We posit that if the social democratic discourse is empowered, it would not replace the predominant Republican discourse, but merely alter its configuration to one that rejects a particular capitalist meaning of work and changes its valence. The values of the Republican discourse can be expected to remain unchanged since they are neither challenged nor in direct conflict with the mass challenger discourses. These value categories are likely to frame the discourses of anti-work should the social democratic discourse be empowered. The meanings and valences of work in the predominant Republican discourse and the social democratic challenger discourse are different. In the predominant republican discourse, the affirmation of meritocracy implies that ability and work are important determinants of self-worth in French identity. In the social democratic discourse, however, it is clear that work is associated with exploitative labor and is thus valued negatively.

Declinist Challenger Discourse

Another challenger discourse of French identity is the declinist discourse. Elements of this discourse include France as old, past its political and economic prime, and in competition with others such as BRICS and Germany. France, according to this discourse, is insecure in the new world order. Identity categories

Table 5.2 **French Identity Topography**

	Speeches	Newspapers (Op-eds)	Newspapers (Letters)	Textbooks	Novels	Movies
Republican						
Egalitarian	+	+		+		
Liberty	++				+	
Justice	++	+			+	
Constitutional		+			+	
Modern	++	+			+	
Meritocratic/ elitist		+			+	
Secular		++	+	++++	+	
Democratic		/				
Cultured, Civilized						
Civilized		++				
Cultural center	++	+			+	
European	+/	/			//	
Western		+			++/	
Old		+	+			
Socioeconomic Values						
Capitalist		−			− − −	
Attitude toward work		−		− −	−	− − − / − −
Social welfare state		− −		++		+−
Pastoral rural, neurotic urban					+++++	+++++
Resistance/ confrontational		+++		+++++	++	+
Respects diversity (aspirational)	+//					− −

(*Continued*)

Table 5.2 (**Continued**)

	Speeches	Newspapers (Op-eds)	Newspapers (Letters)	Textbooks	Novels	Movies
External Others						
Africa/ francophone	+++++	+				
Europe	+/	/			//	
BRICS* (competitive)		/	/		−//	
Britain/ Anglo-Saxon					++−/−	++
America					++−−	+++++
Historical Others						
Catholic/ Christian		−		−−//		
Colonial	− − − − −	−				
Patriarchal	−	−/				

* BRICS stands for the emerging economic powers Brazil, Russia, India, China, and South Africa.

of significant others that touch on the rise of new economies like China, India, and also the dominant leadership of Germany in Europe have led the French to reflect upon the relative languor of their economy, as evidenced in newspaper op-ed columns and even mass sources like the novels. This discourse centers on the glorious past of the country instead of emphasizing the need to adapt and remain competitive and relevant in a globalized world economy.

This discourse rejects the idea of participating more actively in the global economy, as its negative representations of work and capitalism serve as its basis. This and the widespread view that the future outlook is bleak spur a retreat into the past. The absence of rhetoric that mentions the need for greater productivity or that expresses the hope that France or Europe would emerge from the Eurozone crisis as stronger or more powerful supports this French declinist discourse of identity. The French declinist discourse could be combined with the social democratic discourse if both are empowered, with the declinist discourse resonating with the social democratic discourse that unfettered profit-making is not a priority for the country. As such, a combination of these two discourses could lead to a less competitive attitude on the global stage.

If empowered, the mass challenger French declinist discourse would not replace the predominant Republican discourse. Instead, it would alter the Republican discursive formation. The Republican discourse suggests that to be French is to be Western, civilized, and cultured. An empowered French declinist discourse is likely to alter what it means to be civilized and cultured. Recognizing that there are other equally cultured or civilized others, the French declinist discourse would accept that France no longer has an exclusive status as a cultural leader and civilized nation. With an empowered declinist and social democratic discourse, we expect that France would have a severely weakened position at the core, potentially shifting from the core to the semi-periphery in the global economy, although it would still remain democratic through the Republican values that form the core of its identity.

Conclusion

The predominant Republican discourse of French national identity reinforces to some extent the hegemonic global discourse of neoliberal democracy. Although France's social welfare state is an alternative to the neoliberal capitalist model, France is still situated at the core of the world market economy. Elements within the French Republican discourse such as the identity categories of Western, modern, civilized, and European also resonate with the hegemonic liberal democratic discourse. Given that this predominant discourse does not have a strong discursive fit, with neither mass rejection nor mass affirmation; it implies that France's position at the core of the world capitalist economy might potentially be thwarted by the social democratic and declinist mass challenger discourses of French national identity. The social democratic discourse has greater mass support than the declinist discourse. Both the social democratic and declinist discourses of French national identity go against the Western hegemony of democratic neoliberalism and thus could complement each other. We posit that both the social democratic and declinist discourses, if empowered, would reconfigure the Republican discursive formation.

The social-democratic and declinist discourses undermine this hegemonic neoliberal democratic global discourse in several ways. First, it is evident that there is considerable mass derogation of work and capitalism. Instead of aspiring toward the development of a more competitive economy, these identity discourses articulate disaffection for urban life and the neurosis that is a consequence of France's participation in the global capitalist economy. Second, with rural pastoral France as an aspirational other, it suggests that should this alternative discourse of French identity be empowered, France might move from the core of global economy to the semi-periphery. While ceding economic or political influence to the emerging powers such as BRICS, these challenger discourses still perceive France as a cultural leader. The French elites would continue to understand French as republican, since it would not be replaced. French "soft power" coupled with its cultural affinity with other European, Western states might be the few remaining links that prevent France from slipping from the core to the semi-periphery.

Bibliography

Speeches

Sarkozy, Nicolas. "Fête nationale 2010 en France, Nicolas Sarkozy a reçu ses homologues africains à l'Élysée." Paris: Elysee, July 13, 2010.
Sarkozy, Nicolas. "Vœux 2010 de Nicolas Sarkozy—Président de la République." Paris: Elysée, December 31, 2009.

Newspapers

Le Figaro
Le Monde

Textbooks

Aujas, Éric, et al., *Histoire Géographie: Éducation Civique (1re BAC Pro).* 3rd ed. (Paris: Hachette Technique, 2010).
Fugler, Martin, et al., *Histoire Géographie: Éducation Civique (1re BAC Pro)* (Paris: Nathan Technique, 2010).

Novels

Houellebecq, Michel, *La Carte et le Territoire* (Paris: Éditions J'ai Lu, 2010).
Pancol, Katherine, *Les Écureuils de Central Park sont tristes le Lundi* (Paris: Le Livre de Poche, 2010).

Movies

Camping 2. Directed by Fabien Onteniente. Produced by Pulsar Productions, Pathé. Subtitles by Franck Dubosc, Mathilde Seigner, Claude Brasseur, Mylène Demongeot, Antoine Duléry, and Richard Anconina. 2010.
Les Petit Mouchoirs. Directed by Guillaume Canet. Produced by Les Productions du Tresor. Subtitles by François Cluzet, et al. 2010.*BRICS stands for the emerging economic powers Brazil, Russia, India, China, and South Africa.

6

The Politics of Responsibility

German National Identity in 2010

LIM KAI HENG

Introduction

The texts reveal a standard of responsibility to which Germans hold others and themselves. In this chapter, I discuss the politics of responsibility: a master discourse spanning multiple dimensions of German national identity. Threading together seemingly disparate topics such as German history, environmentalism, and the European project, the politics of responsibility provides an overarching framework that highlights the subjects and objects of responsibility. There is also an elite-mass accord of Germany as Western and liberal. This second discourse emphasizes freedom, democracy, and other liberal values. Resistance to the discourse can be seen in traces of DDR nostalgia, and traditional family and gender roles. Although Western and Liberal, the texts reveal some criticisms against Neoliberal tendencies; it is important to note that Germany is a cornerstone of the Neoliberal hegemonic order in Europe.

As the political and economical powerhouse of the European Union, Germany was very much instrumental in the implementation of austerity measures in Europe. Especially in Greece, aggressive privatization of state-owned assets were synonymous with the ravages of neoliberalism. It is thus interesting to note that the texts reveal criticisms against rampant privatization. While rejecting the excesses of the market, Western liberal economies are still firmly upheld as the way forward especially when compared to a historical other in communist East Germany. With clear consensus emphasizing Democratic institutions and liberal values as central to the Germany and the German identity, the findings thus present a nuanced position supporting the Neoliberal hegemonic order.

I. Text Selection

The first political speech selected is the annual New Year's speech.[1] In this important event televised throughout Germany, the chancellor traditionally reviews the past year while highlighting hopes for the upcoming year. The second speech selected is the annual German Unity Day speech.[2] Equivalent to the National Day celebrations of most other nations, German Unity Day commemorates the reunification of Germany after the fall of the Berlin Wall at the end of the Cold War. In this second speech, the federal president traditionally commemorates the historical circumstances and challenges faced in achieving a united Germany.

I included the daily newspapers with the highest circulation numbers,[3] namely, the *Frankfurter Allgemeine Zeitung* (*FAZ*) and the *Süddeutsche Zeitung* (*SZ*). The *FAZ* provides a center-right perspective on national, regional, and international news. The *FAZ* also has one of the world's largest networks of correspondents, making it largely independent from press agencies while boasting a circulation of 382,000. The *SZ*, on the other hand, has a circulation of 445,000. It offers a left-wing liberal perspective on national and international news. It is similarly renowned for its independence. For both newspapers, I sampled the editorial and letters-to-the-editor sections on the 15th of each month.

Sampling German novels was more difficult. A comprehensive list comprising only German novels by German-speaking authors is hard to find. Most books that make it to the bestseller lists are international best-selling English books translated into German. Furthermore, the bestseller list from *buchreport*, the authoritative trade magazine of the German-language book industry, combines readership numbers from Germany, Austria, and Switzerland. Cross-checking the bestseller lists from *buchreport* and Amazon.de,[4] I use Amazon as a close if imperfect approximation of book preferences in Germany. The two best-selling fiction books on the list are *Hummeldumm: Das Roman* (*Hummeldumm: The Novel*) by Tommy Jaud and *Für jede Lösung ein Problem* (*There Is a Problem for Every Solution*) by Kerstin Gier. Although Thilo Sarrazin's wildly popular and controversial book *Deutschland schafft sich ab* (*Germany Abolishes Itself*) had better sales than both of the books above, I've opted against sampling it as a text. The explicitly political and controversial nature of the book and its author works against any efforts to excavate the unreflexive reproduction of German national identity.

While different *Länder* (states) are generally responsible for the education system within their administration zones, there is some consistency in the history textbooks used in *Gymnasiums* (high school). The year 2009 saw a syllabus change in the standard history textbook used. As such, we've selected both the latest revised version of the text as well as the older version still used in some high schools that have yet to make the syllabus switch.

For the category of movies, we basically selected the two best-selling original-language German films based on the German box-office sale records.[5] This criterion effectively excludes the first eleven films that topped the charts, as they were not German films. The first film selected was *Friendship!*, directed by Markus Goller, at the twelfth position, and the next German film was *Konferenz der Tiere* (*The Conference of the Animals*), directed by Reinhard Kloos and Holger Tappe, occupying the sixteenth position.

II. Identity Categories

Table 6.1 details the raw counts of the top twenty identity categories.[6]

Often attributed to the influx of foreign migrant workers (*Gastarbeiter*) in the 1960s, **diversity** has become a prominent feature of German society. Christian Wulff, the *Bundespräsident*, describes his delight in receiving a letter from students "whose families come from *seventy* different countries." Calling upon Germany to embrace diversity, he affirms that the German identity is "not defined merely by people's passports, family background or faith, but is something broader." He does not, however, discount the need for integration. Similarly, in the editorials, **immigrants**, especially Turkish immigrants, are criticized for their lack of integration into mainstream society while in letters to the editor, immigrants that speak accent-free **German (language)** were praised (König 2010). This "call of **unity**" in speeches for the pursuit of cohesion in light of today's diversity can and should be seen in light of the evocation of "the consciousness of national unity" that recurs in history textbooks.

With regards to European affairs, there is a common understanding that Germany is **leading and driving Europe**. Political speeches talk about Germany rising above the economic crisis unlike any other nation while remaining the economic engine of the European Union; similarly, the newspapers proclaim that "Germany taking the lead" in European affairs (Nonnenmacher 2010). While Merkel takes care to emphasize that Germany is **a part of Europe** with the choice phrase "we Europeans," opinion editorials in newspapers feature articles describing Germany as **apart from Europe**, with Germans not "feeling any solidarity with the Irish or the Greeks" (Kornelius 2010). Restricted by the sample text size, Germany's relationship with Europe, be it a part or apart, in this study remains ambiguous. German perceptions of other significant European others are, however, anything but ambiguous.

Table 6.1 **Identity Category Raw Counts**

Category	Total	Speeches	Newspapers (Op-eds)	Textbooks	Newspapers (Letters)	Novels	Movies
China	54	0	41	9	2	0	2
Western liberal	47	10	22	10	3	0	2
East Germany/ DDR	45	2	8	15	1	1	18
German history	38	8	6	5	7	7	5
France	38	0	17	9	0	0	12
United	38	21	2	10	1	0	4
Environmental responsibility	36	2	10	0	3	1	20
Governmental responsibility	29	0	11	1	14	0	3
Social responsibility	28	12	4	0	8	0	4
Traditional gender roles	28	1	0	6	5	8	8
Diverse	26	17	2	3	0	0	4
Leader of Europe	23	2	9	9	3	0	0
Nazi Germany	22	0	0	20	1	0	1
United States	22	1	5	7	0	1	8
German language	22	3	0	0	14	2	3
Southern Europe	21	0	11	2	5	1	2
Neoliberalism	21	0	0	0	9	0	12
Traditional family	16	0	0	2	1	12	1
Immigrants	16	10	4	0	2	0	0
Total	**560**	**79**	**148**	**106**	**76**	**31**	**120**

France is described as the "second-strongest" nation in the EU after the wake of the Euro financial crisis, and French attempts to "defend its claim to leadership" need to be seen in light of populist claims that France has been "incapacitated by the Euro". In relation to Germany, however, France is understood to being "no longer able to ignore the demands from Berlin" (Wiegel 2010). **Southern**

Europe, on the other hand, is viewed as very much a region of financial instability and irresponsible spending. Newspaper articles alluded to the common
impression of "lazy Greeks financing their sunny retirement plans with German
tax money" with countries like Spain and Portugal being grouped together with
Greece in needing "tough new austerity measures" to ensure that German tax
money was being spent responsibly (Gammelin 2010, Göbel 2010).

Similarly, the texts reveal that Germans expect **responsible governance**.
Editorials comment on the infighting between different political parties and
coalitions in Germany. In the film *The Conference of the Animals*, politicians are
portrayed as hypocritical and largely ineffectual, merely presenting a façade
of competence. Similarly in newspapers, readers write about the "loss of confidence in politicians who fail to account for their promises" (Bosse 2010).
Besides being the primary theme of *The Conference of the Animals*, being **envi-
ronmentally responsible** was also noted in Angela Merkel's speech as she
boasts of Germany's transition to green energy sources. Although some letters to
the editor talk about "responsibility to (our) earth," they do not directly couple
environmental awareness with the German national identity. Nonetheless, it is
interesting to note that one of the newspapers dedicated a substantial segment
of one of their issues exploring environmental considerations involved with veg-
etarianism (Klarmann 2010). Dramatic scenes of industrial excess destroying
nature in one of the movies attributes environmental degradation to irresponsible economic development.

Neoliberalism is criticized in letters to the editor as one reader, Alexander,
declares in no uncertain terms "those who seek to resolve (extant transport)
issues through further liberalization and privatization are wrong" (Tomm
2010). Ludwig warns against the liberalization of state railways, suggesting that
authorities should not take "Neoliberalism as the new Bible," while Wolfgang
lambasts the "radical austerity measures" imposed upon Berlin's S-Bahn (street
trams) demanding that there be "consequences for those responsible" in light
of the transport debacle earlier that month (Koschier 2010, Wagner 2010).
Similarly, Steltzner critiques the "ethical precipices in large corporations," contrasting them with family businesses characterized by **social responsibility**
and regional roots (Steltzner 2010). This emphasis on ethical behavior in order
to fulfill social responsibility is further reinforced by the speeches. Wulff hails
citizens who "contribute what they can to our community" as the ideal citizens,
emphasizing that social responsibility is an important virtue in Germany—a
place where you must not simply "help yourself to everything without giving
anything in return" (Wulff 2010).

A controversial term in the study of post-1945 German literature and culture,
Vergangenheitsbewältigung, quite literally meaning to "coming to terms with the

past," came into popular use in Germany at the beginning of the 1950s. We were thus hardly surprised to see indications of the collective effort by German society to grapple with **German history**, in particular the **National Socialist dictatorship**. We were however intrigued to note that while explicit references to the Nazi past were drawn almost entirely from the historical textbooks, references to German history in the other texts only implicitly acknowledge the Nazi past. To better reflect this feature, we've opted to separate instances where the Nazi past was explicitly invoked from instances where German history is obliquely referred to in a shameful or regrettable manner. Wulff's oblique references such as "given the events of the first half of the last century" were thus sorted under the latter category, while explicit invocations such as "Nazism should be eradicated and Germans should be educated about Democracy" were sorted under the former (Berg, et al. 2000, Wulff 2010).

Mentions of the **Deutsche Demokratische Republik (DDR)** proved to be a particularly interesting means of understanding German national identity as the DDR is used as a foil to establish (Western) German identity. The textbooks described the DDR as characteristically communist, authoritarian, and "backwards," which was diametrically inverted in the characterization of the Bundesrepublik Deutschland (BRD) as anti-communist, liberal, and economically successful. That reunification was essentially the BRD incorporating the DDR on a BRD base is perhaps best encapsulated by the following phrase from one of the history textbooks: "in the memory of many West German currency reform was the 'real' founding date of the later Federal Republic" (Berg, et al. 2000). This is complimented by **DDR nostalgia**, which is prominent in Markus Goller's film *Friendship!*, about the exploits of two friends from the DDR in the **United States**.

The **United States** appeared consistently as another significant external other. Mentioned in the speeches as an actor playing a crucial role in Germany's reunification, the United States was also frequently mentioned in the editorials, albeit in a much more neutral, and sometimes negative, light. For its role in the wars and postwar era of the 20th century, the United States is largely portrayed as a benevolent superpower in the textbooks. In the novels, the United States is less prominent of an other as compared to the movies, which portray the United States as a developed country worth aspiring to and emulating, as well as a significant power that it is the center of world events leading the West. **Western liberal ideals** such as democracy and freedom of speech are often referred to as ideal values that Germans should embrace. Wulff describes these as the German way of life—"freedom of opinion, religious freedom . . . equality between men and women"—values that Germans must rise up to defend. Importantly, the textbooks took pains to describe "fascist parties and regimes (as) anti-democratic, anti-parliamentary, anti-liberal and anti-Marxist" and in general the diametric opposite of Western liberal ideals (Berg, et al. 2000, Vogel 2009, Wulff 2010).

China is the focus of several sampled editorial pieces, in which it is consistently portrayed as negative because it lacks democratic processes and freedom of speech. In the textbooks, China's history in the 20th century is described with similar emphasis on the same liberal deficit. Opinion letters state that "no one need be under any illusions: (the National People's Congress in China) is not a democratically elected parliament" (Fähnders 2010). This serves as yet another foil for the construction of German national identity that is mirrored in the movie, in which China is used as the punch line to a joke involving the Berlin Wall and the USSR, referencing the leaders of the communist world in quick succession.

However, in spite of this German self-identification with Western liberal values, it is interesting to note that **traditional gender roles** and **family structure** are still very much entrenched as seen from the sampled texts. While Merkel herself is an example of how far gender equality has advanced in Germany, the letters to the editor suggest that gender stereotypes might still hold strong at the mass level. Engineering is described as "still, and will be for a long time, a man's world" because in spite of the women's emancipation movements, "women still do not want to get their hands or their beautiful shoes dirty" doing engineering stuff (Breymann 2010). Heterosexual normativity was particularly evident in one of the novels, in which homosexuality is seen as taboo:

> "Simply not normal," my mother said. "You know what I'm talking about, different." "Different from what?" "Oh, now you're just appearing dumber than you are," my mother said. "Different. Different. Different. Different!"[7]
>
> "Lesbian? The family thinks that I'm lesbian?" "Child, I do not like it when you use such expressions." (Gier 2010)

However, this traditional understanding of gender roles and family structures can hardly be generalized across the texts, as Merkel's speech makes special mention of the women's national soccer team even as Merkel herself is a marked instance of the progress of gender equality in Germany.

III. German Identity Topography

In this section I've decided to organize seemingly disparate identity categories into a single cluster based on a common set of words and phrases threading through them. I posit that these German words and phrases, more exhaustively detailed in the following paragraph, invoke a master discourse of **responsibility**.[8] Before proceeding, however, I must raise the caveat that the concept of responsibility (*Verantwortung*) has a rich and complex place in the tradition of German philosophy and language. In this study I will only be proposing semantic links between an overarching discourse of responsibility and textual invocations of responsibility while unpacking the former solely within the timeframe of 2010. Having raised the necessary caveats, Table 6.2 presents the evidence for a master discourse of German national identity as characterized by the politics of responsibility.

To begin, I suggest that the politics of responsibility frames two immediately identifiable components. First, we can clearly identify a subject and an object and the dynamics of responsibility that mediates the relationship between the two. Baldly, the subject is responsible to the object. Thus, *verantworten*,[9] a German infinitive meaning "to accept responsibility," is a useful marker of the politics of responsibility that occurs through the spread of texts. For instance, Klarmann's call for the German public to honor their "responsibility to (our) earth" is an excellent example of how environmentalism is framed by the politics of responsibility (2010). The poignant closing remark by the reporter in *The Conference of the Animals* similarly translates well to "we are finally being held responsible by the animals" for environmental degradation. In political speeches, Wulff upholds social responsibility, citizens beholden to be responsible to society at large, as an important German trait. Reciprocally, politicians and policy-makers are responsible to the public. In letters to the editor, the public reserves special opprobrium for politicians and policy-makers[10] who fail to behave in a "responsible manner" (Fröhlich 2010, Klöckner 2010, Wagner 2010, Hesse 2010). If these invocations are understood as hailing an overarching discourse of responsibility, then Merkel's speech can be framed as a deliberate attempt to leverage upon the politics of responsibility to garner public support for unpopular foreign policy commitments.

In her New Year's national address, Merkel argues strongly that Germany needs to continue contributing financially to the European Union and militarily to the Coalition operations in the Afghanistan War. In the face of growing public discontent over Germany's financing of EU debts and German casualties in Afghanistan, the Chancellor argues poignantly, "we Germans take our responsibilities very seriously—even when it is tough and costly to do so" (Merkel 2010, Pew Research Center 2010). Merkel appeals to a sense of responsibility when she calls for the Germans to work harder (economically) to strengthen the Eurozone just as the editorials that argue for the European project similarly appeal to a sense of responsibility. Astute as Merkel's invocation is politically,

Table 6.2 **German Identity Topography**

	Speeches	Newspapers (Op-eds)	Textbooks	Newspapers (Letters)	Novels	Movies
Historical Others						
Nazi Germany			– – –	–		–
German History	–	–	\	–	– –\	– –
East Germany/ DDR	–	–	– –\\		–	+ – – – –
External Others						
United States	+	\	++		+	+
China		– – – –	– –	–		–
Europe						
France		– –	– \			+ – –
Leader of Europe	+	+	++	+		
European	+	+	+	+		
Apart from Europe	\	+	+	+		
Southern Europe		– –		–		–
Economically Strong	+		+ +		+	
Industrious	+		+	+	+	
Materialism					+++++	– –
Capitalism		+		++		
Technologically advanced	+	+		+	– – –	
Responsibility	+			+		
Governmental responsibility		+ +	+	+ +		+
Social responsibility	+ +	+		+ + +		+
Environmental responsibility	+	+		+	+	++++
Responsibility to the past	+		+		+	

(Continued)

Table 6.2 **(Continued)**

	Speeches	Newspapers (Op-eds)	Textbooks	Newspapers (Letters)	Novels	Movies
Social-Political Values						
Traditional family			+	+	+++\\	+
Traditional gender roles	+ −		+ −	+	++++	+
Western ideals[11]	++++	++++	++	+		+
Diverse	+ + +	+				+
United	+++	+	++			+
Neoliberalism				−		+++
Miscellaneous						
German language	+			++++	++	+
Immigrants (SO)	++	+		+		

the Europe cluster on the topographical chart is revealing of how the politics of responsibility can turn out to be a double-edged sword. While elite opinion of the European project is generally positive, the masses are conspicuously apathetic toward the European Union.

I suggest that the average German does not feel responsible to the European Union and instead perceives certain states within the EU as behaving irresponsibly. Framed within the politics of responsibility, this works against political efforts to shore up the European project, as seen in the negative valence with which southern Europe, primarily Greece, is afflicted. Resistance to the irresponsible governmental spending of southern European states can be noted, as Gammelin argues in an op-ed: "the German taxpayer fears that he/she is footing the bill for irresponsible Greek spending" (2010). Furthermore, Wolfgang Schäuble, the German Finance Minister, in a pointed reference to Greece, demands that members of the European monetary union need to be "responsible for themselves (financially)" (Mussler 2010). Strikingly, Greek sailors are also portrayed as behaving irresponsibly in one of the movies. As such, it is hardly much of a stretch to argue that Merkel's attempt to leverage upon the master discourse of responsibility would backfire unless the impressions of the German public on the ground of southern European governments as behaving irresponsibly undergo a substantial change.

The German national project of *Vergangenheitsbewältigung* can similarly be framed in the politics of responsibility: a responsible Germany is necessarily one that needs to be accountable to its historical legacy. In eloquent phrasing, Assmann describes a collective German cultural memory as remembering "German guilt and the historic responsibility for the atrocities of the Nazi regime" (Zytyniec 2010). The textbooks described how at the end of the Second World War, "denazification, demilitarization, and decentralization were key Germany policy objectives" as the victorious powers sought to hold Germany responsible for the crimes of the Nazi regime (Vogel 2009, p. 513). Similarly, in his speech, Wulff talks about "the events of the first half of the last century" taking responsibility for "the terror and havoc caused by Germany" (2010).

While I argue that the politics of responsibility similarly frames German perceptions of national history, the question of what "taking responsibility" actually entails in terms of practical prescriptions is not within the scope of my analysis. After all, *Vergangenheitsbewältigung* is a negotiated and ongoing process by which Germany grapples with its responsibility to a complex past. I will however examine in the final section some of the political corollaries of the remarkable consensus among the elite and masses.

Conclusion

Exhibited clearly in the master discourse of responsibility, an integral part of German national identity discourse, the elite-mass consensus can similarly be seen in other areas in Table 6.2. There is, for example, clear consensus that to be German is to be Western, Liberal, and Economically Strong. Described by the German president as the German way of life, the Western liberal discourse enjoys strong elite-mass consensus throughout the sampled texts, although some resistance can be seen in the undercurrents of DDR nostalgia and traditional family and gender roles. Furthermore, this elite-mass consensus can be corroboratively seen in the almost uniform negative perceptions of the DDR as a historical other commonly associated with Communism and non-democratic governance. With national history in mind, it is hardly surprising that democratic governance holds a sacred place in German national discourse.

If Western hegemony is to be defined as democratic neoliberalism, it is clear that the strong elite-mass consensus affirming democratic institutions reveals staunch support for Western hegemony. This is further bolstered by the negative connotations that are attached to China, represented as illiberal in German discourses. However, German economic identities relate to economic aspects of Western hegemony in a more nuanced way. There are some points of resistance to neoliberalism in the mass discourses that emphasize the negative social impact of privatization and do not express unconditional support for free markets. Although Germany remains firmly within the Western neoliberal hegemony, nevertheless it challenges the potentially irresponsible excesses of neoliberalism.

These areas of strong elite-mass consensus are essentially entrenched social mores. They paint a map of social structures relatively set in stone that constrain and sometimes obstruct policy-makers in Germany. As seen in the earlier section, the perception of southern European states as irresponsible can significantly affect attempts by politicians to sway the public using a sense of responsibility toward the political project of the European Union. I suggest that politicians and political scientists alike can glean useful insights from a topographical map of German national identity, particularly in light of the 2014 German European Parliament election.

Alternative für Deutschland (AfD; Alternative for Germany), Germany's "first Eurosceptic party in decades," was putatively founded in February 2013 "as a protest movement against Germany's decision to bail out Greece" (Lamparski 2014). In the recent European Parliament election, they (AfD) won 7% of the vote despite capturing only 4.7% in the 2013 German federal elections. A relatively young party, AfD managed to tap into existing undercurrents of frustration and dissatisfaction with Germany's decision to bail out Greece. This observation is simple and obvious. An appreciation of German national identity through a topographical chart would, however, offer a more elucidative and nuanced explanation.

The decision to bail out the Greek economy was politically costly *because* there is a perception of the Greek government as having had irresponsible monetary policies. German politicians seeking to improve public opinion on the EU should thus increase efforts on combatting perceptions of southern European states as behaving irresponsibly. After all, it is as the Chancellor herself stated: Germans take responsibilities very seriously. While the main part of the German public might be convinced of their responsibilities toward the European project, appealing to the German sense of responsibility might become increasingly counterproductive should such perceptions of irresponsibility grow.

Notes

1. The speech is freely accessible online at the Chancellor's homepage (Merkel 2010).
2. The speech is freely accessible online at the President's homepage (Wulff 2010).
3. Press circulation numbers were taken from *Presseurop*, a Paris-based news portal.
4. Two out of the top three books on both lists correspond.

5. German box-office sale records were retrieved from *Insidekino* (2010).
6. The raw counts presented in Table 6.1 were developed using a combined list from two analysts, the author and Hazel Tan Shi Wei. The two analysts independently induced the categories, but worked out differences in naming and interpretation together. Thus, the raw count list represents a cooperative endeavor. Thus, special mention and thanks are given to Hazel Tan Shi Wei, my colleague in this project. In order to check on intercoder reliability, we each went through the list of sampled texts individually before eventually coming together to agree upon common categories. This chapter would not have been possible without her input and efforts.
7. In the original German text, the mother uses five distinct expressions that mean deviance: *"nicht normal," "anders," "andersartig," "andersherum,"* and *"vom anderen Ufer."*
8. Many of the German words and phrases translate well as invoking both either "responsibility" or "accountability," and it must be noted that these two concepts are very much intertwined both in the English and as well in the German language.
9. *Verantworten* is hardly the only German infinitive that is semantically linked to the master discourse of responsibility, simply the one that appears most regularly.
10. The German noun for "public policy-maker" is *"politisch Verantwortliche,"* literally, person responsible for politics.
11. Western Ideals is a gestalt category that consists of the following subcategories: The West, Freedom, Democracy, Liberal Values.

Sources

Speeches

Merkel, Angela. 2010. "Neujahrsansprache der Bundeskanzlerin." http://www.bundeskanzlerin.de/ContentArchiv/DE/Archiv17/Pressemitteilungen/BPA/2010/12/2010-12-30-neujahrsansprache-bkin.html.
Wulff, Christian. 2010. "Rede zum 20. Jahrestag der deutschen Einheit." http://www.bundespraesident.de/SharedDocs/Reden/DE/Christian-Wulff/Reden/2010/10/20101003_Rede.html.

Newspapers

Frankfurter Allgemeine Zeitung
Bosse, Immo. "Unglaublich." *Frankfurter Allgemeine Zeitung* 15 Jan. 2010: 46. Print.
Breymann, Kathrin. "Ingenieure." *Frankfurter Allgemeine Zeitung* 15 Aug. 2010: 32. Print.
Fähnders, Till. "Politische Lähmung in Peking." *Frankfurter Allgemeine Zeitung* 15 Mar. 2010: 1. Print.
Fröhlich, Gregor. "Immer Nur Luxus." *Frankfurter Allgemeine Zeitung* 15 Dec. 2010: 40. Print.
Göbel, Heike. "In Der Schuldengemeinschaft." *Frankfurter Allgemeine Zeitung* 15 May 2010: 1. Print.
Klöckner, Detlef. "Systematisch Blockiert." *Frankfurter Allgemeine Zeitung* 15 Dec. 2010: 40. Print.
Mussler, Werner. "Schäubles Schalmeienklänge." *Frankfurter Allgemeine Zeitung* 15 Mar. 2010: 9. Print.
Nonnenmacher, Günther. "Nur Voran Kann Es Gehen." *Frankfurter Allgemeine Zeitung* 15 Nov. 2010: 1. Print.
Steltzner, Holger. "Vielfalt Statt Einheitskodex." *Frankfurter Allgemeine Zeitung* 15 July 2010: 9. Print.
Wiegel, Michaela. "Sarkozys Wechselnde Allianzen." *Frankfurter Allgemeine Zeitung* 15 Dec. 2010: 1. Print.

SÜDDEUTSCHE ZEITUNG

Gammelin, Cerstin. "Furor Und Unwissen." *Süddeutsche Zeitung* 15 Apr. 2010: 4. Print.
Hesse, Martin. "Er Zündelt Wieder." *Süddeutsche Zeitung* 15 May 2010: 4. Print.
Klarmann, Irmgard. "Wo Bleibt Der Fleischersatz?" *Süddeutsche Zeitung* 15 Jan. 2010: 33. Print.
Kornelius, Stefan. "Der Preis Für Europa." *Süddeutsche Zeitung* 15 May 2010: 4. Print.
Koschier, Ludwig. "Züge Haben Zum Ende Der Knechtschaft Beigetragen." *Süddeutsche Zeitung* 15 Jan. 2010: 33. Print.
Tomm, Alexander. "Immer Ärger Mit Der Bahn." *Süddeutsche Zeitung* 15 Jan. 2010: 33. Print.
Wagner, Wolfgang. "Wer Haftet Für Das Berliner S-Bahn-Debakel?" *Süddeutsche Zeitung* 15 Jan. 2010: 33. Print.
Zytyniec, Rafal. "Die Toxische Version Der Geschichte." *Süddeutsche Zeitung* 16 Aug. 2010: 25. Print.

Textbooks

Berg, Rudolf, Gerhard Brunn, Andreas Dilger, Ute Frevert, Hilke Günther-Arndt, Ernst Hinrichs, and Hans-Georg Hofacker, *Kursbuch Geschichte—Allgemeine Ausgabe: Von der Antike bis zur Gegenwart* (Berlin: Cornelsen Verlag GmbH, 2000).
Vogel, Ursula, *Kursbuch Geschichte: Von der Antike bis zur Gegenwart: Schülerbuch.* (Berlin: Cornelsen Verlag GmbH, 2009).

Novels

Gier, Kerstin, *Für jede Lösung ein Problem* (Cologne: Bastei Lübbe, 2010).
Jaud, Tommy, *Hummeldumm: Das Roman* (Frankfurt: Scherz Verlag, 2010).

Movies

Goller, Markus, dir. 2010. *Friendship!* Berlin: Deutschen Columbia Pictures Filmproduktion.
Klooss, Reinhard, and Holger Tappe, dirs. 2010. *Konferenz der Tiere.* Munich: Constantin Film.

Bibliography

Lamparski, Nina. 2014. "Germany's Youth Rebels against EU." *BBC.* http://www.bbc.com/news/world-europe-27341876.
Pew Research Center, *Obama More Popular Abroad Than at Home, Global Image of U.S. Continues to Benefit, 22-Nation Pew Global Attitudes Survey* (Washington, DC: Pew Research Center, 2010). http://www.pewglobal.org/files/2010/06/Pew-Global-Attitudes-Spring-2010-Report-June-17-11AM-EDT.pdf.

7

Talented Democrats in a Modern State

Indian National Identity in 2010, English Sources

JARROD HAYES

Introduction

As befitting a country as large and diverse as India, identity discourses and markers operate largely at a high level of abstraction and generality. Nonetheless, some significant trends emerge. Perhaps the most dominant identification is as a democracy. In support of this dominant narrative are secondary narratives emphasizing Gandhian or peaceful conflict resolution and constructing India as a progressive, modern, and secular state (albeit one in which linger concerns over unity) aspiring to be socially egalitarian, where regional, caste, and gender distinctions or discrimination belong in the past. There is some contestation over India's economic identity. Some texts emphasize socialist norms and principles while others point to capitalist ideas. Globally, Indians understand their country as a leader, respected and integrated into the international system, and themselves as talented and innovative. Discourses identifying India more regionally (Asian or South Asian) are comparatively weak. In terms of a global democratic narrative, India clearly fits well—democracy is the dominant shared identity discourse for 2010. However with respect to neoliberal narratives, India in 2010 is a conflicted society. As befitting a country that defined itself in contrast to Western neoliberal hegemony and has only relatively recently come to accept some elements of neoliberal economics, socialist and capitalist/neoliberal identities exist in tension at both elite and mass levels.

I. Text Selection

The analysis provided here is based on a collection of 330 distinct English-language texts, ranging from popular Bollywood films to novels to short letters to the editor, producing over 880 identity codings. English plays an important mediating role in India, serving as a bulwark for non-Hindi speakers concerned about the imposition of Hindi as a universal language.[1] Indeed, protests at the planned phase-out of English in the 1960s prompted the federal government to enshrine English as one of the two official government languages indefinitely. Thus, there is significant basis for scholarly attention to Indian identity dynamics as they occur in English. Texts included here fall into five categories: leadership speeches, newspaper editorials, films, novels, and textbooks. I briefly address the selection process for each in turn.

In selecting the leadership speeches for inclusion in the study, I identified two as having the broadest appeal across India as well as the greatest length. The first is Prime Minister Manmohan Singh's August 15 Independence Day speech, commemorating Indian independence from British rule.[2] The second is Singh's address to the first annual conference of the Chief Secretaries of States, a newly developed venue for managing relations between the federal and state governments.[3]

In 2010 the Indian Readership Survey (IRS)[4] identified the Delhi-based, right-leaning *Times of India* as the highest-circulation English-language daily (~7 million readers). The newspaper provides "epaper" archives for all of 2010, making identification of the opinion section straightforward.[5] The second-most-read English-language daily is the Delhi-based, centrist *Hindustan Times* (~3.5 million readers). Unfortunately, subscription services like LexisNexis provide only search-based archives and the *Hindustan Times* provides online archives for only four weeks. Given these difficulties, I turned to Chennai-based, left-leaning *The Hindu*, the third-largest English-language newspaper by circulation (2.1 million). The newspaper has excellent online archives and is based in the south of India, which is in contrast to the *Times of India* and the *Hindustan Times*. The resulting geographic spread provided by sampling the *Times* and *The Hindu* in a country as diverse as India provides additional methodological benefits, notably avoiding reinforcing potentially problematic regional biases. As a consequence, the sampled newspapers offer the potential for a more robust reading of identity discourses.

Attendance figures for India films are not readily available. However, BoxOfficeIndia.com does maintain records of box-office receipts by year, which until January 2014 were free to the public.[6] According to website data, the two top-grossing films in India were both indigenously produced. The first is

Dabangg, a police action film that grossed 1.4 billion rupees (~$30.5 million). The second is a comedy entitled *Gomaal 3*, which grossed 1.08 billion rupees (~$23.4 million).

Assessing the top-selling novels in India for 2010 is a difficult exercise. Unlike in the United States, there is no central aggregator like the *New York Times* best-sellers list. Triangulating across multiple sources including *India Today* (a weekly English-language magazine published in India),[7] Sify.com,[8] and an India-based book review blog,[9] three books appear consistently: *The Immortals of Meluha*, *2 States: The Story of My Marriage*, and *The Palace of Illusions*. However, the data are not consistent enough across the sources to suggest a rank ordering. Accordingly, I randomly chose two of the novels, *2 States: The Story of My Marriage* and *The Palace of Illusions*.

The selection of textbooks proved another challenge. Constitutionally, education is the purview of states. However, the federal government has a central bureaucracy, the National Council of Educational Research and Training (NCERT), tasked with setting a national baseline. The federal textbooks have significant national influence, as debates over efforts to change federal textbook standards suggest,[10] making them an ideal source. The federal-level curriculum specifies that Indian history be taught in Classes Six to Eight, with modern Indian history reserved for Class Eight. Thus the Class Eight textbook (*Our Pasts*) is included in the analysis here, as is a Class Twelve textbook entitled *Themes in Indian History*, which addresses elements of India's modern history within the context of a thematic analytical framework. Both texts are available at NCERT's textbook website.[11]

II. Indian Identity in 2010

As Table 7.1 suggests, aspects of economic identity occupy an important position in the texts. At least at the leadership level, there is a confidence about the country's economic status. The **capitalist** reforms of the past twenty years, Singh claims, have enabled India to "to become one of the fastest growing economies in the world," with "the resilience to deal and meet the challenge of crises, as our response to the recent global downturn shows."[12] Even so, in the same speech Singh also invokes the importance of "**inclusive growth**," which can only come through active government involvement in the economy through "schemes like the Mahatma Gandhi National Rural Employment Programme, the National Rural Health Mission, [and] the Jawaharlal Nehru National Urban Renewal Mission," all of which require "the active participation and commitment of the State Governments." Likewise, in his address to the nation on

Independence Day Singh reiterated the important role capitalism had made in establishing India as a **vibrant economy**, generating "our economic progress in the last many years . . . [t]oday, India stands among the fastest growing economies." At the same time, however, Singh claimed an important role for government in managing the economy and ensuring **equitable growth**, going so far as to ensure that "Every person living in rural areas now has the assurance of 100 days of employment."

This duality of economic identity is not confined to the political leadership. A writer invokes India's colonial history in a rejection of Western capitalism: "India became a slave to East India Company. But in this era of free economy, India has become a slave to many East India Companies in the form of private and multi-national banks."[13] This theme, that India's colonial past is one grounded in exploitation by international capital, also threads throughout the textbooks. Conversely, a *Times of India* editorial lambastes the federal government for failing to pursue capitalism, developing a "faux private sector administration model" for Air India, calling instead for "the real deal."[14] A *Times* op-ed contributor, perhaps unintentionally, identified the conflict between socialism and capitalism in Indian identity when he argues that "for half a century since independence, India has remained away from the world stage, a global backwater, happily complacent in its socialist model," a situation untenable since economic reforms had transformed India into an **economically competitive** place, a "power of some economic consequence."[15] Key here is the author's identification of India as happy with its **socialist** model even as capitalist reforms had turned the country into a **global power**—an identity Indians embrace.

Part of the conflict between capitalism and socialism arises from a general concern that India is **incompetent** and **corrupt**. An op-ed in the *Times*, discussing the opening of a new terminal at Delhi's Indira Gandhi International Airport (which "zoomed us into the airspace of superpowerdom"—a clear reference to India's global power status), noted that capitalism in the form of the new terminal "offer[s] everything and more that we have been demanding in vain from the municipal corporation, the metropolitan development authority, and the corner cop."[16] The advent of the Commonwealth Games, hosted by India in 2010, and the failure of the government to prepare adequately gave rise to apparently pervasive concerns about the ubiquitous presence of corruption in Indian society and politics. Indian corruption had "shamed" India, pushing Delhi into crisis mode rather than benefiting it.[17] For some, corruption in India is a manifestation of "society's falling values":

Corruption has become rampant and almost a norm in every walk of life. No wonder India ranks high in many international corruption

Table 7.1 **Identity Category Raw Counts**

Category	Total	Speeches	Newspapers (Op-Eds)	Newspapers (Letters)	Textbooks	Novels	Movies
Democratic/free	76	7	25	24	19	0	1
Progressive/advancing/ modern	51	10	16	5	11	8	1
Socially inclusive/ diverse/equal	51	5	11	9	21	3	2
Divisive/racist/ exclusive/ regional/caste	50	0	9	13	17	11	0
Rule of law/rights	44	4	15	12	8	5	0
Ineffective/ incompetent/corrupt	42	0	14	20	0	1	7
Capitalist	38	0	7	2	19	6	4
Strong/cohesive/ community	36	6	2	2	16	8	2
Ancient/historic/ tradition/spiritual	33	2	10	7	7	7	0
Economically inclusive/ equitable	27	15	3	5	3	1	0
Economic growth/ vibrancy/competitive	27	18	4	4	1	0	0
Capable/competent/ effective	25	8	5	8	2	2	0
Talented/skilled/ educated/advanced	25	1	6	1	11	6	0
Gender equal	22	0	4	9	4	4	1
Non-democratic/ authoritarian	21	0	8	1	10	0	2
Peaceful/harmonious/ non-violent (domestic)	21	6	4	4	5	1	1
Western	16	0	3	1	12	0	0
Respected/global power/leader	15	1	10	1	2	0	1
World-class	15	0	5	0	9	1	0
Independent (int'l)	14	0	2	0	12	0	0

(*Continued*)

Table 7.1 **(Continued)**

Category	Total	Speeches	Newspapers (Op-Eds)	Newspapers (Letters)	Textbooks	Novels	Movies
Socialist/statist	13	0	5	0	7	1	0
Accountable/responsible	12	3	4	4	0	0	1
Good neighbor	12	1	11	0	0	0	0
Gender unequal	10	0	0	2	2	6	0
Innovative/creative	10	3	5	1	0	1	0
Regressive/backward/medieval	8	0	1	6	0	1	0
Religious	8	0	2	3	3	0	0
Secular	8	1	4	1	2	0	0
Economic stagnation/underdeveloped	7	0	3	2	1	1	0
Forceful/dominant	7	0	0	0	2	0	5
Globally integrated/cosmopolitan	7	1	3	2	1	0	0
Unequal	7	0	0	4	3	0	0
Resilient/resolute/determined	6	2	1	0	3	0	0
Neoliberal	5	0	2	0	3	0	0
Peaceful/harmonious (int'l)	5	1	1	1	0	2	0
Anticapitalist/materialist/	4	0	0	0	0	4	0
Gandhian	3	0	2	1	0	0	0
Powerful	3	0	0	1	0	2	0
Total	**784**	**95**	**207**	**156**	**216**	**82**	**28**

indices. Even worse, corruption goes unpunished in most cases. Poor governance has further contributed to the hopelessness of millions of citizens.[18]

This sentiment, that corruption is an outgrowth of Indian identity and culture is echoed in other letters: "individual and institutional corruption has become a contagious phenomenon in our country."[19] In both of the films sampled in this chapter, government (embodied by the police) is corrupt or incompetent, or both. Particularly in *Dabangg*, the protagonist is a hero because he gets things done.

Another profound insecurity in Indian identity lies in concerns over **social inclusion** and the potential for **divisive** social forces to take hold. The texts show a consistent concern with India as **socially cohesive** with a **strong community**. The novel *2 States: The Story of My Marriage* uses fundamental religious, linguistic, and regional tensions as the central plot device. In brief, the protagonist—a man from Delhi—meets and falls in love with a woman from Chennai (a major city in south India). While the couple—**young, modern, progressive**—have no problem with their different regional backgrounds (interestingly, language is not an issue as both speak English), their parents have deep misgivings about the regional and, to a lesser extent caste, differences. The novel details the trials the couple go through to reconcile their respective families to the marriage. In the end, modernity wins over tradition, but it is a close-run thing. *The Palace of Illusions* also draws deeply on the theme of communal unity through the vehicle of warfare between members of a single extended Indian royal family. Indian Prime Minister Singh underlines the pressing need to be socially inclusive and overcome divisiveness based on **regionalism** or **castes** in his Independence Day speech:

> Our society often gets divided in the name of religion, State, caste or language. We should resolve that we will not allow divisions in our society under any circumstance. Tolerance and generosity have been a part of our traditions. We should strengthen these traditions. As we progress economically our society should also become more sensitive. We should be modern and progressive in our outlook.[20]

Singh's invocation of tolerance and modernity is particularly striking, because it suggests these are key elements of Indian identity. In the same speech Singh also invokes the **secularist** foundations of Indian political identity as a counterpoint to sectarian tendencies:

> Secularism is one of the pillars of our democracy. It has been the tradition of our country and society to treat all religions with equal respect. For centuries India has welcomed new religions and all have flourished here. Secularism is also our constitutional obligation. Our Government is committed to maintain communal peace and harmony.

The reliance on secularism as a basis for countering divisiveness also appears in mass opinion. One letter writer explicitly invoked it as a basis for countering communal violence: "Communal politics is a virulent reality and a major threat to the secular fabric of India."[21] In an op-ed, V. R. Krishna Iyer also explicitly invokes secularism as a core part of Indian identity in the context of addressing the Naxalite insurgency: "The sovereign Republic of India stands for socialism, egalitarianism, trans-religious secularism and national unity based on the principles of fraternity."[22]

The underlying existential concern with a core Indian identity is widespread. The textbooks pay significant attention to the fractured nature of Indian society—notably through discussions of the communal violence that accompanied Indian independence—and highlight Gandhi's important role in grounding Indian identity in norms of tolerance, social inclusiveness, and **equality**. Letters show similar concerns. In response to efforts by a sectarian organization to ban the film *My Name Is Khan* (a controversial film dealing with Islam and terrorism), one letter writer argues, "The singular denouncement by one and all of the mission of communal groups shows how to a man Mumbai stands for a united India. With this victory, the communal factions should realize that India is for **peace** and **harmony**."[23] An editorial in the *Times of India* also commenting on the film controversy links factionalism with "old" or **ancient** India and progressivism and community with "young" or modern India: "It was a moment to savour, a victory for civility. A moment when young India pushed back against old politics and the sowers of division."[24]

Despite these concerns—or perhaps because of them—**democracy** is a profound and fundamental pillar of Indian identity (also the most coded identification). Manmohan Singh traces India's clout in the international system in large part to its democracy:

> As the world's largest democracy, we have become an example for many other countries to emulate. Our citizens have the right to make their voice heard. Our country is viewed with respect all over the world. Our views command attention in international fora.[25]

If there was any doubt as to the importance of democracy to Indian political identity, Singh goes on to give it pride of place as the foundation for a "new" India:

> We are building a new India in which every citizen would have a stake, an India which would be prosperous and in which all citizens would be able to live a life of honour and dignity in an environment of peace and goodwill. An India in which all problems could be solved through democratic means. An India in which the basic rights of every citizen would be protected.

Democracy is also factored into Indian assessments of their country's rightful place as a **global power** on the United Nations Security Council: "Islamabad's stand [that India] doesn't deserve to be a permanent member of the UNSC is ridiculous, if not illogical. India is the world's largest democracy and a responsible, peace-loving nation . . . It should rightfully be made a permanent member of a reformed and expanded UNSC."[26] Some writers point out that "ultimately people are the real masters in a parliamentary democracy,"[27] while others fret about the possible peril posed to Indian democracy arising from parliamentary dysfunction.[28] The latter author condemns the federal government in Delhi in the context of the ongoing contention in Kashmir for failing to recognize that "power, not democracy, comes out of the barrel of a gun."[29] The importance of democracy for Indian identity also emerges clearly in consideration of other countries. Reacting to events in Myanmar, Indian letter writers were effusive in their praise of Aung San Suu Kyi, who would "be forever remembered for her pro-democracy struggle. Her name will find a mention with the names of Mahatma Gandhi and Nelson Mandela in history books. Long live the spirit of democracy."[30] Others assess and condemn Myanmar in terms of the failure of democracy to take root,[31] fret about the frail and unraveling democracy in Thailand,[32] and worry about the rise of a China antagonistic to democracy.[33]

III. Indian Identity Topography

As the topography chart in Table 7.2 suggests, democracy is more than just an identity category—it ties together a number of themes into the dominant discourse of Indian identity. Democracy itself is a central and foundational pillar of Indian identity—one of the few shared ties binding the fractious imagined community of India together and overcoming divisiveness. In the texts, the democracy element of identity occasionally interacts with the economically oriented elements of identity, speaking directly to the question posed by the project organizers regarding the influence of global neoliberal discourses. For example, one letter writer suggests a socialist, or social democratic, flavor to Indian democracy when he holds that "Democracy does mean equal opportunity, but how can there be equal opportunity if some socio-economic groups are handicapped to begin with?"[34] Others hold that government is incapable of mounting effective economic interventions, suggesting a more neoliberal perspective: "The dilemma of our democracy is that even the best of projects fail to produce intended results due to the vested interests of those obstructing reforms."[35] These contrasting perspectives typify the tension in India's economic identity.

In support of the democracy discourses and in counterpoint to concerns over corruption is a focus on rule of law. In addressing the states' Chief Secretaries, Manmohan Singh notes that ensuring rule of law is the primary responsibility of government.[36] Singh also notes the importance of rule of law in his Independence Day speech. Coming from a government official, such a declaration is on its face anodyne. But, given that rule of law is such a commonly accepted obligation of government, it is remarkable that Singh felt it necessary to explicitly mention it in *both* sampled speeches. In doing so, he echoes an ongoing discourse defining an aspirational identity for Indians. Editorials and letters invoke rule of law in support of judicial transparency,[37] in opposition to threats and violence driven by parochial politics,[38] in opposition to unelected village councils,[39] and in admiration of the West for deterring serious crime.[40] In all of these contexts, writers are lamenting the absence or weakness of rule of law, and the desire to see rule of law strengthened. In light of the apparent assessment noted earlier that corruption is fixed in institutional culture as well as in broader popular culture, the process of strengthening rule of law necessarily requires a redefinition of appropriate social, economic, and political behavior—and in turn what it means to be Indian.

Another major aspirational identity for Indians appears to be that of a modern or progressive state and society, a theme often attached to discourses of parochialism or communalism. As mentioned earlier, Prime Minister Singh in his Independence Day speech claimed the government was building a "new" India, one where factionalism and communal strife are absent, and admonished India's citizens to be "modern and progressive in our outlook."[41] Similarly, the theme of a new or modern India appears in both works of fiction sampled here. In *2 States*, the generational dynamic sets up a clear dichotomy between "old" India (the parents of the couple) with parochial world views and suffocating social norms against "new" India (the couple) with a more cosmopolitan, flexible, and open-minded perspective. In *Palace of Illusions*, the idea of moving forward into a new India is also powerfully present. The novel culminates with a massive battle between factionalized members of the same extended royal family. The death toll is so significant and the experience so traumatic that it marked the end of an era in India and the start of a new one, which was also accompanied by a generational shift in leadership. An op-ed in the *Times of India* notes that the main rival to the governing Congress Party coalition (the Bharatiya Janata Party) had a chance of electoral success because of the party leader's "progressive" image.[42] Also, recall that in response to the controversy over the film *My Name Is Khan*, commentators wrote that the resistance to efforts to ban the film was "a moment when young India pushed back against old politics and the sowers of division."[43] Strongly associated with the modernity/progressive identity is the discourse on gender equality. Op-ed contributors note that educated women are key to

Table 7.2 **Indian Identity Topography**

	Speeches	Newspapers (Op-eds)	Newspapers (Letters)	Textbooks	Novels	Movies
Economic Identities						
Capitalist		+	+	−	/	+
Economic growth/ vibrancy/competitive	+++++	+	+	−		
Economic stagnation/ uncompetitive		−	−	−	−	
Inclusive/equitable (economic)	+++++	+	+	+	+	
Innovative/creative	+	+	+		+	
Neoliberal		+		−		
Protectionist		+	+			
Socialist/statist		−		+	+	
Talented/skilled/ educated/advanced	+	+	+	+	++	
Democracy and Political Identity						
Accountable/ responsible	+	+	+			+
Capable/competent/ effective	+++	+	+	+	+	
Democratic/free	+++	+++	++++	+++		+
Ineffective/ incompetent/corrupt		− −	− − − −		−	− − − − −
Unequal			−	−		
Nondemocratic/ uthoritarian		−	−	−		− −
Observes rule of law/ rights	+	++	+++	+	++	
Socially inclusive/ diverse/equal	++	+	++	+++	+	++
Global Power						
Globally integrated/ cosmopolitan	+	+	+	−		

(Continued)

Table 7.2 (**Continued**)

	Speeches	Newspapers (Op-eds)	Newspapers (Letters)	Textbooks	Novels	Movies
Independent (nt'l)		+		+		
Respected/important/ leader	+	+	+	+		+
Good neighbor	+	+				
World-class		+		+	+	
Social Identities and Values						
Ancient/historic/ tradition	–	–	–	+	– –+	
Divisive/racist/ regional/caste		–	– – –	– –	– – – –	
Forceful/dominant				–		++++
Gandhian		+	+			
Gender equal		+	++	+	+	/
Gender unequal			–	–	– –	
Peaceful/harmonious/ non-violent (domestic)	++	+	+	+	+	+
Peaceful/harmonious (int'l)	+	+	+		+	
Powerful			+		+	
Progressive/ advancing/modern	++++	++	+	+	++–	+
Religious		–	–	–		
Regressive/backward/ medieval		–	–		–	
Resilient/resolute/ determined	+	+		+		
Secular	+	+	+	+		
Strong/cohesive/ community	++	+	+	++	+++	++

India's phenomenal economic growth.[44] An editorial in *The Hindu* emphasized the importance of bridging the gender gap for sustainable development and the "urban future."[45] A letter to *The Hindu*'s editors clearly identified the link between gender equality and modern India:

> The gleaming new image of India galloping towards an incredible future will be true only when we weed out the diseases within our country. Dressing up a sick India in bright colours to show the world is like painting a crumbling edifice to make it brand new . . . At a time when India is going to celebrate its 63rd anniversary of Independence, hungry Indians, dying children and illiterate women remain a dark shadow over the jubilations.[46]

The precise indicators of modernity are sometimes contested, as in this comment from a letter on the new terminal at Delhi's international airport: "It's no use joining modern industralised nations with a swanky new airport terminal in the capital. We should also show the same zeal to establish swanky schools, hospitals, roads and railway platforms. The fact is, these are also important 'windows to India'. What's the use of swanky airport terminals if we continue with dirty railway platforms?"[47] Clearly, though, this is not an argument against modernity but rather over what constitutes modernity. Nor is the appeal of modernity and progress universal across the texts. The textbooks in particular are reluctant to embrace progress and modernity, linking it to colonialism and the social, political, and economic disruptions imposed by Britain's East India Trading Company.

Often linked with modernity and democracy and in contrast to sectarian or communalism are discourses invoking harmony or peacefulness. I call the harmony and peace elements of Indian identity Gandhian—a label strongly supported by the textbooks, which spend significant time discussing the impact that Gandhi's ideas on non-violence and inclusive social relations had on India. Interestingly, the specific invocation of Gandhi occurs rarely. A letter to *The Hindu*'s editors implored a peaceful accommodation with Maoist rebels, intoning that a "Gandhian path is the best to follow".[48] Also in the context of addressing the Naxalite rebellion, an op-ed contributor praises "Gandhian non-violence."[49] Nonetheless, harmony and peace as core elements of the Gandhian appear quite regularly. Prime Minister Singh in his Independence Day speech claims, "Our Government is committed to maintaining communal peace and harmony. We also consider it our duty to protect the minorities and provide for their special needs."[50] In Singh's speech, peace and harmony are key elements of India's image of itself internationally as well: "We want prosperity, peace and harmony in our neighbouring countries. Whatever differences we have with our neighbouring countries, we want to resolve them through discussions." Again referring *My Name Is Khan*, a letter writer praises Mumbai for showing peace and harmony as key elements of Indian social and political identity: "The singular denouncement by one and all of the mission of communal groups shows how to a man Mumbai stands for a united India. With this victory, the communal factions should realise that India is for peace and harmony."[51] Recall as well the invocation of India as a "peace-loving country" in support of a belief that India should be on the UN Security Council.[52]

The final major identity discourse emerging from the texts is of India as a world-class state and global leader with an inherently talented society. Recall that Prime Minister claimed as much in his Independence Day speech: "As the world's largest democracy, we have become an example for many other countries to emulate. Our citizens have the right to make their voice heard. Our country is viewed with respect all over the world. Our views command attention in international fora."[53] A *Times of India* op-ed exhorts India to fulfill its proper role as a "global player" by sorting out its relations with neighboring states.[54] An editorial in *The Hindu* claimed India as "a growth pillar in South Asia and the world,"[55] while another noted the special responsibility India bore as leader in global economic recovery.[56] Another contributor argued that India's economic approach provided a much-needed global role model: "The global economy needs the virtues of yesterday's Cinderella economies like India—hard work, no frills, no needless product obsolescence, value delivery at reasonable price, and even commonsense ethics like truth, which are much needed in preparing healthy balance sheets of companies and nations."[57] An op-ed contributor notes that, along with China, India is the preeminent power in Asia.[58] India's global status extends to sports, where India is "No. 1 beyond question"—at least in cricket.[59] India's status is such that it "should rightfully be made a permanent member of a reformed and expanded UNSC."[60] This element of Indian identity is often laced with conceptions of India as charting an independent course for itself. *The Hindu* editorialized that India should rediscover Russia to maintain its foreign policy independence,[61] a theme also shared in an editorial in the *Times of India* on the "old" friendship between India and Russia.[62]

From the Indian perspective, a major driver of their country's international stature is the recognized innovation and entrepreneurial focus of Indians. The innovative drive is deeply sunk in Indian collective identity. They carry it with them to other countries, in one case impressing a local American politician with the "the entrepreneurial nature of the Indian Americans."[63] Another author, referring to the unique nature of Indian innovation as "*jugaad*," argues that, "Over time, jugaad came to mean grassroots innovation to overcome any constraint. In the West, innovation is done by scientists using expensive equipment. In India, it's done by every housewife, farmer, transporter, trader and industrialist. It does not require high-spending R&D: it simply needs creativity and imagination."[64]

In most cases, there is no substantial counternarrative to the constituent elements of this identity. Democracy is supported by discourses praising democracy (in international and domestic contexts) as well as discourses condemning nondemocratic governance. Likewise the conception of Indians as talented and creative does not have any significant challengers. Rule of law is also largely unchallenged, supported both by explicit invocation of the identity and by anticorruption discourses—although there is a slight tension between the rule of law identity with those who fear that corruption has become an integral part of Indian identity. The aspirational identity as a progressive, modern country is supported by strong discourses constructing India as (increasingly) a place of social and gender equality.

That is not to say that all the identity discourses are entirely in sync. There is, for example a significant tension between the Gandhian identity discourses and discourses that emphasize dominance or power as a defining aspect of Indian identity. It is, however, easy to overdraw the significance of this tension. A significant portion of the power/dominance narrative comes from the films *Dabangg* and *Gomaal 3*, both of which are escapist films. The modernist identity likewise experiences some tensions, particularly in the context of how it is framed in the history textbooks. In those texts, modernism is treated much more skeptically than in popular media. Another slight tension in the modernist identity lies in the ways social changes are affecting familial relations, fraying relations between generations and shifting the structure away from extended to nuclear families. Within the global power identity, tensions also exist between some speakers who understand India to be a global power already and others who view it as an aspirational identity.

Other identities are more contested. Of the major identity groups identified, the greatest tension exists between the two economic identities: socialist/statist and capitalist. From the data, both identities are strong, although the capitalist identity appears the stronger of the two. Moreover, the socialist/statist identity is grounded less in a belief that the state should manage the economy directly and more in a belief that the state must actively work to ensure the economy is inclusive and development is equitable, usually in terms of redistribution. The socialist/statist identity operates in synergy with elite-level competency/capability discourses, while the capitalist identity is strengthened by mass-level concerns over corruption.

The distribution of how identities are held (elite versus masses) is not equal across the emergent identities. Economic identities, both capitalist and socialist/statist, are overwhelmingly concentrated in elite discourses. This is not surprising, since elites, particularly the prime minister, spend much more time talking about India's economy in a concentrated way. Also not surprising is the more mass-based nature of political identities, particularly democracy. Conceptions of India as modern are roughly equal in terms of percent of discourse at the elite and mass levels even as concerns over gender equality strongly favor the masses. Conceptions of Indians as skilled and talented are roughly balanced. Peace and harmony (Gandhian) discourses favor the elite level, while concerns over India as an imagined community are roughly split.

Conclusions

Some clear patterns emerge about India's identity in 2010. Indians see themselves as talented, entrepreneurial democrats living in a major global country who aspire to build a modern, progressive, and harmonious society based on the rule of law. In 2010, Indians had every reason to feel confident in the future of their country. US President Barack Obama clearly called for India to join the UN Security Council, and while major developed economies stumbled badly in the wake of the 2008 financial crisis, India was leading developing countries in taking responsibility for the global economy. That said, not all was smooth sailing. The Naxalite rebellion and re-emerging problems in Kashmir undermined Indian confidence in the competence of their government, as did ongoing dysfunction in the Parliament. Rampant corruption, most clearly manifested in the Commonwealth Games, led Indians to express profound concerns about the ways in which corruption was grounded in broader Indian society. Underneath all of this is a pervasive anxiety about the nature of the imagined Indian national community and concerns that the ties that bind are frail, although the strong stance by the citizens of Mumbai in favor of the showing of a controversial movie gave hope that norms of inclusiveness and community would prevail.

In terms of how India is situated in terms of a global discourse emphasizing neoliberal/capitalist democracy, the answer is a mixed one. Indians at the elite and mass levels clearly are deeply vested in the identity of India as a democracy. It is a core element of the shared imagined community at home and believed to be a basis for India's respect and great-power status internationally. The economic identity is dichotomous. No doubt arising out of India's colonial history and Nehru-influenced post-independence development model, socialist and statist identifications—as evidenced in the positive valence of the socialist/statist and inclusive/equitable (economic) identities—retain an important role in how Indians understand their general economic identity. I include the inclusive/equitable (economic) identity in this assessment because it requires active state intervention in the economy and prioritizes equality of outcomes—a socialist or social democratic norm. Nonetheless, capitalist norms are strongly present as well, likely the product of global discourses as well as liberalizing reforms undertaken by Manmohan Singh when he was finance minister in the 1990s. Thus, in economic terms India in 2010 continues to chart an independent course, understanding itself in socialist *and* capitalist terms.

Notes

1. A 2010 *Times of India* article positions English as the second most widely spoken language after Hindi, with more than 125 million who speak English as either a first, second, or third language (Times News Network, "Indiaspeak: English Is Our 2nd Language" in the *Times of India* (March 14, 2010) available at http://timesofindia.indiatimes.com/india/Indiaspeak-English-is-our-2nd-language/articleshow/5680962.cms?referral=PM).
2. Manmohan Singh, "PM's Independence Day Speech, 2010" (August 15, 2010) available at http://archivepmo.nic.in/drmanmohansingh/speech-details.php?nodeid=917.
3. Manmohan Singh, "PM's address at the First Annual Conference of the Chief Secretaries" (February 1, 2010) available at http://archivepmo.nic.in/drmanmohansingh/speech-details.php?nodeid=856.
4. Available at http://hansaresearch.com/dload/Output.pdf.
5. For 2010, microfilm and hard-copy archives of India's top newspapers are unavailable within a reasonable (~100-mile) radius, necessitating a turn to electronic records.
6. Available at http://www.boxofficeindia.com/Years/years_detail/2010.
7. Available at http://indiatoday.intoday.in/gallery/bestsellers-of-2010/1/3970.html.
8. Available at www.sify.com/news/the-top-10-bestselling-books-of-2010-news-national-km2lkeefhfd.html.
9. Available at http://thebookloversreview.blogspot.com/search/label/%27Crossword%20Bestsellers%27.
10. See Randeep Ramesh, "Another Rewrite for India's History Books" in *The Guardian* (June 25, 2004) available at http://www.theguardian.com/world/2004/jun/26/india.schoolsworldwide; Sylvie Guichard, *The Construction of History and Nationalism in India: Textbooks, Controversies and Politics* (London: Routledge 2010).
11. http://www.ncert.nic.in/ncerts/textbook/textbook.htm.
12. Singh, "PM's Address at the First Annual Conference."
13. Subhash Chandra Agrawal, Letter to the editor in the *Times of India* (August 15, 2010).
14. *Times of India*. "Get It Right: Divestment is Only Solution for National Airline" in the *Times of India* (March 15, 2010).
15. Gautam Bhatia. "The Power Of Ideas: More Than Just Good Intentions, We Need Imagination to Reinvent India" in the *Times of India* (May 15, 2010).
16. Bachi Karkaria. "Erratica: Terminal Wellness: If Our Cities Don't Work, Let's Go and Live in Our New Airport" in the *Times of India* (July 15, 2010).
17. P. G. Menon, Letter to the editor in the *Times of India* (August 15, 2010); S. S. Venkata Subramanian, Letter to the editor in the *Times of India* (August 15, 2010).
18. Chandrahas Kiran Singh, Letter to the editor in the *Times of India* (September 15, 2010).
19. Sanjay Dev, Letter to the editor in the *Times of India* (November 15, 2010).
20. Singh, "PM's Independence Day Speech, 2010."
21. Vaibhav C. Ghalme, Letter to the editor in *The Hindu* (March 15, 2010).
22. V. R. Krishna Iyer, "An Appeal to India's Conscience" in *The Hindu* (July 15, 2010).
23. S. Bhanu Prasad, Letter to the editor in *The Hindu* (February 15, 2010).
24. Editorial, "Ghetto Blasters: Defiance of Sena Ban on Film Is a Defeat for Divisive Politics" in the *Times of India* (February 15, 2010).
25. Singh, "PM's Independence Day Speech, 2010."

26. Nalini Vijayaraghavan, Letter to the editor in *The Hindu* (November 15, 2010).
27. R. K. Kutty, Letter to the editor in *The Hindu* (January 14, 2010).
28. Jug Suraiya, "Second Opinion—Total Brake Down: Changing the Stalled Car of Parliament Won't Help; We Have to Change the Driver" in the *Times of India* (December 15, 2010).
29. Jug Suraiya, "Second Opinion—Force of Arms: Power, not Democracy, Comes out of the Barrel of a Gun" in the *Times of India* (September 15, 2010).
30. N. Jayaraj, Letter to the editor in *The Hindu* (November 15, 2010).
31. Editorial, "A Fraud of an Election" in *The Hindu* (March 15, 2010).
32. P. S. Suryanarayana, "Thai Crisis in a Globalised Scene" in *The Hindu* (March 15, 2010).
33. Nayan Chanda, "Global Eye—Shadow Boxing In Beijing" in the *Times of India* (May 15, 2010).
34. Shridhar Shukla, Letter to the editor in the *Times of India* (March 15, 2010).
35. Harish Kumar Prajapati, Letter to the editor in the *Times of India* (July 15, 2010).
36. Singh, "PM's Address at the First Annual Conference."
37. S. Mekala, Letter to the editor in *The Hindu* (January 14, 2010).
38. Editorial, "The Show Does Go On" in *The Hindu* (February 15, 2010).
39. Shreegiri Hiremath, Letter to the editor in *The Hindu* (April 15, 2010).
40. Aishwarya Vijaychandran, Letter to the editor in *The Hindu* (July 15, 2010).
41. Singh, "PM's Independence Day Speech, 2010."
42. Tuhin A. Sinha, "Race for the Crown: In Revival Mode, Can the BJP Successfully Challenge the Congress on the National Stage?" in the *Times of India* (December 15, 2010).
43. Editorial, "Ghetto Blasters."
44. Sylvia Ann Hewlett and Vishakha N. Desai, "Women and the Workplace: Educated Women Are One of the Chief Engines of the Dynamic Economies of India and China" in the *Times of India* (September 15, 2010).
45. Editorial, "Gender & Urban Development" in *The Hindu* (July 15, 2010).
46. Deepa Kylasam Iyer, Letter to the editor in *The Hindu* (August 15, 2010).
47. N. Nagarajan, Letter to the editor in *The Hindu* (August 15, 2010).
48. V. K. Raghunathan, Letter to the editor in *The Hindu* (April 15, 2010).
49. Iyer, "An Appeal to India's Conscience."
50. Singh, "PM's Independence Day Speech, 2010."
51. S. Bhanu Prasad, Letter to the editor in *The Hindu* (February 15, 2010).
52. Vijayaraghavan, Letter to the editor.
53. Singh, "PM's Independence Day Speech, 2010."
54. R. K. Pachauri, "Seek the Peace Dividend: To Achieve Full Potential as a Global Player, India Must Engage Its Neighbours" in the *Times of India* (November 15, 2010).
55. Editorial, "Seizing the Moment" in *The Hindu* (January 14, 2010).
56. Editorial, "Asia's Global Responsibility" in *The Hindu* (June 15, 2010).
57. Satya Saurabh Khosla, "Goldilocks to Cinderella" in the *Times of India* (February 15, 2010).
58. Siddharth Varadarajan, "Time to Reset the India-China Relationship" in *The Hindu* (December 15, 2010).
59. Editorial, "No. 1 beyond Question" in *The Hindu* (October 15, 2010).
60. Vijayaraghavan, Letter to the editor.
61. Editorial, "Rediscovering Russia" in *The Hindu* (March 15, 2010).
62. Editorial, "Old Friends: New Realities Must Define Indo-Russian Ties" in the *Times of India* (March 15, 2010).
63. Narayan Lakshman, "An Unusual Indian-American Icon" in *The Hindu* (October 15, 2010).
64. Swaminathan S. Anklesaria Aiyar, "Jugaad Is Our Most Precious Resource" in the *Times of India* (August 15, 2010).

8

The World's Largest Democracy Between Two Futures

Indian National Identity in 2010, Hindi Sources

SHIVAJI KUMAR

Introduction

In 2010, India's dominant discourse strongly supports the ideology of democratic capitalism and emphasizes transparency and competence. This is reinforced by a discourse of India's place in the future. However, two counter-discourses suggest that the ideal of liberal hegemony is constrained by corruption and divisive politics. Democratic discourse portrays India as a country that takes pride in sustaining democracy, allows popular participation, ensures citizens' rights and responsibilities, and nurtures an open, competitive society. This discourse produces consensus across the elite-mass divide. Indian democratic discourse in 2010 also positions itself as superior to other Asian and African states, states who have shorter experience with democracy and weaker democratic roots. This aligns India closely with Western liberal hegemony.

The corrupt society challenger discourse reflects widespread anti-corruption disposition in mass texts. The lack of accountability, corrupt political class, state failure, and political violence are negatively contrasted with transparency. One salient marker is the divergence of opinion between the elite and masses on the extent of corruption. The second challenger discourse of divisive politics suggests that India lives with two significant others: a constant threat of Balkanization and the memories of country's partition. This predominantly mass discourse seriously challenges India's claim to be a leader of liberal democracy in developing regions and it undermines the country's ability to strengthen liberal hegemony in world politics. If these two challenger discourses grew stronger, they may adversely affect India's standing as an emerging power in international politics and would undermine its self-understanding as a supporter of the democratic capitalism. This would also negatively impact one of the salient features of India's dominant discourse in 2010: its path to modernization, Western or Asian.

I. Text Selection

This report of India's identity topography for the year 2010 analyzed approximately 280 texts. All texts were in Hindi, India's official language. Hindi is the most popular language in India: approximately 40% of the population uses it as the first language and about 25% as the second.[1] It is thus used widely among even non-native speakers of Hindi and serves as a salient element in the formation of India's identity. Toward recovering identity discourses of Hindi-speaking population, this report used two newspapers, two leadership speeches, two high school textbooks, two novels, and two Bollywood movies (see Sources).

I selected two leadership speeches for the year 2010. The first speech was of President Pratibha Patil. She delivered this speech on the eve of Republic Day, January 25, 2010.[2] Republic Day commemorates the formal operationalization of India's democratic constitution in 1950. This speech is now used to highlight where India is and where it should be going in scientific, defense, and cultural achievements. The second speech was of Prime Minister Manmohan Singh, delivered on the occasion of Independence Day, August 15, 2010.[3] On Independence Day, the Prime Minister addresses the nation, highlights the achievements of the government, and lays out the future agenda. I also selected two Hindi daily newspapers: the *Dainik Jagran* and the *Dainik Bhaskar*. According to the 2010 Indian Readership Survey, the *Dainik Jagran* had the largest circulation, followed by the *Dainik Bhaskar*.[4] I read op-eds, letters to the editor, and other editorial pieces appearing on 15th of every month in these newspapers. In total, I read and analyzed about 270 texts from these newspapers, ranging from single-sentence letters to the editor to the full-page editorial pieces.

Next I selected 11th- and 12th-grade high school textbooks. They were, respectively, *Vishva Itihas ke Kuch Vishay* (*Themes in World History*) and *Bhartiya Itihas ke Kuch Vishay* (*Themes in Indian History*). They were selected partly for their focus on India's 20th-century history and partly for their large circulation. NCERT (the National Center for Educational Research and Training) prepares these texts, which are used by various educational boards. CBSE (the Central Board of Secondary Education) is the largest educational board in India that uses these textbooks even in states that have their own boards. The next set of texts was the two most-attended popular Hindi movies. *Dabangg* and *Golmaal 3*[5] were, respectively, the first- and second-most-attended movies in the year 2010. I inferred attendance for these two movies from the revenue earned in the first five weeks of the release, as well as the annual revenue.[6] Finally, I selected two popular Hindi novels. The first novel was a collection of short stories entitled *Bhook ke Teen Din* (*Three Days of Hunger*) by Yashpal. The second was the novel *Aangan mein ek Vriksha* (*A Tree in the Courtyard*) by Dushyant Kumar.[7] Both texts were published in 2010 and were selected based on their availability in the online catalogs of various bookstores. The availability of *Bhook ke Teen Din* (*Bhook* hereafter) in diverse bookstores indicates its fairly high popularity.[8] *Aangan mein ek Vriksha* (*Vriksha* hereafter) appeared in a number of online bookstore catalogs.[9] I adopted this selection criterion because of the absence of a consolidated bestseller list in India, generally available in many other countries. While online book sales may have been low in 2010, the available trends indicate an upward trajectory.[10] Given these constraints, it is difficult to rank these books according to their readership. Following this selection strategy, section II presents India's salient identity elements.

II. Indian Identities in 2010

Democratic Rights

Democratic rights refer to social attributes of democracy that cut across mass-elite, caste, and generational divides (see Table 8.1). It is a positive value for Indians and presents several significant others. India's young generation appears as a significant future other. A letter to the editor in *Jagran* suggests, "We should impress upon children's clean minds the values of rights and responsibilities" (November 15); these children, in turn, will make India's democracy strong in the future. This is reinforced by their awareness of constitutional prerogatives of exercising democratic rights in which constitution-makers emerge as significant historical others. "Our constitution makers were very conscious of giving all citizens equal rights" (NCERT, 11th grade, pp. 406, 421) and "As the world's largest democracy we have become an example for many other countries to emulate. . . . Our people have {a} right to make their voice heard" (Singh 2010).

Democracy

Democratic identification cuts across the elite-mass divide, but the elite role as trustees of democracy is salient. "We must take all decisions in the spirit of trusteeship, our people are poor and illiterate" (NCERT, 12th grade, pp. 407–408). This understanding of democracy is further reinforced in popular imagination.

Table 8.1 **Identity Category Raw Counts**

Category	Total	Speeches	Newspapers (Op-eds)	Newspapers (Letters)	Textbooks	Movies	Novels
Democratic rights	25	4	3	0	13	0	5
Lack of accountability	20	2	5	6	0	1	6
Democracy	16	9	1	0	6	0	0
Modernization	15	1	0	0	7	0	7
Popular participation	14	3	5	0	1	1	4
Economic disparities	13	0	1	0	3	0	9
Religious and linguistic differences	12	2	2	3	5	0	0
Claim to be a developed nation	11	2	4	0	1	0	4
Corrupt political class	11	3	2	0	0	1	5
Neoliberal market reforms	11	0	3	2	3	3	0
State failure	10	1	2	3	0	0	4
Divisiveness	8	0	3	3	2	0	0
Bright future	7	3	0	0	4	0	0
Equal opportunities for all	7	1	1	0	2	0	3
Hard work	7	0	0	0	0	1	6
Political violence	6	0	2	0	0	4	0
Economic relations & outsourcing	5	0	2	3	0	0	0
Distortion of democratic values	4	0	0	3	0	1	0
Transparency	4	0	1	0	0	0	3
Total	**214**	**31**	**39**	**26**	**50**	**12**	**56**

"Prajatantra (government of the ruled) mainly depends on the enlightened decisions of the chosen few" (*Dabangg*). The political class prides itself in taking this democracy to people. "We have ably demonstrated that we are a functioning democracy, by time and again, choosing our government through our ballot and by taking democracy to the grassroots" (Patil 2010).

Popular Participation

This category captures references to Indians' capacity to affect state policies, which appears as an ambivalent identity element. This identity element cuts across the elite-mass divide, but the mass-based sentiment about its effectiveness is more salient. When an overly confident politician inquires about who the village villain was, the ordinary citizens respond, "You are the villain" (*Dabangg*). An aspect of this discourse is the ineffectiveness of democratic means to resolve citizens' problems. "Our government ignores all opposition, even positive opposition; {if you} strike to protest against the petrol price hike, the government does not change its mind" (*Jagran*, September 15). However, another quotation turns popular participation into a virtue. One of Prime Minister Singh's goals in 2010 was to allow caste census for increasing popular participation. "Caste is the most critical glue that binds people together, it is also that motivates people to vote for one of their own" (*Jagran*, November 15).[11]

Modernization

Modernization refers to Indian aspirations to achieve rapid industrialization, distinguishing the country's past experiences from future expectations. This is an aspirational element in which two significant others are salient. Indians look forward to a modern country in 2010, marked by a generational gap and attraction to two different paths of modernization. The future significant other appears from India's own present aspirations. "India had reached a definitional stage" (Patil 2010) from where it would start to lead in the next few decades. This was elevated in 2010 to a new self-understanding: a "new imagination," according to the two sets of brothers in *Golmaal*, "that will bring a future different from the past." Modernization also presents a historical significant other. Indians learn that "the Japanese rise as an industrial, developed nation within a few decades in the 19th century is inspiring" (NCERT, 11th grade, p. 232). Further, Chinese development in the 20th century is spectacular (Ibid., pp. 238–240).

Corrupt Political Class

Corrupt political class is a negative identity element and emerges as a fact of contemporary Indian life, providing a constant source of disillusionment. "I cannot keep everyone happy," says the Environment Minister Jayaram Ramesh (*Jagran*, February 15). This failure to keep others happy is explicitly in reference to the pressures Ramesh felt from different sources to allow marketing of large genetically modified (GM) seed companies' products at the expense of locally preserved seeds. Corrupt political class identity becomes weaker with some positive steps to remove corruption from the society. "Praiseworthy beginning" is one such initiative (*Jagran*, April 15). Another example from elite discourse highlights this. According to the Prime Minister Singh: "In the last few years, we have taken many significant steps in this direction."

Lack of Accountability

This category refers to the absence of measures to hold state officials **accountable** for their failure in performing their responsibilities, a negative element of Indian identity. "Peoples' confidence is eroding because of the lack of accountability and state failure," which has a very different meaning for rural India (*Jagran*, January 15). Bundelkhand[12] women face droughts and famines and carry water buckets on their heads (*Jagran*, July 15; also *Bhook*). Lack of accountability also tells many Indians their powerlessness to fulfill their most basic needs. "Your hunger makes you do everything. You do not know where you are going or what you are doing" (*Bhook*). Indians also understand the problem of lack of accountability as a denial of justice. An editorial raises this problem thus, "janata ke sath anyay kyon?" (Why injustice with people?) (*Jagran*, July 15).

Religious and Linguistic Differences

Religion and language differences appear with both positive and negative valences in Indian identity. The negative valence appears thus, "British left India but sowed seeds of mischief" (NCERT, 12th grade, p. 377; *Jagran*, May 15). Jawaharlal Nehru, Pundit Govind Pant, and Sardar Patel are the heroes. They saved India from the ultimate consequences of the religion-based politics: the Balkanization of the country (NCERT, 11th grade, p. 216). In this context, religious values have positive connotations. Indians know that religion brings out a spirit of charity and empathy in people. A textbook excerpt entitled "Repaying my father's debt" (NCERT, 12th grade, pp. 377–378) recounts the ways in which a Hindu saved a Muslim from his extremist coreligionists at the time of India-Pakistan partition:

> My father was saved by a Hindu woman by hiding him under the pile of dead bodies. When they {Hindu extremists} came back to see if anybody still had life, my father pretended dead until they were gone. The next morning he ran for the border and crossed over. I help you and other Hindus because I feel an obligation to repay my father's debt.

Economic Disparities

The category **economic disparities** refers to a deep divide between rich and poor Indians and appears as an aversive element. "Your hunger makes you do everything. You do not know where you are going or what you are doing" (*Bhook*). Economic disparities defined individual status in reference to the state. "Census of poor" will do nothing to improve plight of the poor, echoes *Jagran* (July 15). Economic disparities also become result of the misuse of state resources. A reader writes to the *Jagran* editor (January 15): "Our government sends officials to international conferences on hunger eradication where they spend money on lavish parties and live in luxurious hotels while the food grains go to waste in warehouses. Millions would benefit if we could fix our food storage system here at home."

Neoliberal Market Reforms

Neoliberal reforms appear mainly positive and refer to opening up of the market to others and making money. The sentiment that "A business requires a good strategy" became salient for individual success. "If you want to be successful, you need to make money" (*Golmaal*). India's prospects of hosting the 2012 ASEAN meeting also reveal a new meaning for this identity. "ASEAN will offer a much larger market to us than signing of preferential free trade agreements with single countries" (*Jagran*, February 15). Western countries are suffering from downturn because of the mismanaged economies. "The Conservatives will bring more fiscal prudence than Gordon Brown's Labor Party" (Ibid., May 15). The "danger of protectionism" against Indian goods is particularly negative because it stems from a country that is the beacon of open market practices. America's withdrawal of incentives for outsourcing is certainly bad for India "because [such measures] take away millions of our IT jobs, but they also undermine open market principles" (*Jagran*, September 15).

Developed Nation

The identity **developed nation** is primarily an aspirational identity that refers to India's desire to be counted among developed states and to achieve the status of a respectable country. "Our achievements and experiences have, indeed, brought the nation to a definitional stage, where the promise of a bright future as a developed and progressive nation is for us to claim, as we all work together with courage and commitment" (Patil 2010). Commanding international respect is another aspect to this identity as evident from this speech. "Our country is viewed with respect all over the world. Our views command attention in international fora" (Singh speech). Empowering of citizens also emerges as another Indian identity element. "We are building a new India in which every citizen would have a stake, an India which would be prosperous, and in which all citizens would be able to live a life of honor and dignity" (Ibid.). "This will occur," the Prime Minister continues, "in an environment of peace and goodwill."

State Failure

State failure refers to India's lack of institutional capacity to deliver services to citizens and has negative connotations. "The medical regulatory body was in deep slumber while hospitals and doctors carried on with their malpractices" (*Jagran*, May 15). State failure also undermines provision of other basic necessities. A quote from movie *Dabangg* clearly highlights this: "India had focused on five basic necessities of bread, clothes, home, electricity, and water since independence but did not deliver them to people even in 2010." Deprived classes have historically been particularly dissatisfied with state failure and continue to be so. "It is not enough to hold meetings, organize conventions, or form organizations. We need help to climb the economic ladder" (NCERT, 11th grade, p. 420).

Divisiveness

Divisiveness is a negative identity marker denoting a general environment of distrust and fear of others. "Himanchal is deprived off its due share of electric generation," which adversely affects its infrastructure development (*Jagran*, April 15).[13] Division of society into men and women adversely affects family and social unity. A newspaper quotation highlights this attitude. "Reservation for women in politics and jobs would divide our society to no end and would undermine their self-confidence and self-realization" (*Jagran*, April 15). Community and individual stereotypes are also salient. "Muslims are rude, boorish, and dirty, descendants of those who attacked Indian civilizations" (NCERT, 11th grade, p. 381). In contrast, "Hindus are clean, liberal, and people who have been under attack from Muslims" (Ibid.).

Equal Opportunities for All

This refers to Indian commitment to making opportunities for progress available to all in a highly unequal society and it is a positive value. "Equal opportunities for all will establish a socialist state in India" that will "make our society progressive" (NCERT, 11th grade, p. 412). Indians know that equality of opportunities for all also implies giving equal access to education. "Shiksha ka adhikar" (right to education) "makes available all other rights to people" (*Bhaskar*, May 15). A salient part of this identity trope is equality of opportunities to earn a decent living. "We are building a new India in which every citizen would have a stake, an India which would be prosperous, and in which all citizens would be able to live a life of honor and dignity" (Singh 2010).

Bright Future

This is an aspirational identity in which Indians are looking forward to a bright future. "The day when our dreams will come true is not far off" (Singh 2010). The idea of a bright future also animated students' imagination. "Writing of our constitution heralded a bright future for India," which was a milestone that marked a break from the past and oriented us to new possibilities (NCERT, 11th grade, p. 406).

Hard Work

Hard work refers to Indian aspirations to work without obstacles of caste, class, or locational divides. Indian citizens desired to work for realizing their potential and dreams but faced various constraints, which contrasted with what people faced in other countries: "Japanese in the 19th century put in tremendous hard work to overcome their country's backwardness and to catch up with Europeans" (NCERT, 12th grade, p. 233). Indians are also changing their own attitude toward work. "Berejgari [unemployment] impedes realization of our potential and also hampers our ability to put in our best" (*Bhook*).

Political Violence

Political violence is an aversive category and refers to politically motivated and politically directed violence. A newspaper quotation clearly shows this negative value: "India is gripped by violence in large parts of the country that would defeat democracy and bring us all under rule of the Maoists" (*Jagran*, July 15). Indians also used political violence to demand greater resources. "Jats are now demanding reservation," which is likely to escalate into large-scale violence (*Jagran*, September 15). As a dialogue from the movie *Dabangg* shows, political violence as an important part of Indian political identity: "Violence is a part of life if you are in politics" and "if you have dreams of securing victory."

Economic Relations and Outsourcing

Indians are ambivalent about this identity element, referring to economic productivity as a means to show talent to several external significant others. A newspaper quote shows a positive aspect of it: "India's economy has been thriving for many years because of outsourcing to other countries" (*Jagran*, November 15). Outsourcing allows Indians to show their technological and scientific acumen to the world and thus to relate their country with significant others. Indians relate with one external significant other thus, "East Asia is our natural connection and we can rely on it more than others" (Ibid.). Outsourcing also is a negative element of Indian identity. "American ban on Indian outsourcing" or "punishing those companies outsourcing to India is taking away our jobs" (*Jagran*, May 15). This becomes more salient when Indians reconceptualize their existing identity in connection with some undefined significant others. "We need to find other places to send our talent" (*Bhaskar*, January 15).

Transparency

Transparency is an aspirational element of Indian identity and refers to a desire to open up government functions to public scrutiny. This is mainly a popular aspiration in which elite discourses are conspicuously absent. "I am tired of this bureaucratic inertia; I want to see transparency in the import of daily goods" (*Jagran*, February 15). A strong moral aspiration for transparency also emerges as a virtue. "Your hunger makes you do everything. You do not know where you are going or what you are doing" (*Bhook*). A *Jagran* reader further shows the way in which this Indian identity appears. "We need a new mindset, a new determination to challenge every official decision" (February 15).

Distortion of Democratic Values

Declining democratic values and its negative implications for their lives define Indian identity. "Our politics is all about self-interests of leaders. It is not about us" (*Jagran*, July 15). This also revolves around Indian identity to reject important opposition voices. "Positive opposition voices are silenced and this makes our democracy rule of the few" (Ibid.; *Bhaskar*, May 15). Tolerance becomes a solution to overcome distortion of India's democratic values. "Happiness and bliss" (*Jagran*, February 15) will not come without the "power of patience" (*Jagran*, January 15).

III. Indian Identity Topography

As the topographical table shows (see Table 8.2), the Indian national identities that emerge from the texts I selected are grouped in several clusters. "Corrupt society" and divisive politics compete with each other as influential clusters but only on the margins of identity topography. Elements such as the corrupt political class, lack of accountability, bureaucratic ineffectiveness, and falling standards of public morality form the core of this cluster. Divisive politics, the other contending cluster and more elite-centered than the first, is composed of the misuse of religion and language, divided loyalties, and rejection of special privileges for minorities. There are no entries under movies and novels for this cluster. India's place in the future appears as a minor but positive cluster. However, "democratic state" emerges as India's dominant identity in the year 2010. This discourse shows elite-mass consensus over the country's state of democracy and citizens' sense of rights and responsibilities.

Democratic Discourse

The democratic discourse emerges as a master narrative of Indian national identity in 2010. The main elements are the pride in sustaining democracy, popular participation, citizens' rights and responsibilities, as well as an open, competitive society. This is primarily a popular discourse in which most elements appear in history textbooks and novels. Although this democratic discourse has lower salience in elite discourse, it still appears as an important element in leadership speeches. It is for this reason that one can confidently claim that the democratic identity produces consensus across elite-mass divide and presents sort of an elite-mass discursive fit.

This dominant discourse rejects the idea of erosion of democratic values. These values include the freedom of expression and equal treatment of all. This presents Indians with two positive significant others. First as the "historical other" and second as the "future other." In the narratives I examined, children appear as the significant other in the future who would remove the current distortion of democratic values. This discourse exhorts children, and by extension India's youth, to imprint the values of democracy on their minds (*Jagran*, November 15). This is not an escapist discourse but firmly grounded in the ways in which democratic institutions had become instrumental in pursuing elite self-interests in 2010. In this, children would restore democracy to people. However, as the historical other, Jawaharlal Nehru, Sardar Patel, and other political leaders emerge as significant figures who introduced and strengthened democratic values in the past (NCERT, 12th grade, pp. 407–408). This historical significant

Table 8.2 **Indian Identity Topography**

	Speeches	Newspapers (Op-eds)	Newspapers (Letters)	Textbooks	Movies	Novels
Democracy						
Democratic rights	++++	++		+++++		++
Democracy	+++++	+		++++		
Popular participation	+++	++++		+	++	++
Distortion of democratic values			----		+-	
Equal opportunities for all	+	+		+		+
Corruption						
Lack of accountability	-	----	-----		--	----
State failure	-	-	----			--
Corrupt political class	--~	-			--	--
Political violence		-			-----	
Transparency		-				+
Divisive Politics						
Religious and linguistic differences	+	-	----	++-/		
Divisiveness		--	----	-		
India's Place in the Future						
Modernization	+			++++		+++/
Bright future	+++			++		
Claim to be a developed nation	+	++++		+		++
Economic and Neoliberal Reforms						
Neoliberal market reforms		++	++	+	+++++	
Economic disparities		+		+		-----
Economic relations & outsourcing		+	++/-			
Hard Work					+~	+++/

other appears as escapist because democracy may not have in fact functioned any better than today, but the high stature of Nehru, Patel, and their contemporaries presents their governance much better than in 2010.

Indian democratic identity in 2010 also positions itself as superior to other Asian and African states, particularly in elite discourses. India becomes a shining example of establishing democracy in a developing country: "our citizens have opportunities to make their voices heard" (Singh 2010). In this, political stability and successful coalition politics emerge as being salient. This identity boundary marker in relation to the Afro-Asian states is erased in the context of India's own population over the urban-rural divide (Patil 2010). India's democratic identity appears solid irrespective of its citizens' location. This aligns India closely to the Western liberal hegemony.

Corrupt Society Challenger Discourse

The corrupt society discourse challenges the dominant democratic discourse and has a high salience in the Indian identity topography. The significant values of this discourse include lack of accountability, corrupt political class, state failure, political violence, and transparency. Divergence in elite and mass discourse over the extent of societal-level corruption emerges as a salient marker in 2010. While the declining influence of corruption forms the core of the elite discourse, the pervasiveness of corruption becomes central to the mass narrative. Movies and novels affirm this mass discourse, reinforced by newspapers. Elite speeches do not mention corruption as affecting peoples' lives. Instead, they affirm its declining role through transparency increasing measures and decisions of individual leaders (Singh 2010).

A set of corrupt-society binary relations emerges over gender and class. The concerns of rich and middle-class Indians differ widely from their poor counterparts. To hungry and poverty-stricken Indians, corruption appears as one of the causes of their plight. Novels depict poor Indians' poverty-generating life conditions that emerge from the state failure to deliver welfare services (*Bhook*). On the other hand, to rich and middle-class Indians, daily concerns are not just about their neighborhoods and towns but also about appearing competitive and efficient at the international level (*Jagran*, January 15). Corruption renders these concerns visible to all to see. This binary is also present in discourses on gender. Females in India experience corruption differently from their male counterparts. To be an Indian female in 2010 is to deal with a set of adverse socioeconomic conditions, combined with her vulnerable physical body (*Jagran*, July 15). Corruption leads to the absence of infrastructure which forces many women to carry water on their heads, limiting their economic contribution to basic activities. This also leaves them vulnerable to antisocial elements, which further limits their contribution to the social and economic development of the country. This discourse constrains India's participation in liberal hegemony. As long as this challenger discourse has a high salience inside India, it weakens the country's claim to support liberal hegemony and follow the capitalist model of development. This discourse mainly occurs in newspapers, novels, and movies, and is predominantly mass-based with a negligible salience in elite discourse.

Divisive Politics Challenger Discourse

Another Indian discourse is that of divisive politics. The main elements of this discourse include riots, separate electorates, divisiveness in the name of language and religion, as well as sociolinguistic complexity and caste politics. India, according to this discourse, runs the risk of Balkanization. This threatens integrity of the country and risks returning India to the colonial past. Two significant aversive others emerge salient in this discourse. Contemporary disintegration of the Balkan states (NCERT, 11th grade, p. 216) and the historical memories of India's partition (NCERT, 12th grade, p. 377; *Jagran*, May 15). This discourse focuses on avoiding these significant others and thus uses to country's sociolinguistic complexity to explain away divisive politics. In 2010, Indians also blamed political elites for using divisive politics to pursue their selfish interests. Riots of the recent past appear as benefiting one or another set of the political class (*Jagran*, September 15). Perhaps for this reason, India's political elites scarcely engage publically in this and thus divisive politics has very low salience in this discourse.

In this discourse, masses are ambivalent toward the significance of religion. Religion appears both as a negative and positive force. It leads to violence and riots (NCERT, 11th grade, p. 381; *Jagran*, September 15) but also promotes interreligious harmony (NCERT, 12th grade, pp. 377–378). Caste becomes yet another point over which India was split in 2010. Practices traditionally associated with caste need to be shunned, but caste could be mobilized for electoral politics. Divisive politics discourse seriously challenges India's claim to be a leader of liberal democracy in the developing regions of the world, and thus undermines the country's claim to strengthen liberal hegemony in world politics. This discourse appears to be narrowly limited to newspapers and history textbooks with no entries under movies and novels, making us question its wider appeal. It also appears to be of only very low salience in elite discourse.

India's Place in the Future Discourse

The final salient discourse, "India's place in the future," my label, is the most global in content. It consists of modernization, a bright future, a claim to be a developed nation, and projection of future expectations. As a reinforcer of the dominant democracy discourse, this narrative has salience across the elite-mass cleavage, and is particularly strong within the mass discourse. In 2010, India was surging ahead in capitalist development and participated in strengthening the global liberal order (*Jagran*, February 15). This participation was driving India toward becoming a developed nation within a few decades. India's position as one of the fastest-growing economies in 2010 features prominently in this discourse (Singh 2010). India's inspired young generation appears as the agent of removing the remaining brakes on country's growth (Patil 2010). This discourse further emphasizes Indians' desire for an improved future. This bright future, and the claim to developed nation status, emerge as salient Indian identity elements. Restraining counsels about the obstacles to get to that future place also appear as important aspects. Modernization, not just economic but also social and cultural, acquires significance. Even though there is no entry for this India's place in the future discourse under movies, across other texts there appears a fairly strong elite-mass discursive fit.

In this discourse, several of India's significant others appear. Indeed, the developed Asian states of Japan and China emerge as India's Aspirational historical others. Among them, India possesses greater cultural affinity with Japan than China. The Japanese rise as an industrial, developed nation a few decades after its industrial development is not only inspiring but also admirable (NCERT, 12th grade, p. 233). Although China appears even more spectacular, but it is culturally distant (Ibid., pp. 238–240). However, Britain and the United States emerge as the symbols of Western modernity and India's future Aspirational others. American capitalism appears not only attractive but also promising (*Jagran*, September 15). India's democracy further pulls it closer to the West. In 2010, British coalition politics became one of the clear connections between the two (*Jagran*, May 15). India emerges as an important part of the liberal world and has a lot to contribute to it. Indians are stewards of coalition politics in this discourse and extol its virtues to rest of the liberal world (Ibid.). However, the mass discourse appears to challenge the consensus over India's path to the future: Asian or Western. Mass discourse favors the Western path to liberal order.

Conclusion

The 2010 Indian identity topography this report reconstructed indicates that corruption and divisive politics are impediments to India's support for Western hegemony, but it was largely comfortable with its other aspects of democratic expansion and capitalist development. Democratic hegemony, centered on India and Western states, was salient. India emerged as a significant component of worldwide expansion and consolidation of global liberal hegemony. Although mass-elite agreement over liberal democracy was unanimous, masses were more optimistic about the liberal hegemonic success at home than abroad. However, elites emerged decidedly more sanguine about this success abroad and India's role in it.

Western liberal hegemony was salient as a model of capitalist modernization, but corruption and divisive politics at home constrained India's participation. India nonetheless faced two models of modernization, Western and Asian, of which mass discourse favored Western. In conclusion, India's identity topography in 2010 on balance supports global liberal hegemony despite the elite-mass differences over promoting liberal democracy at home or supporting it abroad.

Notes

1. http://www.thehindu.com/todays-paper/tp-opinion/think-rationally-about-learning-hindi-and-it-will-make-sense/article3943957.ece. Accessed March 16, 2014.
2. This speech is available at the following website:
   http://republicday.nic.in/2010/pspeech10wd.html. Accessed January 19, 2014.
3. See the Prime Minister's speech at the following website: http://www.ndtv.com/india-news/complete-text-of-pms-independence-day-address-427385. Accessed October 30, 2015. January 12, 2014.
4. I collated data from different quarterly results to arrive at a consolidated figure for the year 2010. This data available with the author.
5. The 2010 *Golmaal* movie is the third in a series. In this report, I will refer to this movie simply as *Golmaal*.
6. This data is available here: http://www.boxofficeindia.com/Years/years_detail/2010#.VjfE4ZVdHIU. Accessed October 30, 2015. January 18, 2014.
7. All translations from original Hindi sources are mine.
8. *Bhook ke Teen Din* was available at the following websites:
   http://www.amazon.in/Bhookh-Ke-Teen-Din-Yashpal/dp/8180314308
   http://www.homeshop18.com/bhookh-ke-teen-din-1st-hindi/author:yashpal/isbn:9788180314308/books/miscellaneous/product:27248080/cid:14567
   http://www.ebay.in/itm/Bhookh-Ke-Teen-Din-Yashpal-/261297767083#ht_500wt_1156
   http://www.homeshop18.com/bhookh-ke-teen-din-1st-hindi/author:yashpal/isbn:9788180314308/books/miscellaneous/product:27248080/cid:14567/. Accessed January 24, 2014.
9. This novel was available at the following websites:
   https://www.goodreads.com/book/show/15785354-aangan-mein-ek-vriksha
   http://www.rajkamalprakashan.com/index.php?p=sr&Uc=9788171197418
   http://pustak.org/home.php?bookid=7865. Accessed January 24, 2014.
10. The leading online bookseller Flipkart claimed to have made available 4 million titles to its 6 million visitors in the years 2009–2010.
    http://publishingperspectives.com/2011/07/publishing-in-india-today-19000-publishers-90000-titles/ Accessed April 29, pp. 2–15.
11. Caste is a social marker that divides Indian society into upper and lower castes. A caste-based electoral system reserves a particular constituency for a numerically dominant caste. The contestants belong to the dominant caste and electorates' voting choices are restricted to electing one of the members from that social group.

12. Bundelkhand is an economically underdeveloped region on the borders of two big states. It is a part of Uttar Pradesh (UP) and shares borders with the state of Madhya Pradesh (MP).
13. Himanchal Pradesh is a mountainous state, located in India's northwest Himalayan region. It has abundant water resources and has one of India's first large hydropower projects, based on the design of the United States' Tennessee Valley Authority.

Sources

Leadership Speeches

President Mrs. Pratibha Patil, Address to the Nation on the Eve of Republic Day, January 25, 2010.
Prime Minister Dr. Manmohan Singh, Independence Day Address to the Nation, August 15, 2010.

Newspapers

The Dainik Bhaskar, 2010.
The Dainik Jagran, 2010.

High School History Textbooks

11th Grade: *Vishva Itihas ke Kuch Vishay* (Themes in World History) (New Delhi: National Center for Educational Research and Training, 2010).
12th Grade: *Bhartiya Itihas ke Kuch Vishay* (Themes in Indian History) (New Delhi: National Center for Educational Research and Training, 2010).

Bollywood Movies

Dabangg, 2010.
Golmaal 3, 2010.

Novels

Dushyant Kumar, *Aangan mein ek Vriksha* (New Delhi: Radhakrishna Prakashan, Raj Prakashan, 2010).
Yashpal, *Bhook ke Teen Din* (Alahabad, New Delhi: Lokbharti Prakashan, 2010).

9

Conflicted Identities

Japanese National Identity in 2010

NANAHO HANADA

Introduction

The dominant discourse of Japanese national identity of the year 2010 supports the preservation of democratic hegemony. This support is derived not from the public's satisfaction with the current system but from the prevalence of peaceful values and the virtues of mutual aid and self-sacrifice. Although there is widespread consensus that state power is corrupt, the aforementioned values and virtues bolster the belief that the Japanese people can solve the country's problems without resorting to government actions or attempting to overthrow the democratic system.

The lack of popular confidence in the government and the prevailing belief in mutual aid and self-sacrificial actions as virtuous pose a challenge. After all, economic recovery and the creation of more gender-equal and family-oriented society consistent with Japanese values cannot be achieved without some level of state involvement.

I. Text Selection

There were two prime ministers in 2010. Yukio Hatoyama of the Democratic Party of Japan (DPJ) served until June 2010 and his successor Naoto Kan served until September 2011. In this study, one speech delivered from each prime minister was examined for the analysis of political elites. Hatoyama's Administrative Policy Speech in the 174th Diet session was used to represent the Hatoyama administration, as it was the most extended speech during his time in office. When Hatoyama resigned, he discussed what he believed he had achieved and his thoughts on what remained to be realized by successive administrations. Meanwhile, Prime Minister Kan had delivered two speeches during his time in office. However, his first speech is analyzed since it was believed to reflect his administration's perspective on policy more accurately in contrast to the former Prime Minister's speech. Both of these selected speeches can be downloaded on the homepage of Prime Minister of Japan and His Cabinet.[1]

Textbooks used in Japanese elementary, junior high, and high schools have to be authorized by the Ministry of Education, Culture, Sports, Science and Technology (MEXT). Japanese history classes in high school are divided into two courses: Japanese History A and Japanese History B. While Japanese History B covers the entire history of Japan, Japanese History A focuses on the modern history.[2] The textbooks used in 2010 were difficult to obtain; however, the Japanese History A revised edition published by Sanseido[3] and Contemporary Japanese History revised edition published by Yamakawa[4] were available through the Textbook Publisher's Association. In the most populated prefecture, Tokyo, these publishers' share was around 20%, which was about the same level as other History A textbooks by other publishers.[5] Therefore, the selection of these textbooks is believed to pose no selection bias on the results.

According to newspaper companies' websites, the two most widely read newspapers in Japan are *Yomiuri* and *Asahi*.[6] *Yomiuri* and *Asahi* issue around 9.1 million and 8.0 million morning papers every day. Of the 9.1 million *Yomiuri* newspapers, the Tokyo headquarters circulates 5.6 million. Similarly, the Tokyo headquarters circulates 4.4 million of 8.0 million *Asahi* newspapers. In order to capture the most "available" and "dominant" views of the Japanese people, newspapers issued by the Tokyo headquarters were analyzed. According to the study that examined political orientation of readers of top five national newspapers, the percentage of those who self-identified conservative was the second-highest among the *Yomiuri* readers, and that of those who self-identified progressive was the second-highest among the *Asahi* readers (Kimura 2004). Since *Yomiuri* and *Asahi* newspapers represent both conservative and progressive views, the data obtained from them are believed to be representative. Op-eds and letters to the editor on the 15th day of each month were used.[7]

For the novels, I chose the fourth-best-selling novel, Sosuke Natsukawa's *Kamisama no Karute*, as well as all three volumes of *1Q84*, which placed first through third.

For movies, *Alice in Wonderland* was the most-watched movie in 2010. *Toy Story 3* and *The Borrower Arrietty* ranked second and third, respectively. Both *Alice in Wonderland* and *Toy Story 3* are American movies.[8] However, while *The Borrower Arrietty* is a Japanese animation, it is based on English writer Mary

Norton's 1952's novel *The Borrower*. Therefore, the fourth and fifth-ranked movies, *The Last Message Umizaru* and *Odoru Daisousasen the Movie 3: Yatsura o Kaihouseyo!*, were also analyzed.

II. Japanese National Identities in 2010

The raw identity counts are shown in Table 9.1. Twenty-three prominent identity categories were identified.

It is interesting to note that identity counts in the speeches by the two prime ministers account for 37% of the total counts, while each of all the other types of texts accounts for between 9% and 17%, respectively. This shows that the Japanese politicians try really hard to frame identities for the masses. This is not so surprising provided that a prime minister is supposed to talk about what this country is about, where it should go, and how the party will lead the country to achieve the goals. Whether or not their articulation of Japanese identity resonates with the views among the masses will be discussed later in the chapter.

Capitalist

In Prime Minister Hatoyama's speech, he explains that although Japan has become wealthy in the 20th century, Japan currently faces the decision whether to preserve capitalism, and if so, how a capitalist society could alleviate its negative effects. One negative impact of a capitalistic society is the prioritization of profit over quality of life. The scandal of pharmaceutical companies highlighted in the newspapers is one case in point. In the 1980s, three CEOs were charged with permitting HIV-contaminated blood for transfusion that caused patient deaths. In a more recent scandal, these pharmaceutical companies manipulated experimental data in order to obtain the ministry's approval of a new drug.[9] This concern with the negative impact of capitalism coexists with Japan's status as an economic giant in the world.

The rapid growth of the **Japanese economy** after WWII is a source of Japanese pride. An entire chapter in a Japanese history textbook is devoted to Japan's economic growth after WWII. In addition, the movie *The Last Message Umizaru* has its setting in the world's largest natural gas plant heavily supported by the Japanese economy and technology. However, the story does not end there. The main message of the movie is not about Japan's economic miracle or technological advancements. It is about the struggle of the people to balance between the search for profit, national pride, and human lives.

Table 9.1 **Identity Category Raw Counts**

Category	Total	Speeches	Newspapers (Op-eds)	Newspapers (Letters)	Textbooks	Novels	Movies
Capitalist	35	9	8	1	4	7	6
Pro–strong economy	30	16	1	1	8	1	3
Anti-corruption	25	3	10	5	0	5	2
Cooperative	21	11	0	3	0	0	7
Hierarchical/ unequal	21	3	0	1	2	10	5
Bureaucratic	18	11	1	0	1	5	0
Exclusive	18	4	1	4	2	5	2
Aging	16	9	2	5	0	0	0
Family-oriented	12	4	1	3	0	0	4
Liberal (insufficient welfare)	10	3	9	1	1	5	0
Ecological	10	4	2	3	0	1	0
Balanced (West & East)	9	5	0	0	4	0	0
Financially unhealthy	9	5	3	1	0	0	0
Individualistic	9	2	1	0	2	2	2
Welfarist	9	8	1	0	0	0	0
Economically weak	8	7	0	1	0	0	0
Peaceful	7	1	0	2	0	4	0
Gender equal	7	2	1	4	0	0	0
Hardworking	7	1	0	0	1	5	0
Self-sacrificial	7	0	0	2	0	0	5
North Korea	6	2	4	0	0	0	0
Korea	3	0	1	2	0	0	0
United States	3	2	0	0	1	0	0
Total	**300**	**112**	**37**	**39**	**26**	**50**	**36**

Anti-corruption

Numerous op-ed articles condemn Ozawa's violation of the Political Funding Regulation Law and other high-ranking politicians for breaching the law. There is a pervasive view that politicians and bureaucrats in political circles are corrupted. In the novel *1Q84*, the female protagonist, Aomame, is an assassin. All her victims are male with a high social status, and are often linked to politicians, bureaucrats, or economic gurus. In *1Q84*, it is heavily implied that the only way to punish those who unduly benefited from capitalistic order is through assassination. Although Aomame is depicted as tough, her character is also portrayed with much humanity and weakness, leading readers to readily identify with her.

Cooperative

In his speech, Hatoyama called for a society where no member of the community is isolated. The plot of the movie *The Last Message Umizaru* is notably centered on the idea of **mutual aid**. In *The Last Message*, marine safety officers and civilians trapped on a collapsing natural gas plant caught in a typhoon successfully escape after risking their lives for each other. A heavy emphasis on emotional ties among those trapped was continuously depicted through the film. An op-ed article also illustrates the importance of mutual aid *between* generations. It states:

> [The] pension system is a manifestation of mutual aid between generations. In the spirit of mutual aid, we need to discuss pension system to which both the younger and the older generations can agree.[10]

Hierarchical/Unequal

A letter addressed to Yomuiri from a part-time employee argues:

> I think an educational gap is partly led by a wealth gap. Children in wealthy households can learn at cram schools at early age, and they can go to private schools. I hope that classes will be reorganized so that each classroom will hold a smaller number of students, and the number of teachers will be increased. In that way, I hope an educational gap due to a wealth gap will be prevented.[11]

In response to such concerns, Hatoyama proposes waiving tuition for high school education in compliance with the International Covenants on Human Rights.[12] Inequality is not limited to the gap between rich and poor. A critique of gender inequality (hierarchy) is also illustrated in the novel *1Q84*. In *1Q84*, Aomame's secret career as an assassin is supported and justified by characters who condemn domestic violence.[13] In addition, the plot of *Odoru Daisousasen* criticizes inequality/hierarchy within Japanese capitalistic society. The story is set within a police department and features a young detective's effort to organize a horizontal network to oppose the strict hierarchy of the system.

Bureaucratic

If hierarchy exists among the three branches of government, the executive branch certainly comes out on top. "Bureaucrats do *amakudari*,[14] and they are inclined to protect the benefits of their own ministries."[15] Hatoyama argues that hierarchy was prevalent when the open budgetary process of post-WWII Japan was replaced. The budget was subsequently written by high-ranking bureaucrats in a closed room at the Ministry of Finance. Citing political scientist Keiichi Matsushita, Kan argues that Japan should be—and is—a parliamentary democracy in which people elect the members of parliament, who in turn choose the Prime Minister. The Prime Minister then forms his or her own cabinet. Thus, decision-making at the initiative of politicians was one of the five pillars of the DPJ's manifesto.

Exclusive

The texts portray Japan as an exclusive, homogeneous society, friendly to those who are similar to the Japanese, but hostile to the outsiders or those with different features or opinions. During the Great Kantō Earthquake of 1923, over 6,000 Korean residents were slaughtered. The Yamakawa history textbook argues that the slaughter of 6,000 Korean residents during the Great Kantō Earthquake in 1923 and other mass killings of Chinese people during the war against China were due to the xenophobic nature of Japanese society.[16] Outsiders tend to be ostracized. Newspapers suggest that the bullying and social exclusion of "transferred students as well as conflicts between groups" is common in Japanese schools.[17] Exclusiveness is also rampant in the bureaucratic system. "Sectionalism was at the core of ministries," and now "it is necessary to work beyond the boundary."[18]

Aging

A 62-year-old man who wrote to *Yomiuri Shimbun* argues that rapid rates of aging and depopulation have resulted in numerous marginal villages around the country. While this is lamentable, Japanese society needed to utilize the skills and experiences of the elderly people to see an aging population as something positive.[19] The imbalanced demographics not only shake the foundation of the pension system but also increase expenses spent on nursing care. Consequently, group homes where elderly people live together are often run on a tight budget, and the lack of safety measures and personnel can and has caused tragedies. Commenting on such incident at group homes, a reader wrote: "[the] government only responds when a tragedy occurs."[20]

Family-Oriented

One report detailed the head of Tokyo's ward government taking paternity leave. In response to this report, a letter to editor article reads:

> No male ward workers have taken paternity leave in the ward, and I think it is great that he took the initiative. I think both men and women should participate in child-rearing. It will lessen mothers' burden and help strengthen family ties.[21]

A grandmother of two children, who expects a third, "wishes that it will be easy for people to raise children."[22] To some extent, the DPJ seemed to have realized that one of the factors explaining why the population is aging so rapidly and fertility rates are declining is the lack of **family-oriented** environment. The DPJ has introduced cash child allowance as one solution to this problem, although its effectiveness remains unclear. In his speech, Hatoyama called this "the first step to support child-rearing by the society as a whole."

Liberal (Insufficient Welfare)

Numerous sources suggest that liberal economic policies mean that Japan does not provide its citizens with enough welfare. The current state of medical care in Japan is described in the novel *Kamisama no Karute*. In the novel, a skillful physician, Ichito Kurihara, works at a hospital in Nagano. The author, Sosuke Natsukawa, uses his background as a doctor to describe the healthcare situation in Japan. Many doctors prefer to stay in big cities, where excellent equipment and facilities are available, and where they can devote their time to research instead of patient care. However, "even at big hospitals in a big city, patients are sent from one place to another and admissions are often rejected to them."[23] Dr. Kurihara turned down an offer to work at a big university hospital and stuck to taking care of patients at a local hospital. He describes the lobby of his hospital as "more crowded than bus terminal at rush hour,"[24] and he and two resident doctors are the only ones to take care of all of them. He continues saying "Do you think it is impossible? Sure, it is, but this is the reality at a local hospital."[25]

Ecological

References to Japan as ecological appear in speeches and newspapers. Kan declares that Japan will reduce CO_2 emissions by 25% by 2020. The government will also encourage technological development and programs in transportation, especially in areas related to daily life, energy, and community development to boost ecology. The area of ecology is considered a strategic advantage of Japan to boost its economy. Commitment to ecology may sound postmodern; however, how it is discussed and what it is associated with suggest a persistent pride in Japan's strong economy.

Balanced (West and East)

History books depict Japanese culture as uniquely fused with Western culture. The textbook goes on to explain that in Japanese culture, "such fusion can be seen in daily life such as clothes, food, and furniture." This can also be seen in the Japanese political system. Such fusion began in the Meiji era, when the national isolation policy ended and Western influence flooded into the country. The fusion between Japanese and Western culture is illustrated in the Yamakawa history book, in which the humanity declaration by Showa Emperor in 1946 was depicted as an effort to introduce democracy while maintaining traditional values.[26] Hatoyama also argues that Japan is the country that has most successfully mixed traditional and contemporary cultures, and suggests this uniqueness is the foundation upon which Japan can become a revered country in international society.

Financially Unhealthy

Despite Kan's pledge to continue cash allowances introduced by the Hatoyama administration, the government was in a dire financial situation. In order to cover the aforementioned cash allowances for children and other programs, the government had to issue national bonds, the total amount of which would be larger than the total tax revenue.[27] Such concerns were reiterated by an op-ed article in *Yomiuri Shimbun* calling for the overhaul of the party's manifesto a day after an intraparty election that re-elected Mr. Kan as the head of DPJ. Referring to the fact the government was to issue national bonds greater than annual tax revenue, it argued that the Japan's financial performance was the worst among the major powers.[28] A mother of a sixth-grader wrote to *Asahi Shimbun* to report that her daughter is concerned with the mounting national debt and she is studying English harder so that when the worst comes, she can escape Japan.[29]

Despite these concerns, the government has been able to avoid default thanks to the vast financial assets of households and the current account surplus. Provided that the rating of the Japanese national bond is in the same level of those of Spain and Ireland, "a market havoc caused by a fall in bond value and rising interest rates can happen anytime."[30]

Individualistic

Japan's rapid economic growth in the 1960s meant that TV, TV games, audio equipment, and automobiles became widely used. Some texts demonstrate concern that this has had an adverse effect by atomizing society. For example, a Japanese history book attributed the increase in domestic violence and bullying to an increasingly individualized childhood, in part facilitated by technological devices.[31] "Our society is now completely different from what it was in the Showa[32] era due to the collapse of family and communities."[33] Hatoyama and Kan argue that a vertical society tends to facilitate isolation and individualism, and that a society whose horizontal network is stronger than the vertical one is superior.

Welfarist

For Hatoyama, an economic situation in which it is difficult for the working poor to make a living is life threatening. He promises to strengthen safety nets for non-regular employees by expanding unemployment benefits. Kan also argues that the economy, finance, and social welfare should not be seen as in a zero-sum relationship. Instead, they should be considered in a win-win relationship where each can mutually benefit. In terms of elder care, an *Asahi* op-ed article writes:

> [I]t is the responsibility of the country as a whole to make sure that the elderly can live comfortably. There is no need to be hesitant to pay the necessary and sufficient cost to do so.[34]

Economically Weak

A 22-year-old unemployed college graduate who claimed to represent the voices of young college graduates wrote in to *Asahi Shimbun*. He disagreed with the argument that the high unemployment among college graduates could be attributed to college graduates' preference to work at big, opposed to small, companies. Rather, the writer argued, it is unavoidable for those who experienced the "lost decade" to privilege stability and hence seek employment in bigger corporations. Students should not be blamed. Instead, it is society's responsibility to reduce unemployment with policies that enhance economic activities.[35]

Peaceful

The violence of student movements over the Japan-US security arrangement in the 1960s, which resulted in a large number of arrests, was highly successful in instilling into society the idea that "a violent revolution is not an acceptable method in Japan."[36] A housewife wrote into *Asahi Shimbun*:

> I am proud that Japan would never sell weapons to make profit in a war. Japan does not have to be a "big country" which takes pride in its military power and runs economy by a military industry. Japan should preach arms control instead of militarily competing with neighboring countries.[37]

Gender Equal

On Kiyoko Okabe's nomination as a member of the Supreme Court, an op-ed article argues, "It is said that this nomination was due to the strong support by the Hatoyama administration. It cannot be denied that it was too little too late, but it still reflects changes in society."[38] In Japanese society, there is still a "tendency to say men should be this way and women should do that. However, children have unlimited possibilities, so they should experience as much as possible"[39] regardless of their gender. The Space Shuttle Discovery in 2010 was the first time a Japanese female astronaut entered space, to the surprise of many. For some, this marked a new era of gender equality in Japan. A 62-year-old businessman said:

> I was moved that Japan has come this far. Now capable women like Ms. Yamazaki can work with Ms. Noguchi who has been working on the space station.[40]

Hardworking

In a column of a history textbook entitled "Immigration to USA and anti-immigration movement," Japanese people are described as hardworking and overworked. Because Japanese immigrants who left for California and Hawaii were industrious and willing to work long hours at low wages, they became the target of anti-immigration movement since they threatened jobs of white people.[41] In *Kamisama no Karute*, doctors at a local hospital were described as "deprived of sleep and hypoglycemic"[42] and only thing that keeps them working is "a handful of conviction and a sense of mission that may be easily blown off."[43]

Self-Sacrificial

Related to the characterization of Japanese people as hardworking is the valorization of **self-sacrifice**. In the movie *Odoru Daisousasen*, detective Aoshima was falsely diagnosed with cancer. Aoshima believed he would die when he began to feel ill. Meanwhile, the police headquarters were attacked and many of his colleagues were held hostage inside the building. The leader of the group demanded that the prisoners on the list they had given be released or the hostages they held were to be gassed to death. Despite his "failing health," Aoshima grabbed a scrap piece of wood and continuously hit it against the fortified door in an attempt to rescue his colleagues. His actions stood in contrast against those of others above his position in the police department who seemed self-centered. Thus, the notion of self-sacrifice is portrayed as a virtue and something Japan should be proud of.

North Korea as a Threat; South Korea and the United States as Allies

In May 2009, North Korea went ahead with its second nuclear test despite vehement opposition from international society. Tensions rose between North Korea and its neighbors. In this uncertain political climate, in October 2010, Japan, South Korea, the United States, and Australia carried out maritime interdiction training in Busan's waters. The notion of North Korea as a perceived threat was similarly echoed in an op-ed article in *Yomiuri Shimbun* a day after the training. The article states that Japan and South Korea had previously participated in the Rim of the Pacific Exercise (RIMPAC) in Hawaiian oceans. More importantly, the article points out both countries had been hesitant to do the same in nearby oceans due to historical conflict between countries. It further states that the North Korean threat had amplified that.

The article also pushes for cooperation between Japan and South Korea in the face of a North Korean threat. It argued for mutual cooperation and trust generated by having a common enemy. In a letter to the editor of *Yomiuri Shimbun*, cooperation between Japan and South Korea was deemed necessary to deal with North Korea. The writer suggested the two countries should cooperate not only in terms of defense but also in economic terms, given that South Korean companies remained resilient even after a financial crisis. It is interesting to note that Japanese-South Korean cooperation is discussed only in the framework of the North Korean threat. Cooperation is considered necessary only when there are perceived benefits, so to speak.

Although Hatoyama ended up causing a fiasco in Japan-US diplomacy by setting up the relocation of Futenma Air Station out of Okinawa on the party's manifesto, Hatoyama viewed the Japan-US security arrangement as having been "essential to the country's defense and world peace and prosperity and its importance will never change."[44]

III. Japanese Identity Topography

Table 9.2 shows the Topography of Consolidated Identities. Twenty-three identities are divided into four categories. Pro-capitalism, strong economy, economically weak, financially unhealthy, and liberal (insufficient welfare) are grouped as Economic Identities because each of these are related to economic system. Welfarist, bureaucratic, and anti-corruption are grouped together as State Power. State involvement in the form of a welfare state, as well as a strong bureaucracy, is a measure of the extent of the state power. Corruption is the condition of such state power. Other identities except for external countries are termed Social Identities because these are not related to either Economic Identities or State Power, but they are about the everyday life of ordinary people.

Neither the elites nor the masses have forgotten Japan's economic achievements and both long for Japan to regain economic leadership, although this appears to be more salient among political elites than the masses. The importance of mutual aid is ingrained in the psyche of the elites and the masses alike. Both elites and the masses see the exclusiveness of the Japanese society as a negative trait. There are other areas of consensus between the elites and the masses. While this has yet to be achieved, there is general agreement that Japanese society should strive to become more gender equal and family oriented. These areas of improvement are, however, much more salient for the masses than for the elites. Inequality/hierarchy is another area where consensus between elites and the masses exists, but to varying degrees. While both view inequality/hierarchy primarily in negative terms, this factor is much stronger among the masses.

The predominant discourse aspires to the creation of a more gender-equal and family-oriented society with a strong economy. However, there are three challenges to the establishment of an ideal society. First, elite texts exhibit an ambivalent attitude toward capitalism and so it is not clear that a strong

Table 9.2 **Indian Identity Topography**

	Speeches	Textbooks	Newspapers (Op-eds)	Newspapers (Letters)	Novels	Movies
Economic Identities						
Capitalist	– +	/// /+	---- / + +	–	----	------
Pro–strong economy	++++	+++++	+	+	+	+++
Economically weak	– –			–		
Financially unhealthy	–		– – –	–		
Liberal (insufficient welfare)	–	/		–	– – –	
State Power						
Welfarist	+++		+			
Bureaucratic	– – –	–	–		– – –	
Anti-corruption	–		– – – –	– – – –	– – –	– –
Social Identities						
Hierarchical/ unequal	–	– – –		–		– – – – – – – –
Gender equal	+		+	++++		
Cooperative	+++			+++		+++++
Exclusive	–	– – –	–	– – – –	– – –	– –
Aging	– – –		– /	– – – –		
Family-oriented	+		+	+++		++++
Ecological	+		++	+++	/	
Balanced (West & East)	+	/ ++++				
Individualistic	–	– /	–		–	– –
Peaceful				++	– / +	
Hardworking		–			– – – +	
Self-sacrificial				/ +		++++
Significant Others						
North Korea			– – – –			
Korea			+	++		
United States	+	+				

economy needs to be a capitalist one. Second, while establishing a more gender-equal, family-oriented society probably requires some state support, the public does not trust state power. The third factor hampering the establishment of this ideal society is the prevalent national identity that emphasizes the importance of mutual aid and views self-sacrifice as a virtue.

First, the discourse exhibits ambivalent attitudes toward capitalism. Capitalism is mentioned thirteen times in novels and movies, all of which are negative. Blind devotion to one's company and an emphasis on profit over family is a thing of the past. While masses wish for economic recovery, they are not simply longing for a "distant past" during the bubble era or the economic miracle of the 1960s.

On the other hand, elites express mixed attitudes about capitalism. Although neither the elites nor the masses are satisfied with capitalism, neither has come up with alternatives. However, both the elites and the masses see ecological action as positive. It seems they both view ecological technology as a possible niche for the Japanese economy.

Clearly, the interests of the elites also differ from the masses. The predominant identity discourse of the elite focuses on economic matters while the masses are concerned about social identities. Indeed, as much as 30.8% of total of 175 identity categories found in political speeches, textbooks, and op-ed articles are devoted to economics, while only 21.6% of total of 125 identity categories in letters to the editor, novels, and movies are on economics.

Second, the public does not trust state power, which is necessary to support a gender-equal and family-oriented society. Mass texts express the belief that state power is corrupted. The lack of trust in state power among the masses also manifests itself in the common view that recognizes and laments capitalism as a broken system and its negative effects, i.e., its lack of welfare. And yet there is no mention of a welfare state in the mass discourses, probably because of the lack of trust in state power and the sense of mutual aid and self-sacrifice mentioned below.

Third, mutual aid and the idea of self-sacrifice might conflict with capitalism and family-oriented values. The importance of mutual aid is prevalent both among the elites and among the masses. To some extent, the current state of gender inequality and lifestyles that undermine family values can be said to have flourished under capitalism. This suggests that the public will attempt to alleviate what they see as negative through mutual aid and the emphasis on self-sacrifice can even work to prevent discontent from growing. A case in point is Chief Officer Yoshida at Fukushima Daiichi nuclear plant. He suggested leading a "suicide mission" in order to address the aftermath of the earthquake and tsunami disaster at the nuclear plant, and later died of cancer. Such sacrifice is viewed as a virtue, but can never be good for the family.

In short, the establishment of a more gender-equal and family-oriented society that predominant discourse speaks to seems to be difficult due to the elites' focus on the economy, persistent public distrust of state power, and their emphasis on mutual aid and self-sacrifice.

Conclusions

Discourse analysis of various texts have found that while the Japanese—both the elites and the masses alike—express pride in the country's strong economy, market-driven and profit-seeking processes are negatively viewed by the masses. The public does not prioritize economic matters. Instead, they are primarily concerned with social issues. Japanese discourse articulates a vision of a more gender-equal, family-oriented society based on values of mutual aid and self-sacrifice.

While the support for neoliberal capitalism is rare in mass texts, neoliberal democratic hegemony is unlikely to be threatened in Japan. The discourse on democracy is almost absent in both groups. The only references to democracy are found in history books, limited to the ones on democratization after WWII. Despite the lack of democratic discourse, neoliberal democratic hegemony is unlikely to be threatened as of yet due to the Japanese tendency to emphasize the importance of mutual aid and self-sacrificial attitudes and behaviors and their identity to see themselves and their society as peaceful. A sense of grievance in Japanese society attributable to the grim byproducts of neoliberal capitalism can be alleviated by reciprocal assistance among the masses. In the first place, grievance itself seems difficult to surface in a country like Japan because the masses view self-sacrifice as a virtue. Moreover, even if the level of grievance reaches a tipping point, the Japanese identity as a peaceful nation is more likely to prevent the masses from resorting to undemocratic means, let alone contribute to the collapse of the democratic system.

Notes

1. "Policy Speeches and Others by Historical Prime Ministers," Prime Minister of Japan and His Cabinet, accessed January 18 2014, http://www.kantei.go.jp/jp/96_abe/statement2/archive/index.html.
2. Ministry of Education, Culture, Sports, Science and Technology, "On the Required Subjects and Classes in High Schools," accessed January 18, 2014, http://www.mext.go.jp/b_menu/shingi/chukyo/chukyo3/028/siryo/06081106/002.htm#001.
3. Aoki, Michio, Katsumi Fukaya, Shigemitsu Kimura, Shumbu Jubishi, Takashi Umemura, Kiyoshi Ito, Hiroko Ikegami, Takaaki Ikai, Nobuo Ogawa, Hideo Kobayashi, and Masaru Kaneko, *Japanese History A: Revised Edition* (Tokyo: Sanseido, 2008).

4. Toriumi, Yasushi, Hiroshi Mitani, Akio Watanabe, and Noro Takaoi, *Contemporary Japanese History* (Tokyo: Yamakawa, 2006).

5. *The Market Share of High School and Junior High School Textbooks in Tokyo for the Use in 2010* (In Japanese), accessed April 22, 2015, http://www.kyoiku.metro.tokyo.jp/buka/soumu/choho/556/page5.htm.

6. "Circulation" Newspapers Ads Data Archive, accessed January 18, 2014, http://www.press-net.or.jp/adarc/data/data03/01.html.

7. When articles were not available on that day, ones on the following day (16th) newspapers were used.

8. "Box Office Ranking 2010," Oricon, accessed January 18, 2014, http://www.eiga-ranking.com/boxoffice/japan/yearly/total/2010.html.

9. "Administrative Sanction on Pharmaceutical Firms. Demand for Trust in Drugs," *Yomiuri Shimbun* [Op-ed], April 15, 2010, p. 3.

10. "Decreased Pension: Time to Share Burden," *Asahi Shimbun* [Op-ed], December 14, 2010, p. 3.

11. "Equal Learning Opportunity," *Yomiuri Shimbun* [Letter to Editor], January 16, 2010, p. 8.

12. This is composed of International Covenant on Economic, Social and Cultural Rights, International Covenant on Civil and Political Rights, and Optional Protocol to the International Covenant on Civil and Political Rights. The right to free secondary education is mentioned in the International Covenant on Economic, Social and Cultural Rights. While Japan ratified it in 1979, it reserved the part on free secondary education. It was not until 2012 when Japan lifted the reservation.

13. Haruki Murakami, *1Q84 Book 1-1* (Tokyo: Shincho, 2012), p. 203.

14. *Amakudari* is a practice where bureaucrats find post-retirement employment in private or quasi-public organizations with which their ministries had close relationship while they were in office.

15. "65th Anniversary Commemorating the End of the War: A Clean Break from the Showa Era System," *Asahi Shimbun* [Op-ed], August 15, 2010.

16. Aoki et al. 2008, p. 81.

17. "We Should Talk to Transferred Students," *Asahi Shimbun* [Letter to Editor] May 15, 2010, p. 18.

18. "Six Months Have Passed since the Establishment of Consumer Agency. They Should Take More Initiatives," *Asahi Shimbun*, [Op-ed], March 15, 2010, p. 3.

19. "Utilization of Skills and Experience of the Elderly People," *Yomiuri Shimbun* [Letter to Editor], October 16, 2010, p. 12.

20. "Need for Tightened Safety Measures at Care Home for Demented Patients," *Asahi Shimbun* [Op-ed], March 15, 2010, p. 3.

21. "Men Should Take Paternity Leaves," *Yomiuri Shimbun* [Letter to Editor], March 15, 2010, p. 11.

22. "Wishing for the Safe Birth of Grandchild," *Yomiuri Shimbun* [Letter to Editor], June 16, 2010, p. 10.

23. Natsukawa, Sosuke, *Kamisama no Karute* (Tokyo: Shogakukan, 2011), p. 23.

24. *Kamisamano no Karute*, p. 12.

25. *Kamisamano no Karute*, p. 12.

26. Toriumi et al. 2006, p. 140.

27. "Kan Was Reelected. Call for United Party for Measures for Economy and against Highly-Valued Yen," *Yomiuri Shimbun* [Op-ed], September, 2010, p. 3.

28. "Reelection of Kan. Call for Party Unity for Overvalued Yen and Economic Measures," *Yomiuri Shimbun* [Op-ed], September 15, 2010, p. 3.

29. "Even Six-Grade Daughter Is Concerned about Debt-Heavy Japan." *Asahi Shimbun* [Letter to Editor], July 15, 2010, p. 14.

30. "Debt-Laden Public Finance. Cannot Take Irresponsible Government Anymore," *Asahi Shimbun* [Op-ed], May 15, 2010, p. 3.

31. Aoki et al. 2008, p. 160.

32. Years corresponding to Emperor Hirohito's reign. It lasted from 1926 to 1989.

33. "65th Anniversary Commemorating the End of the War: A Clean Break from the Showa Era System," *Asahi Shimbun*[Op-ed], August, 15, 2010, p. 3.

34. "Group Homes for Demented Patients," *Asahi Shimbun* [Op-ed], March 15, 2010, p. 3.

35. "College Students Are at the Mercy of Policies of Grownups" *Asahi Shimbun* [Letter to Editor], May 15, 2010, p. 18.

36. *1Q84 Book 1-2*, p. 260.

37. "Proud of Japan—Preaching Arms Control," *Asahi Shimbun* [Letter to Editor], September 15, 2010, p. 26.

38. "Supreme Court Justice: More Diversity, More Clarity," *Asahi Shimbun* [Op-ed], April 15, 2010, p. 3.

39. "We Should Not Categorize What's Masculine and What's Feminine," *Asahi Shimbun* [Letter to Editor] February 15, 2010, p. 9.

40. "After 11 Years. Astronaut Yamazaki Went to Space," *Yomiuri Shimbun* [Letter to Editor], April 15, 2010, p. 12.

41. Toriumi et al. 2006, p. 67.

42. Ibid., p. 23.

43. Ibid., p. 28.

44. Hatoyama's Administrative Policy Speech in the 174th Diet session.

Sources

Speeches

"Policy Speeches and Others by Historical Prime Ministers," Prime Minister of Japan and His Cabinet, accessed January 18 2014. Available at: http://www.kantei.go.jp/jp/96_abe/statement2/archive/index.html.

Newspapers

Yomiuri Shimbun
Asahi Shimbun

Cited Newspaper Articles:

"Administrative Sanction on Pharmaceutical Firms. Demand for Trust in Drugs," *Yomiuri Shimbun*, April 15, 2010, p. 3.

"After 11 Years. Astronaut Yamazaki Went to Space," *Yomiuri Shimbun* [Letter to Editor], April 15, 2010, p. 12.

"College Students Are at the Mercy of Policies of Grownups" *Asahi Shimbun* [Letter to Editor], May 15, 2010, p. 18.

"Debt-Laden Public Finance. Cannot Take Irresponsible Government Anymore," *Asahi Shimbun* [Op-ed], May 15, 2010, p. 3.

"Decreased Pension: Time to Share Burden," *Asahi Shimbun* [Op-ed], December 14, 2010, p. 3.

"Equal Learning Opportunity," *Yomiuri Shimbun* [Letter to Editor], January 16, 2010, p. 8.

"Group Homes for Demented Patients," *Asahi Shimbun* [Op-ed], March 15, 2010, p. 3.

"Kan Was Reelected. Call for United Party for Measures for Economy and against Highly-Valued Yen," *Yomiuri Shimbun* [Op-ed], September, 2010, p. 3.

"Men Should Take Paternity Leaves," *Yomiuri Shimbun* [Letter to Editor], March 15, 2010, p. 18.

"Need for Tightened Safety Measures at Care Home for Demented Patients," *Asahi Shimbun* [Op-ed], March 15, 2010, p. 3.

"Proud of Japan—Preaching Arms Control." *Asahi Shimbun* [Letter to Editor], September 15, 2010, p. 26.

"Reelection of Kan. Call for Party Unity for Overvalued Yen and Economic Measures," *Yomiuri Shimbun* [Op-ed], September 15, 2010, p. 3.

"Six Months Have Passed since the Establishment of Consumer Agency. They Should Take More Initiatives," *Asahi Shimbun*, [Op-ed], March 15, 2010, p. 3.

"Utilization of Skills and Experience of the Elderly People," *Yomiuri Shimbun* [Letter to Editor], October 16, 2010, p. 12.

"We Should Not Categorize What's Masculine and What's Feminine," *Asahi Shimbun* [Letter to Editor] February 15, 2010, p. 9.

"We Should Talk to Transferred Students," *Asahi Shimbun* [Letter to Editor] May 15, 2010, p. 18.

"Wishing for the Safe Birth of Grandchild," *Yomiuri Shimbun* [Letter to Editor], June 16, 2010, p. 10.

"65th Anniversary Commemorating the End of the War: A Clean Break from the Showa Era System," *Asahi Shimbun* [Op-ed], August, 15, 2010, p. 3.

"Supreme Court Justice: More Diversity, More Clarity," *Asahi Shimbun* [Op-ed], April 15, 2010, p. 3.

Textbooks

Aoki, Michio, Katsumi Fukaya, Shigemitsu Kimura, Shumbu Jubishi, Takashi Umemura, Kiyoshi Ito, Hiroko Ikegami, Takaaki Ikai, Nobuo Ogawa, Hideo Kobayashi, and Masaru Kaneko, *Japanese History A: Revised Edition* (Tokyo: Sanseido, 2008).

Toriumi, Yasushi, Hiroshi Mitani, Akio Watanabe, and Takaoi, Noro, *Contemporary Japanese History* (Tokyo: Yamakawa, 2006).

Novels

Murakami, Haruki, *1Q84 Book 1-1* (Tokyo: Shincho, 2012).

_____, *1Q84 Book 1-2* (Tokyo: Shincho, 2012).

_____, *1Q84 Book 2-3* (Tokyo: Shincho, 2012).

_____, *1Q84 Book 2-4* (Tokyo: Shincho, 2012).

_____, *1Q84 Book 3-5* (Tokyo: Shincho, 2012).

_____, *1Q84 Book 3-6* (Tokyo: Shincho, 2012).

Natsukawa, Sosuke, *Kamisama no Karute* (Tokyo: Shogakukan, 2011).

Movies

Hasumi, Ei'ichiro, dir., *The Last Message Umizaru* (Japan: Toho, 2010).

Motohiru, Katsuyuki, dir., *Odoru Daisousasen the Movie 3: Yatsura o Kaihouseyo!* (Japan: Toho, 2010).

Bibliography

"Ad report," Nikkei, accessed October 24, 2015, https://adweb.nikkei.co.jp/paper/data/pdf/nik-keimediadata.pdf.

"Asahi Newspaper Circulation and Areas," Asahi Shimbun, accessed October 24, 2015, http://adv.asahi.com/2010/004/pdf.

"Bestseller Ranking: Novels 2010," Oricon, accessed January 18, 2014, http://www.oricon.co.jp/entertainment/ranking/2010/bookrank1201/index15.html.

"Box Office Ranking 2010," Oricon, accessed January 18, 2014, http://www.eiga-ranking.com/boxoffice/japan/yearly/total/2010.html.

"Circulation" Sankei Shimbun, accessed October 24, 2015, http://www.sankei-ad-info.com/data/index.html.

"Circulation" Yomiuri Shimbun, accessed October 24, 2015, http://adv.yomiuri.co.jp/yomiuri/circulation/index.html.

Kimura, Masafumi, "The Contemporary Japanese Newspaper Readership," *JGSS Research Series* 3 (2004), 59–75.

"Circulation and Distribution of the Mainichi Shimbun" Mainichi Newspapers, accessed October 24, 2015, http://macs.mainichi.co.jp/english/03.html.

Ministry of Education, Culture, Sports, Science and Technology, "On the Required Subjects and Classes in High Schools," accessed January 18, 2014, http://www.mext.go.jp/b_menu/shingi/chukyo/chukyo3/028/siryo/06081106/002.htm#001.

_____, *The Market Share of High School and Junior High School Textbooks in Tokyo for the Use in 2010* (In Japanese), accessed April 22, 2015, http://www.kyoiku.metro.tokyo.jp/buka/soumu/choho/556/page5.htm.

_____, "Textbooks," accessed October 24, 2015, http://www.mext.go.jp/a_menu/shotou/kyoukasho/main3_a2.htm.

Ministry of Health, Labor and Welfare, "Income Redistribution," accessed January 18, 2014, http://www.mhlw.go.jp/toukei/list/96-1.html.

_____, "Non-regular Employment (Termed, Part-Time, and Dispatched Workers)," accessed January 18, 2014, http://www.mhlw.go.jp/stf/seisakunitsuite/bunya/koyou_roudou/part_haken/index.html.

Statistics Bureau of Ministry of Internal Affairs and Communications, "Unemployment Rate since 1953 Labor Force Survey 2013, Appendix," accessed January 18, 2014, http://www.stat.go.jp/data/roudou/sokuhou/tsuki/.

10

America's "Only Friend"

British National Identity in 2010

SRDJAN VUCETIC

Introduction

The dominant discourse of UK national identity in the year 2010, labeled "globalism," strongly supports the ideology of democratic capitalism with an emphasis on openness and competition. A counter-discourse, here called "welfarism," exists but its critique focuses on what it regards as improper neoliberal or "Thatcherite" ideas and policies in the British economy. Both discourses acknowledge the material basis of modern Britain and the importance of wealth creation. Another nearly unanimous understanding concerns the need to maintain some degree of influence in the rapidly changing but nevertheless "American" world order.

I. Text Selection

My archive consists of 588 discrete units of texts, ranging from one-sentence-long letters to the editor to a novel going well over 400 pages (Primary Sources and Bibliography). I include two speeches made by David Cameron, who became the UK prime minister following the general election of May 6 when a coalition government was formed between Cameron's Conservatives and the Liberal Democrats under Nick Clegg. These are the Shipley speech of May 28, entitled "Transforming the British economy: Coalition strategy for economic growth," the prime minister's first major post-election speech, and the keynote speech delivered at the Conservative Party conference in Birmingham on October 6. The newspaper sample includes 214 op-eds and 101 letters to the editor published in *The Sun*, the United Kingdom's largest daily, plus 121 op-eds and 143 letters in *The Times*, the country's venerable "newspaper of record" and the highest-circulating "broadsheet" (seventh overall in 2010). Then there are three high school "set texts" covering aspects of the 20th-century history: *Access to History Britain 1945–2007* by Michael Lynch (2008), *AQA History AS: Unit 1 Britain, 1906–1951* by Chris Collier and Chris Rowe (2008), and the "Britain chapters" in *GCSE Modern World History* (Chapters 2 and 3, focusing on the 1906–1918 period) by Ben Walsh (2001).[1]

For novels, I turned to *One Day* by David Nicholls, which ranked eleventh on Nielsen's "Top 100" for the year and was the highest-selling British novel of the year, and *Twenties Girl* by Sophie Kinsella (aka Madeline Wickham), which ranks eighteenth on the Nielsen list.[2] Both can be said to tackle topics in British history from the perspective of Gen X- and Y-ers. *One Day* takes annual snap-shots of Emma and Dexter and their friendship for twenty years, starting in 1988. *Twenties Girl* centers on the contemporary 27-year-old Londoner Lara and the ghost of Lara's just-deceased Auntie Sadie. But rather than material-izing as an old lady, Sadie arrives as her 23-year-old self, carrying the spirit of Britain's—or rather England's—Roaring Twenties into Lara's 2000s.[3] Last, the two most-attended movies analyzed here as independent units of texts are *Harry Potter and the Deathly Hallows: Part 1* (dir. David Yates), which in 2010 was the second-highest-grossing film internationally (after *Toy Story 3*) and by far the highest "UK film" released in the United Kingdom, and *StreetDance 3D* (Max Giwa and Dania Pasquini), the highest-placed "independent UK film" at the 2010 UK box office.[4]

II. British Identities in 2010

My archive describes a country weathering a terrible recession. While economic woes are blamed on globalized capitalism and business cycles, there is some sense of a profound moral **decline** as well (Table 10.1). The main problem is avarice, and more specifically the selfish and irresponsible behavior of the rich. Special opprobrium is reserved for the City of London bankers, traders, and fund managers—the bosses of the Royal Bank of Scotland (Sir Fred Goodwin) and Northern Rock (Adam Applegarth), for example—and others who enjoy six-figure salaries and bonuses while an unprecedented 27% of the workforce works part-time (*Sun*, July 15; *Times*, July 15 and June 15).

Ambiguities of the **modern** age are also reflected in low-minded consum-erism, best exemplified in the fact that many high street stores sell a "disturb-ing range of sexy children's gear" (*Sun*, April 15). Such social ills are new, but national decline is old. A century ago, Britain was "the richest and most

Table 10.1 **Identity Category Raw Counts**

Category	Total	Speeches	Newspapers (Op-eds)	Newspapers (Letters)	Textbooks	Movies	Novels
Socially progressive	32	2	4	7	9	2	8
Orderly	31	3	4	9	12	1	2
Partisan/ ideological	31	3	4	1	18	0	5
Just, fair, equitable	29	2	5	6	10	2	4
Modern	27	2	5	5	11	0	4
Democratic	26	2	4	6	12	0	2
European	26	2	5	3	10	1	5
Open & competitive	26	5	4	4	9	1	3
Class-based	25	1	5	5	8	2	4
Militaristic	25	2	4	2	15	1	1
Immigrant	22	1	3	7	9	1	1
Balanced (not London)	19	3	5	5	4	0	2
Four-national	18	3	4	4	6	0	1
Multicultural	18	0	3	3	7	2	3
Declining	14	2	2	3	5	1	1
Secular	14	0	3	7	2	0	2
American	10	0	1	1	5	1	2
Contrarian	10	0	1	3	3	1	2
Imperial	10	0	1	2	6	0	1
Western	10	0	1	3	5	0	1
Total	**423**	**33**	**68**	**86**	**166**	**16**	**54**

powerful country in the world." Then came the world wars. The nation played a starring role in both, but it also irreparably drained its coffers. "Britain's imperial decline was symbolised by the events of 1947, with the decision to withdraw from India, and the humiliating dependence upon financial aid from the United States" (Collier and Rowe 2008, pp. 1, 144). **Empire** thankfully expired, and dependence on **America** evolved into the "special relationship" (Lynch

2001, pp. 41, 214–216). No less thankfully, Britain mostly stayed out of the **European** integration project (Ibid., 62–63). In 2010, Britain is still resisting the pull of European integration while carrying a significant **military** burden in Afghanistan, where it is helping America defend the **Western democracy**, this time against Islamic extremism.

On "internal" social and cultural dimensions, the British never emerge as a homogenous group. Let us start with the **"four-nations"** reminders. In *The Times* of June 15th, a Dorset man writes to the editor that "our boys in Afghanistan are British, only some are English. We support our boys with the Union flag not the Cross of St George," while a Fife woman points to the fact that "the English national football team seems to be suffering from the same tendency to confuse England with Great Britain through its use of God Save the Queen as its anthem." The union never seems to have zero problems with its nations; solve one problem (Northern Ireland), another one (Scotland) resurrects. From the perspective of the center, the "Celtic" pride of place is understandable, but this pride does nothing to improve anyone's material well-being. A *Sun* article on Britain's unemployment has this headline: "Scots Need a Lot of Work to Catch Up" (July 15). A powerful sense that England bankrolls, even owns, the union renders the idea of an independent Scotland jejune.

All storylines, even *Harry Potter*, make **London** "the city." It is Britain's center of centers—a place where big decisions are made, both good and bad. It is also a place where the country showcases its **openness and competitive power**, whether in finance or in football. The British people appear to have a love-hate relationship with London. On the one hand, the city is joyful and congenial for the upwardly mobile. "It's so PREDICTABLE, moving to London," howls Emma (from Edinburgh) in *One Day*, while in *Twenties Girl* Lara is annoyed that her American boyfriend "show[s] zero interest in it . . . London is one of the most fascinating, historic, amazing cities in the world!" *StreetDance* agrees: only New York can top London's cool. On the other hand, London is a neurotic and increasingly foreign megalopolis. One of the new prime minister's goals is to make Britain's economy more **balanced**—or less dependent on what goes on in the capital city.

Britishness is also always inflected by **class, ethnoracial**, and **gender** identifications—and it is on these dimensions that the nation truly becomes, or aspires to become, **progressive** and **legal** as well as **orderly**, all at once. Class, which is associated with practices, especially accent, rather than wealth, is obvious at all times. In the novels, cockney, Yorkshire, Geordie, Midlands, and Northern are juxtaposed against more posh voices, like Dexter's "pleasant West Country burr" in *One Day*. An aesthetic point of stability from which to interpret this axis of identification is always the middle class. Upper-class manners are silly, working-class ones are tragic, and meltdown-prone celebrities are in a class on their own (e.g., Dexter, Susan Boyle). Class division is also geo-graphical. "The further away from London you go, it's very different. People are worried," is how the boss of a large grocery chain sees the pace of economic recovery (*Sun*, October 15). In the 1930s, a history textbook explains, "Life in the suburbs had little connection with working-class society . . . The two nations remained separate" (Collier and Rowe 2008, p. 85). In contemporary Britain, full upward mobility is rare: *StreetDance* and the novels are all social dramas that depict unusual forms of sex, love, and/or friendship between the well-heeled and the rest.

Multiculturalism emerges as a fact of modern British life. Multiculturalism is understood as either parallel or subordinate to the four-nations reality but it is a much greater source of "tension." The case of the "Luton louts," five Muslims who abused and harassed the troops of the Royal Anglian Regiment during their homecoming parade, is morally repugnant, and not simply a mat-ter of basic **law and order** or **secularism** (*The Sun*, January 15). As history textbooks explain, what events from the 1958–1959 riots to the 7/7 London bombings demonstrate is that cultural tensions sometimes erupt in **anti-establishment** violence. And no government has yet managed to adequately respond to the challenges of accommodation and integration. "The issue that remained [in the early 21st century] was not a racial but a cultural one. Were all cultures to be regarded as morally equivalent? Was there such an identifi-able concept as British culture? If there was, what were its main features?" (Lynch 2008, p. 222).

Public rejection of overt **racial hierarchies** is one of them. In history text-books Britain stands as significantly less racist than Europe in the 1930s and America in the 1940s (Collier and Rowe 2008, p. 89, 144), while in fictional accounts, it is the middle class, now prefixed as white, that strives for an antiracist, post-racial Britain. In *StreetDance*, a decidedly post-racial group of street dancers succeeds in competition only by uniting with a rather white ballet troupe. In *One Day*, the year 1989 sees Emma working on a state-funded "radical" theater play about the slave trade in Wolverhampton. "It's staggering how little these kids know about their cultural heritage, even the West Indian kids, about where they come from . . . .We're going to banish colour prejudice from the West Midlands, even if we have to do it one child at a time," she writes to Dexter, adding that one of her fellow actors may be "secretly really racist, but apart from that he's a lovely man, a lovely, lovely man."

Are there limits to the antiracist ethos? Absolutely, contends one author in *The Sun* (February 15); affirmative action and racism allegations now "poison" government and the media. As for **immigration**, many agree with the prime minister that it ought to be "capped." "Around three million new citizens arrived and settled in a period of five years—one in 20 of the population. Not a bad voting lobby" (Ibid.). Another *Sun* piece interprets the 2010 student protest thus: "Who does David Cameron represent—the UK or China? It seems to be China after saying an increase in tuition fees here will ease the cost for foreign students. I do not condone violence but no wonder our students are protesting" (November 15). *The Times* is more judicious on the subject: immigration may or may not be high, but immigration controls are decidedly bad news for medical research jobs on which the nation's health depends (October 15).

Another divided area of human difference in which Britain aspires to be ever more socially and politically **progressive** is gender, understood as the binary dichotomy between men and women. Men were understood to have more power, but virtually all texts consulted underline the presence and desirability of exceptions to female disadvantage. To different degrees, the two best-selling novels examined here can both be described as "chick lit" to the extent that their female characters are "chicks" in an ironic sense only. In *Twenties Girl*, Lara and her "glossy and confident" friend Natalie run a headhunting firm, while Sadie, Laura's auntie, travels alone "to the Orient"—and this is back in 1933. Sexuality, a related progressive theme, makes an overt appearance everywhere, even the *Potter* film. The origins of this behavior can be found in the 1960s and, to a lesser extent, in the social upheaval caused by World War II (Collier and Rowe 2008, p. 116). Britain may be oversexed today, but the Victorian alternative is worse, to say nothing of the Islamic one.

The British are wondering whether **traditional politics**, understood in terms of class plus the Labour-Conservative two-party system, *still* matter in 2010. In *One Day*, Emma, a long-time Labour sympathizer, used to always know where she stood at home (housing rights, nuclear power) and abroad (the Sandinistas, Mandela) but now she is often confused. The love of Emma's life, Dexter, also a self-declared "bourgeois," finds all politics a bore, especially Iraq in 2003: "like I'm this right-wing nut because I don't spout platitudes about The War. I swear, if I sit at one more dinner party and hear someone say—It's all about the oil! Maybe it is, so what?" Elsewhere, class, region, and politics are defined through each other in fairly predictable ways. In a weekly readers' review of *The Times* (December 10), which can be read as both an op-ed and a letter to the editor, a reader from greater London area points out to three stories about the country's North-South divide published the previous day that taken together suggest that Labour still dominates the struggling working-class North while Tory priorities still lie in the affluent Home Counties. The implication, shared across a broad swath of texts, is that Britain could be (or once was) a lot more **just, fair**, and/or **equitable** place than it is today.

III. British Identity Topography

The British national identities that emerge in my archive can be consolidated into several clusters (Table 10.2). **"Anti-Britain"** groups identities that question capitalism, materialism, the state and nation, parliamentary politics, and Western modernity more generally. It is sympathetically treated only on the margins of the mass-level texts. In *One Day*, for example, Emma's anarchist proclivities are youthful and only ironic. Opposite to Anti-Britain is a cluster of identities that I label **"modern Britain."** This is a country that values individual freedoms, political stability, and the rule of law. The latter very much includes "basic rights such as the right not to be tortured or to receive a fair trial" which "apply to everyone. That means Iranian protestors or women raped in Darfur as much as it does suspected terrorists in the 'war on terror' "[5] (Letter to the editor, *Times*, February 15). This is a master discourse of sorts: it represents the widest area of the elite-mass consensus on what it means to British in 2010. Within it, I identify two identity sub-clusters, **"globalism"** and **"welfarism."** While both subscribe to the socially progressive ends associated with liberal democracy and capitalist free enterprise, they propose different means for achieving them.

The globalist discourse, which can also be called "competitive," "neoliberal," or even "centrist," believes in free, prosperity-seeking, and competitive individuals. This discourse is well-entrenched and self-confident: a country that once was a great empire and an industrial giant can and should be able to maintain its position as a postindustrial global hub. When Kraft, an American company, made a bid for the candy-maker Cadbury, *The Times* (January 15) expressed worries about the government's reaction. While "protectionist industrial policy no longer seems wildly inappropriate" for some, this thinking is decidedly anti-British:

> saving this one company from a foreign predator is not worth setting a precedent: one that allows a business secretary to interfere in the business of takeovers, based on a whim; one that overturns all notions of free trade; one that could damage our international reputation as a place that values fair business practices and minimum state intervention. These are more important British principles, alas, than a decent bar of chocolate.

The heroes of the competitive Britain are Winston Churchill and, for the card-carrying Tories only, Margaret Thatcher, "the greatest peacetime Prime Minister of the 20th century" (*Sun*, October 15). One of the most important political developments in the country's recent history, suggests one textbook, is the emergence of the Thatcher–New Labour "consensus" on how to deal with the

Table 10.2 **British Identity Topography**

	Speech	Newspapers (Op-eds)	Newspapers (Letters)	Textbooks	Movies	Novel
Anti-Britain						
Contrarian		−	−	−	++	/
Modern Britain						
Democratic	++	++	++	++		+
Four-national	///	//	~	/		/
Declining	− −	−	~	−	− −	− −
Modern	++	+	+	+	++	++
Orderly	++++	++	+++	++	//	+
Secular		+	++	+		+
Socially Progressive	++	++	+++	+	++++	++++
Globalist Britain						
Balanced (not London)	+++	++	++	+		+
Open	++++	++	~	+	++	+
Welfarist Britain						
Class-based	−	− −	−	−	− − −	−
Partisan/ideological	− − −	//	−	− − −		///
Just, fair, equitable	++	++	~~	++	++++	− − −
Western Britain						
American		+	+	+	++	~
European	~~	//	−	~	//	~~~
Immigrant	−	−	−/+	//	//	+
Imperial		/	/	−		/
Militaristic	++	++	+	++/−	//	/
Multicultural		−	−	+	++++	++
Western		+	+	+		+

fast-changing challenges of global capitalism. Cameron, upon winning party leadership in 2005, "made it his task to become more Blairite than Blair. His main line of approach was to offer more of the same" (Lynch 2008, p. 230). The same goes for Nick Clegg, the Lib Dem leader and Cameron's coalition partner (*Sun*, March 15; compare with *Times*, July 15). This discourse claims to go beyond traditional right/left distinctions on economic policy, and for a broad swath of both elite and mass opinion in 2010 (especially those willing to give the new "Con-Lib" coalition government the benefit of doubt), the panacea for this round of national decline is fiscal prudence. This is where the critique of the financial sector coexists with, and occasionally reinforces, the critique of the previous government's Keynesian policy of boosting public spending, which resulted in huge public-sector deficit and growing national debt. A letter to the editor in *The Sun* puts it thus: "To help cut the deficit, how about banks repaying the taxpayers' money Gordon Brown lent them? At the same loan rates they ask of their customers, naturally" (*Sun*, June 15).

The welfarist discourse, which can alternatively be labeled "paternalism," "interventionism," or "statism," challenges this apparent consensus with an argument that the imposition of state authority is essential under the conditions of globalization and climate change. In history textbooks, welfarism stands against both "self-help" ("laissez-faire") and against socialism (Walsh 2001, pp. 51, 53). For example, the common ownership clause in Labour's 1918 constitution, clause IV, was radical, but it only "sounded" socialist (Collier and Rowe 2008, 5). Similarly, in the interwar period "[m]ainstream Labour opinion refused to countenance any deal which involved communists and did all it could to avoid the taint of 'radicalism'" (Ibid., p. 76). And after World War II, "Labour's moves towards a welfare state marked the high point of reforming liberalism. It was very much in the tradition begun by the Liberal governments between 1906 and 1914" (Lynch 2008, p. 12; also see Collier and Rowe 2008, pp. 24, 135). In this discourse, 1951 was as significant for Britain as any year in the previous decade: "the NHS was much admired in western Europe. It seemed to show that universal, comprehensive and free medical care could be provided in a democratic, capitalist society" (Collier and Rowe 2008, p. 139).

This is a very different take on Britain's decline. In 1947, Britain gave up on India and give in to America, but already by 1951 it had reinvented itself as the leading welfare state in the West. In lieu of the market or shareholder power, the welfarist discourse valorizes unions, Keynesian economics, and the civic spirit of past governments, notably those led by Lloyd George, Attlee, and Macmillan. Paradoxically, Britain was more modern then in the sense that its citizens happily worked together, in solidarity even, to improve the common good. A measure of their success is the fact that the social welfare state is now self-evident. "In Britain today, we take it for granted that the state pays for health care, education, social services, unemployment benefit and many other services for whoever needs them" (Walsh 2001, p. 51).

While the welfarist discourse today self-identifies as weak, the prime minister's main worry is that it is far from dead. From his Birmingham speech: "Yes, Labour centralised too much and told people they could fix every problem. But it was the rest of us who swallowed it, hoping that if the government took care of things, perhaps we wouldn't have to. Too many people thought: 'I've paid my taxes, the state will look after everything.'" My archive suggests that "too many people" indeed hold this view. Though welfarism accepts that centralized planning and the nationalization of so many areas of public life were unsustainable over the long term, it also rejects the current globalist orthodoxy as either hopelessly naïve or, more frequently, as vacuous spin and flim-flam that dazzles many but in reality serves only a tiny minority. For example, one area where the British people clearly and energetically reject the globalist view that capital must run free concerns the costs of living in London. Thanks to Britain's laws that allow foreigners to hold their assets tax-free, ordinary families are being priced out of the real estate market by the global rich and super-rich.

The masses are not necessarily more sympathetic to the idea of government intervention than those authored by the elite, but welfarism captures a uniquely mass-level contention that the political classes, the Labour Party included, had long sold out to private economic interests. (But it is that the Tories who most keenly look for solutions to problems that do not exist in order to implement the Thatcherist ideology of the residual state.) In the main welfarism aspires to a new redistribution of wealth, but accepts that current trends cannot be changed without mass effort.[6]

Another clear area of the elite-mass consensus in 2010 is **"Western Britain,"** which is my label for a discourse that anchors "modern Britain" in international society. Its overarching aspiration is the maintenance of the country's influence.[7] It proposed two methods for achieving this goal: the pursuit of global economic integration and active participation in global governance. The second method is the more controversial of the two. A letter in *The Times* (June 15) summarizes the main point of contention:

> Your leading article of June 11 rightly rejects the concept of punching above our weight. Yet you persist in supporting foreign policies based on an unreal perception of Britain's place in the world. This defies the logic of your excellent series on Afghanistan, which is that we are not a world power and our defence commitments should be tailored to our economic situation, not the other way round.

Western Britain allows for diverse meanings of Europe, especially at the mass level. Europe is close in the sense that the British people, seemingly of all classes, hop to the continent and back effortlessly and regularly. But it is far in the sense that Brussels, i.e., the European Union, stands for a centralizing, antidemocratic force that is becoming increasingly unattractive. Germany is regarded as the most important European country, and the prime minister's representation of the same speaks volumes about how Western Britain positions itself in the world. In the Shipley speech, Germany is a model: "I passionately believe we don't have to accept things the way they are. Imagine if Germany had given up after the Second World War, leaving the bombed-out factories on the Ruhr lying dormant." At Birmingham, it is a rival:

> there is another side to life as prime minister. Like being made to watch the England football team lose 4-1 to Germany, in the company of the German chancellor. It's a form of punishment I wouldn't wish on anyone. I have to say, she is one of the politest people I have ever met – every time their players scored another goal, she would turn to me and say: "I really am terribly sorry." It's brought a whole new element to Anglo-German diplomatic relations: whatever you do, don't mention the score.

Cameron's closing remark is a nod to a line from an episode in a popular 1980s BBC sitcom *Fawlty Towers* in which mockery is made of Germans' uneasiness about World War II ("Don't mention the war"). The rest of the statement, however, follows the standard history textbook view of Germany as a worthy and occasionally superior rival. Detailed references to the world wars-era Anglo-German clashes are balanced out with consistent recognition of Germany's power and influence: "In 1908, Lloyd George went to Germany to study the practical details of their system of social insurance" (Collier and Rowe 2008, p. 19); "by delaying its welfare state until it had achieved industrial recovery [Germany] put itself on the path to an economic miracle" (Lynch 2008, p. 24). True, the prime minister also mentions South Korea in his Shipley speech, but the rest of my archive suggest that this reference was not as meaningful as the invocation of Germany.

America, colloquially called the States, is regarded as a leader and a friend, with the partnership going back to World War II: "There was much genuine enthusiasm for the American Way ... these positive attitudes continued into the post-war era" (Collier and Rowe 2008, p. 118). America is always years ahead: "Seen from the standpoint of the early 21st century (or even of Americans at the time), Britain did not appear to be all that 'modern' in 1951" (Ibid., p. 144). Oxbridge and London universities cannot compete with their richer American counterparts, but at least Britain ranks second only to America in most university rankings. The American Way is not always the way. A *Times* (July 15) op-ed on the idea and practice of restorative justice identifies one area:

> Often we're [in this case: England and Wales] closer to our transatlantic cousins in affairs of the law than to those oddly behaved strangers in Europe. Yet levels of imprisonment for youngsters in the United States are frightening, with whole populations consigned to predestined cells, and we can certainly love America without admiring the way she treats her underclass.

The British masses seek sustenance from America on anything from pop culture to democracy. All British celebrities seem to draw some of their artistic analogies in America, but only the best succeed there, one measure of which is appearance on US television shows like *Oprah*. The Americans are also better at democratic ownership of the economy. "America always does things bigger and President Obama's tax is no exception," says *The Sun* in reference to the US government's decision to "spank the banks," including those headquartered in the United Kingdom, with a new profit tax (January 15). Britain's love for America can be unrequited, however. Obama's attempt to spank BP for the accidental oil spill in the Gulf of Mexico pushes the envelope of what is fair, writes one citizen in *The Sun* (June 15): "He shouldn't criticise the only friend the US has in the Western world."

The elite-mass divide on the meaning of America is the clearest in the case of the war in Afghanistan, where Britain is fielding 10,000 soldiers, "second largest force after the US" (*Sun*, May 15). For the elite, the war is waged to "keep British streets safe" or in the prime minister's own words: "Our Forces are in Afghanistan to prevent Afghan territory again being used by al-Qaeda as a base to plan attacks on the United Kingdom or our allies" (quoted in a piece by *The Times*' defense editor, June 15). Mass opinion is divided. On the one hand, there is a clear recognition that Britain fights the good fight in Afghanistan. A letter in *The Times* (May 15) urges to the foreign secretary William Hague to remind his American counterpart about "the need to safeguard Afghan women's rights in any future peace deals with the Taleban. It would be an absolute travesty if these were traded away to the very groups that subjugated a whole generation of Afghan women in the 1990s."

On the other hand, the war is regarded as unnecessary and unwinnable. To continue with *The Times*, consider a string of letters from January 15. The first letter: "Today's British public know full well that the security of our realm is not threatened at all: there is no one plotting to invade our shores nor is there any foreign government aiming to overthrow our own." The second: the British are skeptical about the war in Afghanistan because in Iraq they "had been lied to by the Government regarding the reasons for this invasion." And the third: "In 1940 the cause was obvious. In 2010 the feeling among very many ordinary people is that we should not be risking the lives of our soldiers in a struggle that cannot have a successful outcome." A long opinion piece published in the same newspaper on May 15 goes further still. "Afghanistan has made the military heroic, cool, even sexy," argues the author. It had already changed traditional popular culture representations in which only "American GIs were glamorous action heroes, [while] British soldiers in their inferior uniforms were stupid, mindlessly obedient or pigeon-chested comic Tommy turns." This triumph of style over substance may help military recruitment, she concludes, but it almost certainly impedes our understanding the world.

IV. Conclusions

The UK identity terrain reconstructed in this study suggests that the British struggled with global capitalism in 2010, but were largely comfortable with most other aspects of Western democratic hegemony centered on the United States. Europe was significant as a trading partner and a holiday destination, but EU politics caused annoyance. The material basis of modern Britain was almost unanimously accepted. The same goes for the importance of the rule of law, justice, as well as social progress. A move to characterize British reality as anti-immigrant and anti-multicultural would be simplistic, since most texts, especially those mass-level genres, revel in Britain's diversity. While the loss of empire was seen as good riddance, especially in financial terms, the loss of the great-power status was a source of confusion for British. This is most clearly reflected in the elite-mass differences over the Afghan campaign. In short, in 2010 Britain regarded itself as a modern, democratic, capitalist, and Western follower of the American Way, even if it sometimes leads to a cul-de-sac.

In 2010 Britain also suffered from an imbalanced economy, plus a number of social ills. The political debate on how to deal with the recession and, more generally, with national decline divided modern Britain into two discursive camps. Globalism, the dominant discourse, gave priority to the reduction in the size and scope of the state in order to make Britain more competitive abroad. So viewed, contradictions wrought by capitalism appear to be resolved, as in the case of class struggle, or resolvable, as in the case of the financial sector reform and public-sector deficit. Welfarism, the challenger discourse, decried the neoliberal ideology that had characterized the policy agenda since the Thatcher era. In its view Britain was no longer fair: why must British workers compete against their foreign counterparts by working harder, for less money, and with lower levels of health care, when British bankers can do as they please? Importantly, welfarism debated the nature of state intervention, not the value of individual freedom, property rights, private capital, the market, and the like. On balance, however, most British, whether elite or mass, accepted the necessity of cuts in public spending as a way of maintaining competitiveness in the world and creating wealth. Counterfactually, were a welfarism to prevail in the British society, the country would still stay the course in supporting Western democratic hegemony.

Notes

1. The textbooks studied here were used in 2010 for exam specifications at General Certificate of Secondary Education (GCSE; 15- and 16-year-olds) and A levels (17- and 18-year-olds), which are qualifications for advancement in education. England's "national curriculum" regards history a "foundation" subject and is policed by the Office for Standards in Education. See, for example, OFSTED, "History for All: History in English Schools 2007/10" (March 2011), retrieved on November 23, 2013 from www.ofsted.gov.uk/publications/090223.
2. Apart from my two selections and a single Jamie Oliver cookbook, the top 18 books on the Nielsen list were all foreign-authored. Nielsen's "Top 100 for 2010," published on December 11, 2010, on file with the author.
3. My archive is decidedly England- and even London-centric. For example, while I pay close attention to the fact that Nicholls' novel is partly set in Edinburgh, I ignore the Scottish history curriculum and *The Scottish Sun*. I rationalize this selection bias thus: geographically, socially, culturally, economically, and politically, England is the dominant unit in the Union and London, which in 2010 accounted for a fifth of Britain's economy, is the dominant site for the discursive production of British identity. Suffice it to say, the "plausibility probe" philosophy that drives this collection disallowed a larger-scale study that would examine UK identity in 2010 from a comparative "four-nations" perspective.
4. Both selections received "British Film Certificates," but only *StreetDance 3D* is considered an independent production. In 2010, the Britishness of a film was determined by a "cultural test" administered by a committee convened under the auspices the now-defunct UK Film Council. The test evaluates the storyline, setting, characters, authors, and audiences in terms of national identity, and certification leads to tax relief. The British Film Institute, *Statistical Yearbook 2011* (London: BFI, 2011), p. 139.
5. Always in quotation marks in my archive. More on the representation of this conflict below.
6. At this point, welfarism comes close to discursive elements grouped under the rubric "anti-Britain," the difference being that the latter implies the need for a mass anti-establishment effort undertaken at the international scale.
7. Both globalist and welfarist UKs are equally Western; in other words, while they compete to define modern Britain, they agree that the country must remain an important player in the world.

Primary Sources

Cameron, David, "Transforming the British Economy: Coalition Strategy for Economic Growth," Shipley, May 28, 2010. Retrieved on November 23, 2013 from http://www.webarchive.org.uk/wayback/archive/20100601231418/http://www.conservatives.com/.

Cameron, David, Speech to the Conservative Party conference in Birmingham, 6 October 2010. Retrieved on November 23, 2013 from http://www.telegraph.co.uk/news/politics/david-cameron/8046342/David-Camerons-Conservative-conference-speech-in-full.html.

Collier, Chris and Chris Rowe, *AQA History AS: Unit 1 Britain, 1906–1951* (Cheltenham: Nelson Thornes Ltd, 2009).

Kinsella, Sophie, *Twenties Girl* (London: The Dial Press, 2009).

Lynch, Michael, *Access to History: Britain 1945–2007* (London: Hodder Education, 2009).

Nicholls, David, *One Day* (London: Hodder & Stoughton Ltd, 2009).

The Sun, a British daily tabloid newspaper, owned by News Corp/Rupert Murdoch.

The Times, a British daily national newspaper, owned by News Corp/Rupert Murdoch.

Walsh, Ben, *GCSE Modern World History* (London: Hodder Murray, 2001).

Bibliography

British Film Institute, *Statistical Yearbook 2011* (London: BFI, 2011).

OFSTED, "History for All: History in English Schools 2007/10" (March 2011), retrieved on November 23, 2013 from www.ofsted.gov.uk/publications/090223.

11

The Country upon a Hill?

American National Identity in 2010

KI HOON MICHAEL HUR

Introduction

American Liberal Idealism (ALI) was the dominant discourse in the United States of America in 2010, without any serious challengers. This primary discourse supported three sub-discourses: American Leadership (AL), Social Progressivism (SP), and Neoconservatism (NP). Competition between Social Progressivism and Neoconservatism reflected the deep bipartisan divide within the country—each discourse interpreting the same identity categories differently, while American Leadership and American Liberal Idealism were consensual discourses that were present across all texts—transcending differences in political affiliations or socioeconomic status. In 2010, American Liberal Idealism—as the dominant discourse in the United States—reinforced the Western hegemony of democratic neoliberalism, while American Leadership served as the vehicle for expanding and protecting the hegemony around the world.

I. Text Selection

President Barack Obama's State of the Union Address and his Remarks at Independence Day Celebration in 2010 were selected as the two most important elite speeches. For op-eds and letters to the editor, *The Wall Street Journal* (*WSJ*; the most circulated and the third most popular in terms of website traffic in 2010) and *The New York Times* (*NYT*; the third most circulated in 2010 and the second most popular online) were selected.[1] *American Anthem* and *The American Vision* were selected as two widely used high school textbooks. The best-selling American novels in 2010 were *The Help* by Kathryn Stockett and

The Last Song by Nicholas Sparks. For movies, the highest-grossing blockbusters from 2010, *Toy Story 3* and *Iron Man 2*, were analyzed.

II. Key American Identities in 2010

Protecting American ideals of **liberty, equality, and democracy** appeared in every textual genre examined. In his State of the Union Address, President Obama remarked: "America must always stand on the side of **freedom** and **human dignity** . . . In the end, it is our **ideals**, our **values**, that built America . . . These aren't Republican values or Democratic values . . . They are **American values**." In his Remarks at Independence Day Celebration, the President also noted:

> This is the day when we celebrate the **very essence of America** and the spirit that has defined us as a people and as a nation for more than two centuries . . . 234 years later, the words are just as bold, just as revolutionary, as they were when they were first pronounced: 'We hold these truths to be self-evident, that all men are **created equal**, that they are endowed by their Creator with certain **inalienable rights**; that among these are **life, liberty, and the pursuit of happiness**.'

Op-eds and letters to the editor also evoked these American ideals in regard to various issues (Table 11.1). One letter in *The New York Times* emphasized the **constitutional right** to bear arms as an expression of "**fundamental individual liberty**" (*NYT*, July 16, 2010). Another letter called for combining the Olympics with the Paralympic Games, arguing that such a division violates the true spirit of equality (Ibid., February 15, 2010). Although bipartisan politics has produced different conceptions and types of liberty, all Americans—regardless of their political views—define liberty as an "American value," upholding and invoking it in various issue areas. Both liberals and conservatives also share their belief in the fundamental liberties protected by the American Constitution.

The two American history textbooks also provide ample evidence supporting the importance of liberty and democracy in the United States. They repeatedly label America as the **protector and champion of the free people and democracy** around the world, especially after the Second World War. *The Help*, a novel set in the 1960s, also explicitly deals with the theme of individual liberty and equality, as it tells the stories of three black maids struggling to find their place and to overcome racial discrimination in a small Caucasian town in the South.

Closely related to the ideals of liberty, democracy, and equality, **upholding justice and fairness** is also at the heart of every American discourse. A number of op-ed articles and letters to the editor in 2010 criticized the CIA's inhumane interrogations of terrorist suspects as well as the instances of atrocious treatment at Guantanamo Bay, calling for a swift deliverance of justice. Other articles also pointed out various violations of justice and fairness, including the government's failure to prosecute instances of rape and abuse in juvenile correction facilities (*NYT*, January 15, 2010) and the racial injustice of widespread poverty among African Americans throughout the country (*NYT*, November 16, 2010).

The identity category of **legalistic** plays a crucial role. Americans perceive the ideals of liberty, democracy, equality, justice, and fairness to be enshrined in the Constitution and protected by the Supreme Court. In his State of the Union Address, President Obama remarked:

> We find unity in our incredible diversity, drawing on the promise enshrined in our Constitution: the notion that we are all created equal, that no matter who you are or what you look like, if you abide by the law you should be protected by it; that if you adhere to our common values you should be treated no different than anyone else.

Moreover, a *New York Times* op-ed highlighted the need for the **Supreme Court** to prosecute the government's unconstitutional antiterrorism policies including its warrantless wiretapping of citizens and inhumane treatment of prisoners at Guantanamo Bay—all of which amount to an **unconstitutional** infringement of liberties (*NYT*, May 16, 2010). A letter to the editor also criticized the growing sentiment of Islamophobia in America, denouncing it as a violation of the **constitutional right** to religious freedom (Ibid., August 16, 2010). In addition, the American history textbooks highlight the vital role of the **Supreme Court** and its **legal authority** in interpreting the **Constitution** and guaranteeing the liberties and rights of Americans at various moments in history—e.g., *Brown v. Board of Education* (1954), *Miranda v. Arizona* (1966), and *Texas v. Johnson* (1989).

Lastly, **fighting evil with good** is an important identity produced between the American ideals and the **feeling of fear, doubt, and uncertainty**. One can find this good–versus-evil dichotomy in every genre of textual sources—"good" representing all that embodies and respects the ideals of liberty, democracy, and equality, and "evil" constituted by all that challenges or threatens those values. Such polarized categorization is motivated by the fear of any deviations from and challenges against the American self. In his State of the Union Address, President Obama implicitly portrayed America, its liberal values, and its leadership in the world as good, while condemning terrorists and nuclear proliferation as evil. A *Wall Street Journal* op-ed argued against the Democrats' effort to pass the Affordable Care Act, citing the inherent evil of the central

Table 11.1 **Identity Category Raw Counts**

Category	Total	Speeches	Newspapers (Op-eds)	Textbooks	Newspapers (Letters)	Novels	Movies
Defending national security (fighting terrorism, military supremacy)	**248**	32	65	116	27	0	8
American ideals (liberty, democracy, equality, rights, and human dignity)	**158**	15	36	64	22	12	9
Upholding justice and fairness	**129**	8	25	56	24	9	7
Feeling doubt, fear, anxiety, and uncertainty	**127**	14	24	41	19	13	16
Perseverant through hardship	**126**	14	10	46	15	22	19
Individualist/materialist (money, profit)	**106**	4	17	41	19	11	14
Bipartisan	**98**	9	30	43	16	0	0
Fighting evil with good	**97**	4	14	27	24	11	17
Wary of corruption (government, corporations, and other institutions)	**95**	8	28	28	26	0	5
Undergoing economic instability (financial crisis, unemployment, recession)	**86**	16	25	23	22	0	0
Progressive (reform, welfare, social change)	**84**	19	20	23	18	4	0
American leadership (interventionism, exceptionalism, responsibility)	**83**	13	18	34	11	0	7
Supporting the middle class	**82**	10	11	31	15	13	2

(Continued)

Table 11.1 (**Continued**)

Category	Total	Speeches	Newspapers (Op-eds)	Textbooks	Newspapers (Letters)	Novels	Movies
Legalistic (rule of law, Constitution, the Supreme Court)	**79**	4	20	31	15	7	2
Fearful of a big government	**78**	2	20	37	19	0	0
Protecting American businesses	**75**	11	16	26	14	3	5
In need of government regulation, doubtful of laissez-faire capitalism	**74**	14	25	16	19	0	0
Endorsing free trade and globalization	**74**	7	20	38	12	0	2
Troubled by income inequality	**72**	7	13	24	18	10	0
Dominated by corporations	**59**	6	19	13	14	0	7
Facing a budgetary crisis	**57**	8	21	19	9	0	0
Alert to China	**47**	0	16	25	6	0	0
Protecting the environment	**33**	6	8	13	6	0	0
Christian, believing in God	**24**	4	0	4	1	13	2
Total	**2191**	**235**	**501**	**819**	**391**	**128**	**122**

Note: The novels and the movies have relatively fewer codings, because *The Last Song* and *Toy Story 3* shared few common themes and identity categories with the other textual sources. Instead they produced unique codings such as "rebellious teen" and "accepting a new home," respectively—making little contribution to a better understanding of central American identities and discourses. Lastly, the identity category of "Christian, believing in God" was not evidently present across various textual sources, and it was not a significant American identity in 2010.

government (*WSJ*, September 15, 2010). The history textbooks also provide examples of the good-versus-evil dichotomy, including the American labeling of Soviet communism as evil during the Cold War, the neoliberal condemnation of tariffs, regulations, and state interventions in the economy, and Bush's categorization of Iran, Iraq, and North Korea as the "axis of evil" in 2002. Furthermore, this dichotomy is especially accentuated in popular culture, which often dramatizes it into a struggle or battle between good and evil. In *Toy Story 3*, Woody and his toy friends try to defeat the totalitarian Lotso (an evil teddy bear), in order to win their freedom and happiness.

In 2010, America continues to suffer from **economic instability** and mass **unemployment** caused by the **financial crisis** in 2009. At the macroeconomic level, the government has been unable to manage its soaring **budget deficit. Fear, anxiety, and uncertainty** about the future fill the hearts of many Americans, who continue to **persevere** through **personal hardships**. In his State of the Union Address, President Obama described:

> One year ago, I took office amid two wars, an economy rocked by a severe recession, a financial system on the verge of collapse, and a government deeply in debt... One in ten Americans still cannot find work. Many businesses have shuttered... And for those who'd already known poverty, life has become that much harder.

The elite speeches and the newspapers noted that **middle-class** families had been hit particularly hard by the ongoing recession, forcing many small and medium-sized **American businesses** to close down. They also criticized **corporations** and large **investment banks** on **Wall Street** for their speculative activities that brought about the crisis, their lack of moral and social responsibility, and their large executive bonuses. One *New York Times* op-ed argued: "But there was nothing accidental about the [financial] crisis. From the late 1970s on, the American financial system, freed by deregulation and a political climate in which greed was presumed to be good, spun ever further out of control" (*NYT*, January 15, 2010). A letter to the editor also highlighted the need to criminally prosecute the greedy Wall Street bankers who had caused the crisis and to expand welfare and health-care benefits for "Main Street" (Ibid.). Moreover, President Obama expressed his doubt regarding the viability of laissez-faire capitalism in his State of the Union Address:

> For some on the right, I expect we'll hear a different argument—that if we just make fewer investments in our people, extend tax cuts including those for the wealthier Americans, eliminate more regulations, maintain the status quo on health care, our deficits will go away. The problem

is that's what we did for eight years. That's what helped us into the crisis. It's what helped lead to these deficits. We can't do it again.

Obama thus highlighted the **shortcomings of laissez-faire capitalism** and the dire **need for government regulation**. As a result, **profit-driven individualism**—which has been at the heart of the American capitalist system—faced scrutiny in 2010. In response to various social problems such as ever-increasing **income inequality**, many Americans have expressed the **need for political, economic, and social change**. Yet this call for reforms and regulated capitalism has re-sparked the centuries-old American debate of **big versus limited government**. One WSJ op-ed defended "free enterprise" in this context:

> Because the financial crisis and resulting recession caused so much pain, a bashing of our entire free enterprise system may have been inevitable . . . The free enterprise system, hardwired into this country's DNA, has created more wealth and lifted more people out of poverty than any other system ever devised by human beings . . . It would be a profound mistake to grow government's size in a way that would fundamentally shift its level of involvement in our overall economy (*WSJ*, July 15, 2010).

While the Republicans and the wealthy continue to warn against the dangers of state interventions in the economy, the Obama administration (the Democrats) and many average-earning Americans have stressed the government's ability to implement beneficial reforms and to achieve social justice.

Bipartisan politics in America, however, has created a **political gridlock** in Washington, as the Republicans have repeatedly blocked the Democrats' efforts for reform—especially the Affordable Care Act. One op-ed in *The New York Times* criticized the political stalemate, created by the lack of serious negotiations between the Democratic and Republican parties, and lamented the ineffectiveness of the American government (*NYT*, February 15, 2010). A letter in *The Wall Street Journal* expressed similar concerns:

> We need to think critically and not politically through party affiliation lenses . . . Neither party is addressing the real issue when it comes to spending. I don't think Democrats or Republicans have the backbone to deal with the real situation. All they are concerned about are elections and job security (their own). We need to realize that our government has made promises it cannot keep (*WSJ*, May 15, 2010).

With neither side willing to make compromises and implement necessary reforms, the American government has been severely criticized from both left and right for its **incompetence** and its failure to put its words into action. **Public distrust** of the government and charges of its **corruption** are widespread throughout the country. Despite President Obama's call for the nation's strength as a union, America suffers from deep divisions among its people between the conservatives and the progressivists.

One of the most important of America's identities in 2010 was its status as a **national security state**. President Obama stated in his State of the Union Address: "Throughout our history, no issue has united this country more than security . . . Let's leave behind the fear and division, and do what is takes to defend our nation." America's security concerns include **terrorism**, nuclear proliferation, totalitarianism in foreign countries, weapons of mass destruction, Iran, North Korea, the conflict between Israel and Palestine, global poverty, and the wars in the Middle East (Afghanistan and Iraq). In his State of the Union Address, Obama claimed:

> Since the day I took office, we've renewed our focus on the terrorists who threaten our nation. We've made substantial investments in our homeland security and disrupted plots that threatened to take American lives . . . And in Afghanistan, we're increasing our troops and training Afghan security forces so they can begin to take the lead in July of 2011.

A *New York Times* op-ed claimed that the exacerbating tensions in Lebanon and Hezbollah's rising power in the region were threatening the security of the region, which in turn would "compromise US national security" (*NYT*, November 15, 2010). Op-eds and letters frequently cited global issues such as ethnic violence in Kyrgyzstan and water scarcity in Pakistan as potential threats to US national security. National security was one of the most recurring themes in op-eds and letters to the editor, as well as elite speeches.

Fear and **anxiety** are linked to the country's preoccupation with national security, convincing people that any instability or conflict in seemingly distant parts of the world is a threat to America. In turn, the overwhelming concern for national security, along with the country's mission to realize the American ideals of liberty, democracy, equality, rights, and human dignity throughout the world, has fueled **American leadership** and **interventionism**. Viewing itself as the champion of liberty, democracy, peace, and human rights, the United States has repeatedly highlighted and acted upon its **leadership** and **responsibility** as the protector of the free world.

US military supremacy is another recurring identity. The history textbooks describe that America's unmatched military capacity led the Allies to victory against Nazi Germany and Japan in World War II. They also imply that US military supremacy has allowed America to actively preserve peace and security throughout the world ever since, constantly maintaining military presence throughout the world. President Obama stated in his State of the Union Address: "In the last year, hundreds of al Qaeda's fighters and affiliates, including many senior leaders, have been captured or killed—far more than in 2008."

On another note, **China**—as America's major trade partner—is a very important country for the United States in 2010. In the increasingly globalized world economy, marked by **free trade** and **open capital markets**, the economic and financial interdependence of the two superpowers has grown significantly. In his State of the Union Address, President Obama stated: "We have to seek new markets aggressively, just as our competitors are . . . we'll continue to shape a Doha trade agreement that **opens global markets**, and . . . strengthen our **trade relations** in Asia." In regard to China, he also said:

> How long should America put its future on hold? You see, Washington has been telling us to wait for decades, even as the problems have grown worse. Meanwhile, **China is not waiting** to revamp its economy . . . I do not accept second place for the United States of America.

Op-eds and letters to the editor were also **wary of China**'s rapid growth and its status as America creditor. While some criticized the country for its censorship and suppression of liberties, others worried about China's selfish monetary policies.

Another important American identity in 2010 is **environmental protection**. Many countries including the United States have become increasingly concerned about the dangers of **climate change** and **global warming**, and reducing carbon emission and pollution is a recurring identity category in America in 2010. In his State of the Union Address, President Obama spoke of the dire need to promote **clean energy** and to stop **climate change**. He stressed the need to build "a new generation of **safe, clean nuclear power plants** . . . [investing in] advanced **biofuels and clean coal** technologies . . . and passing a comprehensive **energy and climate bill**." A letter in *The New York Times* also claimed that America as the "leader of developed countries" must take the responsibility of ensuring **sustainable environmental practices** in China (*NYT*, September 15, 2010).

III. Analysis of Central Discursive Formations in the United States

This section organizes the key American identity categories into four main discourses present in 2010—American Liberal Idealism, American Leadership, Social Progressivism, and Neoconservatism. These discourses interact and overlap with one another in different ways. In 2010, American Liberal Idealism (ALI) is the dominant discourse that supports and pervades all other discourses. It defines what it means to be American, and faces no significant challengers or counter-discourses. The other three discourses are sub-discourses that draw on elements of ALI and combine them with other identity categories to form unique discursive formations (Table 11.2).

American Leadership (AL) is a sub-discourse that shapes US foreign policy, predominantly driven by identities of ALI. While ALI and AL represent identities, beliefs, and values of the United States as a whole—thus shared by most Americans, the two opposing sub-discourses of Social Progressivism (SP) and Neoconservatism (NC) reveal a deep domestic division within the country. SP and NC compete with one another, interpreting and drawing on ALI and AL in distinct ways.

American Liberal Idealism is the most dominant and the most pervasive discourse of American society in 2010. It consists of identity categories such as the **American ideals of liberty, democracy, equality, rights, and human dignity**, the principles of **justice** and **fairness, legalistic**, revering the **Constitution, the Supreme Court, and legal authority, dichotomizing good and evil**, and **feelings of fear, anxiety, and uncertainty.** ALI thus characterizes the American essence—a cluster of values and principles shared by all Americans at the root, serving as a strong unifying force within the country against the deep internal division between Social Progressivism and Neoconservatism.

Feeling **fear, anxiety, and uncertainty** is an American identity significant enough to constitute its own discourse. Like the other identity categories within ALI, it pervades all the other discourses and every part of American society. This identity is included within ALI, because it is both a byproduct of and a menace to the American ideals of liberty, democracy, and equality. Considering the vital significance of these values as the "greatest source of strength" and the foundation of the country, any challenge or threat to them undermines the very essence of American society, thus creating a deep sense of fear, anxiety, and vulnerability. The history textbooks describe how fear and paranoia struck at the heart of every American during the series of communist Red Scares during the Cold War. Although fear and anxiety may serve as a positive impetus for America to reinforce its liberal values, they have often resulted in suspensions of those very ideals—especially for certain targeted persons and groups. A clear example of this is the America's response to 9/11—including government activities under the Patriot Act as well as the maltreatment of terrorist suspects at Guantanamo Bay.

Motivated by American Liberal Idealism, **American Leadership** is a sub-discourse that focuses on America's relationship and interactions with the external world, and it reflects the country's sense of duty to proliferate American ideals (liberty, equality, democracy, etc.) around the world. Like ALI, it transcends the divisive pressures of the two opposing sub-discourses of Social Progressivism and Neoconservatism, unifying the American people under the shared ideology of US exceptionalism as well as the issues of national security. Promoting the image of America as the world leader and the champion of liberal ideals and the free world, this discourse is characterized by identity categories such as **American leadership, responsibility, interventionism,** and a robust **national security state.** The national security state features **US military supremacy** and is predominantly engaged in **fighting terrorism.** America is also portrayed as a leader of **globalization and free trade** as well as a potential leader in **protecting the environment.** Finally, **China's** rapid growth has begun to threaten the American economic hegemony.

In his State of the Union Address, President Obama claimed: "the nation that leads the clean energy economy will be the nation that leads the global economy. And America must be that nation." Later he stated: "That's the leadership that we are providing—engagement that advances the common security and prosperity of all people . . . As we have for over 60 years, America takes these actions because our destiny is connected to those beyond our shores." In his Remarks at Independence Day Celebration, Obama also connected the American ideals of liberty and democracy to American exceptionalism and leadership by expressing: "And on this day that is uniquely American, we're reminded that our Declaration, our example, made us a beacon to the world, not only inspiring people to demand their own freedom." Op-eds and letters to the editor reflected similar sentiments, accentuating the need for America to act as the world leader in various issues such as climate change, helping Haiti rebuild, and promoting regional security and peace. The history textbooks also portray America as the "champion of the free world" and the hegemonic power in the postwar order.

The American ideals of liberty, democracy, and equality, the feeling of fear and anxiety, and the preoccupation with national security interact with one another in a paradoxical way. While America promotes liberal values in different parts of the world in order to prevent terrorism, conflicts, and totalitarianism—which it believes to be a critical step for protecting its national security, the ever-present fear of foreign threats has often led the country to take measures that actually undermine the very ideals to be safeguarded. Numerous op-eds

Table 11.2 **American Identity Topography**

	Speeches	Newspapers (Op-eds)	Textbooks	Newspapers (Letters)	Novels	Movies
American Liberal Idealism						
Protecting American ideals (liberty, democracy, equality, rights, and human dignity)	++	++	++++	++		++
Upholding justice and fairness	+	+	++	++	++	++
Feeling doubt, fear, anxiety, and uncertainty	– –	–	/	–	–––	––––
Fighting evil with good	/	/	/	//	///	////
Legalistic (rule of law, Constitution, the Supreme Court)	+	~	+	+	+	+
American Leadership						
Defending national security	++++	++––	++––	+–		+–
Believing in American leadership (interventionism, exceptionalism, responsibility)	++	+	+	+		++
Alert to China		~	~	–		
Protecting the environment	+	+	+	+		
Endorsing free trade and globalization	+	~	+	~		+
Social Progressivism & Neoconservatism		NYT WSJ		NYT WSJ		
Supporting the middle class	+	+ +	/	+ +	+++	+
Perseverant through hardship	––	– –	//	– –	–––––	–––––
Undergoing economic instability (financial crisis, unemployment, recession)	––	– –	/	–– ––		

(*Continued*)

Table 11.2 (**Continued**)

	Speeches	Newspapers (Op-eds)		Textbooks	Newspapers (Letters)		Novels	Movies
Protecting American businesses	+	+	+	+	+	+	+	++++
Troubled by income inequality	−	−	−	−	−	−	--/	
Facing a budgetary crisis	−	−	−	−	−	−		
Wary of corruption (government, corporations, and other institutions)	−	--	--	/	--	--		−
Bipartisan	−	--	--	~	−	−		
Progressivist (reform, welfare, social change)	+++	+	−	/	+	−	+	
In need of government regulation	++	+	−	/	+	−		
Individualist/materialist (money, profit)	−	−	+	/	−	+	−	++--
Dominated by corporations	−	−	+	/	−	+		+−
Fearful of a big government	+	+	−	/	+	−		
Christian, believing in God	+						+++	+

and letters criticized the US government for its torture, inhumane treatment, arbitrary arrest, and extrajudicial detentions of prisoners at Guantanamo Bay. In regard to this issue, one *NYT* editorial explicitly accused the Bush administration of "fear-mongering," claiming that President Obama must rectify the situation and "insist on maintaining the long proven system of trying terrorism cases in federal court [rather than military]" (*NYT*, April 15, 2010). Moreover the history textbooks highlight other examples of instances where individual liberties and rights were suspended for the sake of national security. They criticized McCarthy's "campaign of fear and paranoia" during the Second Red Scare as well as the Supreme Court's ruling in *Korematsu v. United States* that constitutionally allowed the American government to force Japanese-Americans into internment camps during World War II.

In contrast to AL, **Social Progressivism** and **Neoconservatism** are two opposing sub-discourses that deal with various domestic issues in the United

States. They consist of similar identity categories, but each discourse assesses them very differently. The identity categories of ALI such liberty, equality, rights, and democracy play an important role in both SC and NC, and the division between the two sub-discourses arises from their different conceptions of these values. In 2010, Social Progressivism—primarily supported by the Democrats—is the more prominent sub-discourse that expresses the need for systemic change and reforms in America, in order to solve various domestic problems—including mass **unemployment, economic and financial instability,** growing **income inequality,** and **budget deficit.** This sub-discourse is motivated by a belief in positive liberties—the freedom and power to fulfill one's own potential—and positive rights such as economic, social, and cultural rights. Numerous op-eds and letters to the editor emphasize the **inadequacies of laissez-faire capitalism** and the dangers of **profit-oriented individualism,** while condemning the reckless speculative activities of **Wall Street banks** and argued in favor of implementing various **government regulations** of the financial system as well as the economy. Social Progressivism asserts that active government interventions—such as Obama's stimulus policies and increased spending—are key to steady economic recovery. The discourse also alludes to the **personal struggles** and **hardships** of **middle-class families** caused by the **financial crisis of 2009,** and it supports comprehensive **welfare reforms** and tax cuts for those Americans. In his State of the Union Address, President Obama stressed the need for far-reaching healthcare, Medicaid, and Medicare reforms, and he proposed a fee on the biggest Wall Street banks to increase unemployment benefits for middle-income families and to extend credit to small businesses. Thus Social Progressivism purports to build a system of regulated welfare capitalism, in which the central government uses its expanded power to carry out beneficial reforms for a better American society.

In contrast to Social Progressivism, Neoconservatism is a sub-discourse that fears the **dangers of a big government,** supporting the **neoliberal tradition of unfettered capitalism** and rejecting any **financial or economic regulations.** Unlike SP, this sub-discourse emphasizes negative liberties and rights such as the freedom from government interference. Many *WSJ* op-eds and letters to the editor expressed that the ongoing crisis was only a natural and temporary stage of the boom-and-bust cycle, and that the Wall Street bankers—who failed to predict the bursting of a bubble—should not be held responsible. Believing in the market to correct itself in time, they claimed that belt-tightening, tax cuts for all income levels, and deregulation of the economy would lead to speedy recovery. In contrast to Social Progressivism that focuses on **middle-class families,** the NC discourse emphasizes the importance of creating an unrestricted environment in which **profit-driven American corporations** could thrive. It also seeks to cut Social Security, Medicaid, and Medicare benefits for the purpose of reducing the government's **budget deficit**.

Despite their antithetical views on various political, economic, and social issues, Social Progressivism and Neoconservatism share a few commonalities: a negative view of **bipartisan politics** and **political gridlock**, criticisms of **government incompetence** and **corruption,** and **distrust of the government** and its failure to put words into action.

IV. Conclusion

This report found one dominant discourse and three sub-discourses in the United States of America in 2010. American Liberal Idealism was the dominant discourse that served as the foundation for the three sub-discourses, and it was shared by all Americans, regardless of the elite-mass divide and differences in political views. No counter-discourses to ALI were found. In 2010, political leanings and party affiliations had a significant influence on how different identity categories were assessed; however, the disjuncture between the elite and mass discourses was minimal. This attests to the deeply entrenched partisan politics prevalent in America.

The report's finding that American Liberal Idealism was the predominant discourse is consistent with the Western hegemony of democratic neoliberalism. In fact, elite speeches and history textbooks claim this hegemony as fundamentally American—portraying the United States as the protector and champion of democracy, capitalism, and the free world. American Leadership endorses US internationalism and responsibility to promote and secure Western hegemony throughout the world. Although the financial crisis of 2009 and the Great Recession have greatly debilitated the American economy and threatened its ideological influence, the country's commitment to liberal values and democracy both at home and abroad is unwavering. Elections, the rule of law, the Constitution and legal processes, liberties, equality, justice, and fairness are upheld and respected by all Americans. However, America's faith in neoliberal laissez-faire capitalism has eroded, due to the financial collapse, mass unemployment, and the soaring budget deficit. Social Progressivism reflects the growing support for state regulation of capitalism and expansion of welfare programs in America—a sharp break from the country's deregulatory, free-market tradition endorsed by Neoconservatism. Yet individualism and competitiveness continue to serve as important values for all Americans, and the United States as a whole is still committed to open markets, free trade, and many fundamental aspects of a capitalist market economy. Thus, the four American discourses found in this report largely bolster and reproduce the Western hegemony of democratic neoliberalism, although various efforts to reform capitalism via state interventions were ongoing in 2010. While the "democratic" component of the hegemony is quite rigid and robust, the definition and scope of neoliberalism are continuously evolving and changing—perhaps to allow more room for necessary state regulation and interventions.

Notes

1. *USA Today*, the second-highest-circulating daily and most popular online newspaper, was not selected because the online database does not allow sampling of op-eds and letters to the editor.

Sources

Elite Speeches

President Obama's State of the Union Address (January 2010).
President Obama's Remarks at Independence Day Celebration (July 2010).

Leading Newspapers

The New York Times
The Wall Street Journal

High School History Textbooks

Appleby, J., A. Brinkley, A. Broussard, J. M. McPherson, and D. A. Ritchie, *The American Vision* (New York: Glencoe, 2010).
Ayers, E. L., R. D. Schulzinger, J. F. de la Teja, and D. G. White, *American Anthem* (New York: Holt, Rinehart and Winston, 2010).

Best-Selling Novels

Sparks, Nicholas, *The Last Song* (New York: Grand Central Publishing, 2009).
Stockett, Kathryn, *The Help* (New York: Penguin Books, 2009).

Top Blockbuster Films

Toy Story 3
Iron Man 2

PART THREE

CONCLUSIONS

12

"Making Identity Count" beyond IR

SRDJAN VUCETIC

How nations construct themselves is a question that has catalyzed literally tens of thousands of scholarly articles and books.[1] In the present chapter, I address the implications that the "making identity count" project raises for existing conceptual, theoretical, and methodological approaches within this vast literature. If we accept that nations and their identities can and should be studied in a more valid and systematic manner introduced in this volume, then it also stands to reason that "making identity count" offers up an opportunity to advance other fields of inquiry, not just International Relations (IR).

In what follows, I explore renderings of the link between national identity and political order in anthropology, history, social psychology, sociology, and IR. Of course, such an exercise will only scratch the surface of this voluminous literature, but I aim to form enough linkages and relations to indicate the wider relevance of the framework advanced in this volume. I begin below by looking at how anthropologists first essentialized and then de-essentialized nations. In the next two sections I examine some paths by which this project can enter into a dialogue with social psychology and sociology, respectively. Turning to history, I show how "making identity count" could contribute to the knowledge production in this field. In the final section I go back to IR once again, suggesting the ways this project could help overcome current limitations in analyzing the construction of national communities within a broader global society.

I. Anthropology

When it comes to national identity, social and human sciences have come a long way. This is how this volume's empirical chapters might have been done in the mid-20th-century US anthropology:

As she wrote in her own job description, for each national character that she was asked to analyse, her task was to survey all of the existing secondary literature in all disciplines (including translations of those in foreign languages), to collect all relevant information from other government agencies (including cables, intercepts, news and intelligence, and specially tailored information from [Office of War Information]'s own outposts), interview first-and second-generation immigrants and refugees to get at "the rearing of the child in the home," then to prepare a fifty-page memorandum covering the culture pattern, its rewards and sanctions, and attitudes relevant to the war (such as authority, violence, fate), and finally to sum up with "suggestions for psychological warfare."[2]

The "she" in this paragraph is American anthropologist Ruth Benedict. Funded in the 1940s and early 1950s by the growing US national security state, Benedict, Margaret Mead, and their colleagues produced a whole library of national character reports, all of which have had a remarkably short shelf life in scholarly circles. The fundamental problem, as many critics pointed out even then, was a bizarre assumption that one could grasp the cultural essence of large, diverse, and rapidly modernizing societies such as, to cite one of more infamous Benedict's case studies, early-1940s Romania.[3]

National character studies are a large warning sign about the pitfalls of attempting to study what makes nations tick. To begin with, it is unclear that forms of national (un)consciousness exist as such.[4] Even if they do, nothing suggests that nations should be studied as whole-culture entities. Anthropologists, ever concerned about false generalizations, focus their attention to localized events—a festival or a factory in Romania, rather than Romania itself. This approach was in fact pioneered in other contexts by scholars like Benedict and Mead: attention to ethnographic detail is what helps researchers appreciate the inherent complexity, heterogeneity, flux, multiplicity, contingency, and contestability of the national, while also forcing recognition that findings always depend on the temporal and spatial location of the observer. This is why in anthropology today one does not even talk about nations so much as the practices of nationhood.[5]

The ethnographic sensibility is one of the main intellectual drivers of "making identity count." As Hopf and Allan explain in their chapters 1 and 2, the empirical goal of this volume was to capture the elusive "overheard conversations" about who we are and who they are. Ethnographers may raise questions about this project's print-centric methods, but they will probably be familiar with the underlying methodological principles (Adams 2009).[6] This spells potential for two-way validity cross-checks: ethnographers working on contemporary Brazil or China may be as interested in this project's "global" findings as the authors of the Brazilian and Chinese identity reports are in the "localized" ethnographic knowledge.

II. Social Psychology

Social psychologists have long studied national identity as a cause of political action. Good illustrations of this approach, to use the US context as an example, are studies of how national identity influences attitudes toward immigrants and minorities, the likelihood of voting and other form of political engagement, or levels of support for government institutions and policies, including foreign policy.[7] This scholarship is characterized by the use of diverse and mixed methods, but its overarching methodology remains committed to the subjective dimensions of nationhood—that is, on what goes on inside people's heads when they think about what it means to be American. In surveys, for example, the salience and valence of national identity are typically measured by asking people how "close" or "attached" they feel to their country or how "proud" they are about their country's achievements and history.[8] The contrast with the approach undertaken in this volume is sharp, and it stems from ontology: social psychologists conceive national identity as the experience of categorization and evaluation at the individual and subjective level, rather than an intersubjective phenomenon embodied and embedded in the stock of social knowledge about what being a nation or national is like.[9]

Despite this fundamental difference, social psychological and constructivist approaches have long influenced each other's research practices. For example, many of those who draw on the teachings by Tajfel, Turner, Moscovici, and others to study the link between the psychology of national identification and political action acknowledge that collective experiences and history impact this process in consequential and remarkably sticky ways.[10] The same scholars also recognize that national identity formation is always structured by power relations for many reasons, including the fact that all modern states work hard to define membership and belonging in explicitly national terms. After all, one of the main purposes of the modern state is to distinguish the in-group from the out-group and to promote the former's security, positive social evaluation, attractiveness, and esteem.[11]

What "making identity count" might contribute to social psychology–inspired research into the political consequences of national identity is a repository of real-world intersubjective meanings that people attach to nationhood in different geographical and historical contexts. For example, the discursive topographies of the eight national identities presented in this volume show that the elites and masses differ in defining group boundaries, especially with respect to immigration or the dynamics of minority-majority encounters. Similarly, my own report on the UK national identity in 2010 suggests that being British means different things in London and in Edinburgh. Jarrod Hayes and Shivaji Kumar's respective analyses of the meanings of India suggest that national identity depends not only on class or region, but also on language—or intersections with language. These types of findings could be used by social identity theories in two ways. First, they could provide an external validity check on their own research on the nexus between national attachment or pride on one hand and behaviors such as tolerance of minorities or tax compliance on the other. This is valuable considering that the most fundamental trade-off in different approaches to measuring social identity concerns the decision to use preordained identity categories as opposed to specifying them as inductively as possible.[12]

Second, the data from the national identity reports could be used to devise more fine-grained survey questionnaires involving dimensions of national identity such as the nation's main achievements or key shared norms. For example, if there is reliable discourse analytic evidence that the masses consistently define their country in terms of lasting social hierarchies and ongoing class-based political struggles, then there is a case to be made for including questions about disaffection and detachment as well as negative values when surveying people about what their country means to them. In fact, a research design that employs inductively generated insights about the social psychology of nationhood in order to improve the validity of closed-ended surveys grappling with the same phenomenon might well become an exemplar of multimethod research on national identity.[13]

III. Sociology

Though it originates with sociologists Renan, Marx, Durkhem, and Weber, the study of nations, nationalism, and ethnicity is today thoroughly multidisciplinary, bringing together scholars trained in anthropology, economics, geography, history, law, and political science. It is also thoroughly socially constructivist in the sense that few researchers still contend that nations and ethnic groups are anything but social constructions.[14] What is more, a large portion of these constructivist approaches uses the same building blocks as the framework presented in this volume: identity, discourse, and habit. Consider the literature on the social construction of nationhood: while classical studies sought to explain the rise of nations from a macro-historical point of view—how and why they were "imagined" or "invented"[15]—the current research focuses on how nations are reproduced and "engrained" via quotidian activities like, for instance, the daily weather report or the official and unofficial displays of national flags.[16]

"Making Identity Count" shares with this literature a number of assumptions, including the idea that the modern social and political world is in significant ways made intelligible through discursive indices of national identity.[17] Similarly, while the early studies focused on elite-driven institutional reinforcement of nationalism and ethnic identity, scholars today are deliberately turning toward the more demotic practices of "everyday nationhood" such as watching (sub-titled) films, going to (international) sports performances, reading (translated) harlequin romance novels, sending kids to (minority and/or foreign language) schools, perusing (exotic) cookbooks, and the like.[18] As Prasenjit Duara puts it, the purpose of the study of nations is not simply to demonstrate that nations are imagined but also to analyze "who imagines what and when"—that is, how and why "different views of the nation contest and negotiate with each other."[19]

Students of the social and cultural foundations of nationhood might be attracted to the framework developed in this volume for several reasons. To begin with, this framework pays more or less equal attention to both elite and mass agency. What this move accomplishes is a systematic comparison of ideas about the nation operating among narrowly construed elites with those circulat-ing among the masses, providing empirically grounded answers to who imagines what and when. For instance, the empirical chapters in this volume demonstrate a considerable degree of the elite-mass consensus on who we are or who others are. On the surface, this finding supports the idea that a standardized national culture achieved in the modern industrial era may be hard to dislodge even in the era of technologically advanced means of global mass communication. Rendered sufficiently cross-national and longitudinal, this type of analysis could be used to trace macro-historical vagaries of nationhood in ways that may help inform long-standing theoretical debates on the relationship between nations and nationalism such as, for example, the one on whether nations precede nationalism or the other way around (or whether they arise simultaneously).[20]

I will turn to history in the next section, but for the moment let us propose that sociologically inclined researchers may be particularly attracted to this project's attempt to inductively recover identity categories. The rationale for this perspec-tive was addressed by Hopf and Allan in the introductory chapters: induction forces an examination of local particulars that might otherwise be lost in a top-down, theoretically prefabricated approach. To use the above example, students of nations and nationalism interested in the constitution and signification of rela-tionships of similarity and difference between national collectivities, including those who worry that research on how nations become themselves overempha-sizes the role of self-other interactions. Indeed, the national identity reports pre-sented here intimate that not all others are the Other, much less the antagonistic

Other. In analyzing the UK national identity in 2010, I discovered that only Islamic fundamentalism qualifies as a living oppositional Other. An inductive recovery of identity categories eliminates or at least minimizes the risks posed by fixating on, for instance, the French Other as the discursive engine of British national development.[21]

The same point applies to political sociological research. Following the "cultural turn" that began in the mid-1970s, cultural approaches to state formation, institution building, policy-making, social movements, and other political phenomena have turned to concepts such as discourse, habitus, cognitive frames and schemas, national repertoires, and so on—concepts that purport to capture the active and interactional nature of culture.[22] The approach presented here overlaps with these efforts, but it goes a step further to provide a theory and methodology for examining culture from the ground up—as that which is not only fluid, multiple, contingent, and contestable, but also the stuff of habit and practice. What this does in analytical terms is to allow for the coexistence of multiple and competing cultures within a single country as well as for the interaction of institutional and cultural forces in conditioning political possibilities in a given historical context. Last but not least, a more inductive recovery of intersubjective meanings and contexts may also sensitize researchers to avoid Eurocentrism, Americentrism, and related myopias when interpreting social and political life.[23]

IV. History

The theoretical background, methodological dilemmas, and even analytical themes appearing in this volume are likely to be very familiar to some historians—and perhaps just as useful. To begin with, the comparative method deployed in the project allows for a better understanding of the specificity and generality of historical phenomena—the primary goal of much of transnational and, indeed, global history.[24] Although the main theme of this volume is the hegemony of neoliberal democratic capitalism, the archives generated for the empirical chapters could easily be mobilized to analyze other substantive subject of interest to historians. For example, those interested in cross-border movements and events under headings such as terrorism, multiculturalism, or the social media could analyze and compare them as everyday social knowledge items within American, Brazilian, British, or Chinese society as well as examine the degree to which the dominant meanings attached to each of these phenomena vary between the elites and masses. More specific historical subjects such as soccer, the Haiti earthquake, or the "official mind" of G20 governments in 2010 would of course require a different sampling strategy, but what this volume demonstrates is that a relatively small group of researchers (albeit one equipped with diverse linguistic skills) working with relatively small amount of historical documents (for the most part assembled via mass-digitized databases) can relatively swiftly reconstruct many key aspects of the global past.

In recovering the stocks of social knowledge around the world, this project is in many ways following in the deep footsteps made by the "history of mentalities" approach first used the proponents of the French *Annales* school,[25] whose members sought to produce "total history" by, among other things, piecing together and comparing the deeper layers of social structure, including the presuppositions and beliefs unconsciously held by the actors situated across a variety of sociocultural contexts.[26] Although intellectually committed to positivist philosophy and methods, the annalistes and their fellow travelers revolutionized historical research everywhere, trailblazing numerous new routes in historiography, including some idiosyncratic ones.[27] These developments not only changed the practice of history—objectivity, casual reasoning, and generalization now coexist with social construction, the knowledge-power link, and discourse analysis—but they also opened up space for historical research that challenges disciplinarity. IR's own historical-sociological turn—one label for scholarly production that finds inspiration in the work of sociological theorists-cum-analytic historians like Mann, Tilly, or Wallerstein—is arguably a byproduct of this revolution, too.[28]

An interdisciplinary approach to history that shares more than a few theoretical and methodological parallels with "Making Identity Count" is the 1989 work by Marc Angenot entitled *1889: Un état du discours social.*[29] Much like the present volume, Angenot offers a theory of "hegemony" based a conceptual relationship between "social discourses" (practices of communication that are structured, implicit, and taken for granted and that serve in a given sociocultural context to authorize certain beliefs, tastes, opinions, and themes while repressing others) and "society" (an entity that can be historically reconstructed by an analysis of certain texts).[30] The empirical results take a familiar form: Angenot's book is a topography of the discourses (and interdiscourses) of identity in the European *Francophonie* in the year 1889, presented and synthesized across what the authors calls themes (narcissism, patriotism, etc.) and fields (politics, literature, etc.).

Angenot's project relies on a gigantic archive: 1) 1,200 book- and booklet-length works of fiction and nonfiction (roughly one in three of all francophone volumes published in Europe that year); 2) a selection of newspaper items from 157 dailies published in Paris, plus a dozen dailies published in Lille, Lyon, Marseille, and Brussels; 3) items from 487 French, Belgian, and Swiss periodicals, ranging from prestige Parisian weeklies to small special-interest publications; and 4) several hundred miscellaneous materials like poems, shopping catalogues, burlesque monologues, and political pamphlets.[31] (In other words, while Angenot did not follow Foucault's infamous advice to "read everything," this archive is as exhaustive as anything assembled by the annalistes, to say nothing of Foucault himself.) For Angenot, social discourse analysis requires a large archive because the researcher must delineate the realm of the "sayable" and "thinkable" in as precise terms as possible; all ideas and all discursive formations, no matter how marginal, matter. For example, in 1889, the main challenger discourses to the hegemony of "bourgeois Gallocentrism" (my label, with apologies to Angenot) are "socialism" and "feminism" (the latter was not an actor category at the time). Below the surface and on the margins, the identity of the francophone Europe is torn in many more directions: "anarchism," "radical internationalism," "royalism," and so on.

Relative to Angenot's, the archive or archives used on this volume look slim, but given the collections' aims, this can be forgiven. Focusing only on the most widely consumed forms and media of communication, they are designed to be manageable yet sufficient to grasp the everyday thinking and activities of both the chattering classes and the silent majorities in each political community under study. Put in methodological terms, the size and composition of the archive should follow the research question, not vice versa.[32] Thus, if one aims to recover historically constituted collective meanings in a community in "totality," then an Angenotian archive may be necessary to identify ideas that are truly exceptional or marginal in the sense that they cannot be categorized as an element of any collective discourse. Conversely, if the research goal is a big-picture view of what it means to be France or French in 1889 or, for that matter, an analysis of how different discourses of French identity underwrite, ignore, resist, or modify major ideologies of the age, then a slimmer archive is likely to suffice.

It should also be said that social, cultural, and intellectual histories are all extremely valuable to this project in the sense that they provide a potential validity check or even an opportunity to investigate how a change in values of the input impacts the output. It would thus be interesting to see if a historian using the sampling and analytical rules laid out in this volume to uncover the identity of France in 1889 would produce knowledge that harmonizes with Angenot's findings about, say, the hegemony of "bourgeois Gallocentrism" (or some equivalent discourse that posits that all peoples must gravitate toward the French model of social, cultural, and political organization) or, for that matter, France's place in the world.[33]

The "story-of-the-year" approach, whether Angenot's or the one developed in this volume, may appear woefully ahistorical to some—especially to those who insist that history requires analysis of diverse historical documents appearing in succession over the *longue durée* of centuries. This criticism is misplaced: the rationale for selecting *any* chronological section, whether a year, a minute, or five centuries, is to examine the synchronicity, convergence, and divergence in historical developments.[34] Building on what I said above, when applied across multiple calendar years or other predetermined blocks of time, "Making Identity Count" could conceivably contribute to the *Annales*-style international histories as well.[35] Suppose that the present volume is a part of a larger collection that includes twenty annual national identity reports reconstructed in ten-year intervals between 1810 and 2010 on what it means to be a member of the political communities headquartered in Berlin/Bonn, London, Moscow/Saint Petersburg, and Paris. For one thing, this collection would almost certainly help historians better navigate the vast ocean of the historical material by identifying the mainstream forms and media of communication in a large part of Europe over the last two hundred years. For another thing, and far more importantly, it would help researchers trace the various twists and turns in the ideas about being aristocratic, British, civilized, democratic, European, et cetera, over successive generations of people—ideas that operate beneath the surface of the everyday life, whether at the elite or mass level. Such a "constructivist data set" would not constitute an actual social history of modern Europe, but it may well be turn out to be its first draft.

V. Back to IR

Although IR has now gone through a series of vertiginous turns—not just cultural, but also discursive, ethnographic, interpretive, linguistic, practice, and others—the field is yet to fully emerge from the shadows of the mid-20th-century characterology.[36] As Hopf notes in the introductory chapter of this volume, studies in this field still have a tendency to reduce national identity to easily quantifiable proxy measures.[37] "Making identity count" shows that quantification need not result in simplification, much less in essentialization and reification. Staying true to the core constructivist teachings, it conceives national identities relationally and processually. This volume thus shows that Brazil, China, France, Germany, India, Japan, the United Kingdom, and the United States became themselves in 2010 by interacting with other subjects—with their societies above all, and through their society, with other states and nations, with international institutions and transnational norms, and with collectively constituted notions of selfhood at the systemic level.

In their concluding chapter, Hopf and Allan discuss how "making identity count" can be fruitfully deployed toward research problems other than the global power of neoliberal democratic capitalist ideology. To further their discussion, let us consider identity-based explanations of foreign policy decisions and orientations—the bread and butter of the first wave of constructivist IR.[38]

A good illustrative foray into this literature is the now-standard constructivist argument that the governments of the United States and its key allies legitimated the 2003 invasion of Iraq by invoking the war-on-terror identity.[39] Put differently, absent a particular understanding of the 9/11 attacks and the subsequent intervention in Afghanistan, the Iraq War would not have happened, at least not in the same "coalition of the willing" form.

As convincing as sounds, this argument has only partial empirical grounding. To what extent does the Iraq War hinge on the war-on-terror identity? What other discourses (and "interdiscourses") might have been implicated in the invasion, how, and with what impact? These questions are valid since many researchers have already pointed out to the causal role of ideas emphasizing moral and political leadership[40] and even to religious and racialized identities.[41] What "making identity count" could contribute to these studies is a procedure for a more systematic assessment of how the invading nations defined themselves in the run-up to the war.

Allow me to illustrate by way of a look at the excellent work by Stuart Croft, *Culture, Crisis and America's War on Terror*.[42] To trace the "power and spread of the war on terror as a discourse" from the moment it became articulated by the US President George W. Bush on the evening of September 11, 2001, Croft relies on discourse analysis and uses an archive of texts drawn from the local and national media, novels, pop songs, the commercial landscapes, jokes, and so on.[43] This "new common sense," he finds, was challenged on two fronts. A counter-discourse on "freedom" questioned the emphasis of counterterrorism measures over the nation's civil liberties throughout 2002, as did, in early 2003, a "no war for oil" discourse. Neither, however, impacted a sufficiently wide range of social and political institutions to change the discursive topography. The fact that the opposition Democratic Party, to mention one of the key political institutions in this context, never challenged any of the premises of the war-on-terror discourse can help explain both the passage of the Patriot Act and the Iraq invasion.[44] While Croft's main argument is eminently plausible, it would have been more convincing had closer attention been paid to the procedures for text selection and interpretation. In a related manner, Croft's analysis of the discursive means by which the post–September 11 world came into existence attributes a remarkable staying power to the war-on-terror discourse. However, the methods he uses to reach this conclusion are never made explicit. Viewed from the perspective of "making identity count," Croft could made his analysis more systematic had he compared two discursive maps of American society based the analysis of key best-selling, must-read, highest-circulating, and/or most-watched texts: one corresponding to what appears to be a crucial three-month period following Bush's speech to a joint session of the US Congress on September 20, 2001, and the equivalent period of time leading up to the presidential election of November 2, 2004.[45] Not only would this comparative set-up help generate more precise knowledge claims about the continuity and change in the war on terror discourse, but it would also help evaluate the author's theoretical argument about the cycle of institutional structuring, stabilization, contestation, and adaptation in the social construction of crises.[46]

One distinct benefit of using the topographical approach in constructivist investigations of foreign policy concerns the argument, often implicitly made, that the success of a particular legitimation strategy depends on its "resonance" or "fit" with the underlying discourses of national identity.[47] A similar concept appears in social psychology–inspired theories of identity management, namely, in the argument that ruling elites seek to "reframe" national identities as a way of achieving a more positive social evaluation.[48] Here, too, success appears to be a function of the frame's "match" or "congruence" with the prevailing attitudes and opinion of the public or publics.[49] Securitization theory hinges on a similar theoretical move, too.[50] There, the framing of issues or events as security ("existential") threats depends on the willingness and ability of the target audience to accept the claim that their reality has changed such that extraordinary or emergency measures may be implemented (although audience acceptance of securitizing moves is not a sufficient condition for emergency action).

All of these theories share the same challenge: in order explain why an audience or audiences supported some argument, frame, or securitizing moves but not others, the researcher needs to reconstruct the sociopolitical and sociocultural context in which this process occurs; this includes, among other things, the intersubjective background knowledge and discourses of identity through which claims and counterclaims are processed. Without an independent account of said discourses or prevailing attitudes, however, a claim that a particular line of reasoning constituted a fit or match in a given context is not set out in a way that can be empirically evaluated. The knowledge produced through "making identity count" might help overcome this limitation. To the extent that they specify what different audiences (nations, elites, masses) know about the world in a given context, national identity reports can be utilized to explain why some issues and events become privileged legitimatized, or securitized while others do not.[51]

IR scholars studying the construction of international communities within a broader global society—various zones of peace, conflict, free movement, or religiousness—could use this archive, too. To use the somewhat hackneyed example, one of the central questions in the literature on Europeanization is the extent to which post-national identity narratives associated with the European integration project are impacting the elite- and mass-level identity discourses at the national level.[52] Survey-based studies have thus found that while the member state elites habitually cue the mass public opinion about the value of integration, the latter still set the overall "policy mood"; (it may also be that these two pro-cesses are occurring simultaneously).[53]

One way to begin to disentangle the complex interface between Europe and the nation would be to supply more national identity reports that would allow us to examine how nations become themselves via historical feedback loops. A series of national identity reports would this generate a new and qualitatively dif-ferent body of evidence about elite- and mass-level attitudes and moods about Europe—one that taps into intersubjective meanings as opposed to information generated by Eurobarometer survey series. Also note that the Eurobarometer covers the post-1973 period and focuses on the member states. In contrast, not only could the national identity series proposed here go back to the years of the Schuman declaration or Churchill's Zurich speech, but they could conceivably also cover both "insiders" and "outsiders"—founding and new members, candi-dates and neighbors, big and small states[54]—enabling far more ambitious cross-national and longitudinal studies of Europeanization.

As indicated in the previous section, the research methodology and tech-niques introduced in this volume could conceivably be used to map out the dynamics of identity formation—national and otherwise—in multiple countries over long stretches of time. This could advance IR knowledge in many ways, but the most immediate impact would be on the constructivist research program since it would enable, arguably for the first time, a system-atic evaluation of key constructivist teachings on what makes the world hang together.

Notes

1. For comments on this draft, I am grateful to Thierry Balzacq, Jarrod Hayes, and the editors of this volume. All errors remain mine exclusively.
2. Mandler 2013, p. 78.
3. The "joke of Washington" is how political scientist Harold Lasswell described these studies (Mandler 2013, p. 174). Top U.S. government officials, including Roosevelt and Kennan, were more sanguine (Reeves 2005, pp. 96–97).
4. For discussions, see, for example, Mandler 2006, Margalit 1997, and Özkirimli 2010.
5. Eriksen 2010.
6. Adams 2009.
7. See, for example, Paxton and Mughan 2006, Transue 2007, Huddy and Khatib 2007, Schildkraut 2005, Theiss-Morse 2009.
8. These are becoming more and more sophisticated and internally reliable: respondents are now increasingly being given considerable latitude over expressing their in-group experi-ences. Huddy and Khatib 2007, for example, measure national identification with the fol-lowing questions: "How important is being American to you?"; "To what extent do you see yourself as a typical American?"; "When talking about Americans how often do you say we instead of they?"; and "How well does the term American describe you?" Others have devel-oped scales that tap into divisions between civic, cultural, and ethnic dimensions of national identity (Pehrson et al. 2009) or symbolic, blind, and constructive patriotism (Theiss-Morse

2009). For more on measurement issues, see Herrmann et al. 2009, Theiss-Morse 2009 (esp. pp. 44–54), McDermott 2009, Lee 2009, Citrin and Sears 2009, and Kuo and Margalit 2012.

9. As per the constructivist ontology, it is redundant to describe identities as social because defining oneself and others is a relational meaning-making practice, which, to various degrees, must be shared. Put differently, without (some) mutual intelligibility, there can be no identity. For more on this issue from an IR theory perspective, see, among others, Hopf 2002, pp. 4–7; Hopf 2012, pp. 6–7; Shannon 2012, pp. 3–6; and McDermott and Lopez 2012, p. 208.

10. Huddy 2002, p. 826. Also: Huddy 2001 and Reicher 2004. Note that social identity theory inspired more scholarly production on identity than any other theory of identity in any field (Abdelal et al. 2009, p. 9). For overviews, see Brewer 2001, Hogg 2006, and McDermott 2009. For a recent IR application, see Hayes 2013.

11. I use the Tajfelian language here, but the point applies to other social psychological approaches to identity as well (McDermott and Lopez 2012; cf. Ashton, Deaux, and McLaughlin-Volpe 2004, Burke and Stets 2009). Also note that not all psychological theories of identity formation treat the individual or intrapsychic as the unit of analysis (Billig 1985, Billig 1996, Potter and Wetherell 1987).

12. Sylvan and Metskas 2009 p. 93.

13. Ibid., pp. 95–96; also see Kowert 2012, pp. 216, 227.

14. For overviews, see Eley and Suny 1998, Chandra 2012, Fearon and Laitin 2000, and Özkirimli 2010.

15. Anderson 1983, Gellner 1983, Hobsbawm and Ranger 1983.

16. Billig 1995, Eriksen and Jenkins 2007.

17. E.g., Billig 1995.

18. Fox and Iddiss 2008, Brubaker et al. 2006.

19. Duara 1998, p. 152.

20. Özkirimli 2010.

21. For a critique, see Mandler 2006.

22. For retrospective manifestos, see Lehman 1972 and Laitin and Wildavsky 1988. For contemporary examples, see Adams et al. 2005 and Hall and Lamont 2013.

23. *Inter alia*: Beck 2006, Bourdieu and Wacquant 1999, Hanchard 2003, Urry 2003, Young 2001.

24. Iriye 2004, p. 213, and Hughes-Warrington 2008, p. 754. These new subfields may be seen as a byproduct of a broader, cross-disciplinary spatial turn. See, for example: http://spatial.scholarslab.org/spatial-turn/.

25. E.g., Braudel 1958, 1966 [1949], Duby 1961.

26. On how the annalistes stole history, see Tendler 2013 and Armitage 2012. The concept of *mentalité*, introduced by Durkheim alongside his *conscience collective*, has influenced Foucault's idea of discursive formations.

27. Vucetic 2011b.

28. For more on this epistemic community, see http://historical-sociology.org/about.

29. Angenot's 1898 project straddles a variety of fields of inquiry, but it comes closest to (francophone) sociocritique—a mix of social theory, literary history, and cultural sociology. This particular research project yielded three more books, one each on anti-Semitism, sex, and socialism. For the closest thing to an English-language version, see Angenot's brief summary, translated by Robert F. Barsky, and the essays authored by Angenot's critics in Barsky 2004.

30. Angenot, too, builds on Gramsci's *common sense*, Foucault's *épistémè*, and Bourdieu's *habitus*, among other concepts and theories (including Claude Duchet's *déjà-dit*; "culture" in the sense of Jean-Pierre Faye and Raymond Williams; the semiotics of Mikhail Bakhtin, Luis Prieto, and Roland Barthes; the Zeitgeist school in the history of ideas; various approaches to "ideology"; and so on). Angenot 1989, pp. 20, 26–29, 36; Angenot 2004, pp. 199–200, 203.

31. Ibid. 1989, pp. 41–47; also see Chs. 3, 4, 21, 22, and 41–48.

32. LaCapra 1989, p. 55, puts it more bluntly: "an archive itself may become a fetish when it is seen not as a repository of traces in the inferential reconstruction of historical processes but as a surrogate for the missing thing itself—*l'histoire totale*."

33. The following derives from Angenot 1989: Chs. 10–14: "The Germans are *the* enemy—and not just Bismarck's 'vampire' state across the Rhine, but also those 200,000 German-speaking workers in France" (Ibid., p. 250). The English and the Americans are annoying; the former

because of their hypocrisy and trickery (the likely Anglo-German alliance being an example), and the latter because of their vulgarity (Ibid., pp. 273–276). As for the roots of France's friendship with Russia, this is not simply a matter of the common Teutonic threat, but also the "heart" (Ibid., p. 256). Indeed, if the centerpiece of the French superiority in 1889 was the novelistic expression of a Mallarmé or a Zola, then the Russia of Tolstoy and Dostoyevsky might have been evaluated—by segments of the nation's elite—as a natural ally to France.

34. Angenot 1989, pp. 1081–1084. Historical annualizations have now become a popular form of history-writing, both scholarly and popular. For more, see North 2001.
35. Students of politics could use this approach to more systematically examine how nations constitute themselves over centuries (e.g., Neumann and Pouliot 2011, Somers and Block 2005).
36. For example: Broderson 1961. For a history of essentializing culture in IR, see Reeves 2005.
37. Guilty as charged: Vucetic 2011a. For critical reviews of identity-based scholarship in IR, see Berenskoetter 2010 and Hynek and Teti 2010.
38. For a review, see Kowert 2010.
39. E.g., Jackson 2005, Krebs and Lobasz 2007, Holland 2012.
40. E.g., Sjöstedt 2007, Widmeier 2007.
41. Domke 2004, Thobani 2014.
42. Croft 2006.
43. Croft 2006, p. 36. While Croft follows the ethos of cultural studies to conceptualize discourse in "an eclectic fashion" (Ibid., p. 44), his focus is still on discourse as a means of "thinking about identities and the world" (Ibid., p. 12).
44. Ibid., pp. 167–168, 187, 193–198, 274, 277.
45. See Croft 2006, Chs. 3 and 6, respectively.
46. Ibid., pp. 271–275.
47. E.g., Krebs and Lobasz 2007, p. 428.
48. Larson 2012, p. 67.
49. Anstee 2012, p. 81.
50. For more on this point, see, among others, Balzacq 2005; Balzacq 2011a, pp. 15–16, 22–28; Balzacq 2011b, pp. 36–37. Securitization theory was first promulgated by Ole Wæver in 1989. See the special issue on "The Politics of Securitization," *Security Dialogue* 42:4–5 (2011), 315–480.
51. Given the wide reach of securitization theory alone, this means that national identity reports could find application in the studies of societal security and other sectors that tightly connect to the politics of identity such as immigration (Wæver and Kelstrup 1993), health (Elbe 2010), and environment (Floyd 2010). On why securitization by default involves both the elites and the masses, see Balzacq 2005.
52. Herrmann, Risse, and Brewer 2004, Checkel and Katzenstein 2009, Wæver and Kelstrup 1993.
53. E.g., Haller 2009, Hooghe and Marks 2005, Steenbergen, Edwards, and de Vries 2007.
54. This intersubjective data set would overlap on some dimensions with the EU-funded Integrated and United (IntUne) project. Survey-based data collected via IntUne tap into both mass- and elite-level attitudes toward European integration in both member and candidate countries, while also paying close attention to media discourses. (For more, see www. intune.it.)

Bibliography

Abdelal, Rawi, Yoshiko Herrera, Iain Johnston, and Rose McDermott, eds., *Measuring Identity: A Guide for Social Scientists* (Cambridge: Cambridge University Press, 2009).

Adams, Julia, Elizabeth Clemens, and Ann S. Orloff, eds., *Remaking Modernity: Politics, History, and Sociology* (Durham: Duke University Press, 2005).

Adams, Laura L., "Techniques for Measuring Identity in Ethnographic Research." In Abdelal, Rawi, Yoshiko Herrera, Iain Johnston, and Rose McDermott, eds., *Measuring Identity: A Guide for Social Scientists* (Cambridge: Cambridge University Press, 2009), 316–341.

Anderson, Benedict, *Imagined Communities: Reflections on the Origin and Spread of Nationalism,* rev. ed. (London: Verso, 1991).

Angenot, Marc, *1899: Un état du discours social* (Montréal/Longueuil: Éditions du Préambule, 1989).

Anstee, Jodie, "Norms and the Management of Identities: The Case for Engagement between Constructivism and the Social Identity Approach," in Shannon, Vaughn and Paul Kowert, eds., *Psychology and Constructivism in International Relations: An Ideational Alliance* (Ann Arbor: University of Michigan Press, 2012), 76–90.

Armitage, David, "What's the Big Idea? Intellectual History and the *Longue Durée*," *History of European Ideas* 38:4 (2012), 493–507.

Ashmore, Richard D., Kay Deaux, and Tracy McLaughlin-Volpe, "An Organizing Framework for Collective Identity: Articulation Significance of Multidimensionality," *Psychological Bulletin* 130:1 (2004), 80–114.

Balzacq, Thierry, "The Three Faces of Securitization: Political Agency, Audience and Context," *European Journal of International Relations* 11:2 (2005), 171–201.

Balzacq, Thierry, "A Theory of Securitization: Origins, Core Assumptions, and Variants," in Balzacq, Thierry, *Securitization Theory: How Security Problems Emerge and Dissolve* (Oxon: Routledge. 2011a), 1–30.

Balzacq, Thierry, "Enquires into Methods: A New Framework for Securitization Analysis," in Balzacq, Thierry, *Securitization Theory: How Security Problems Emerge and Dissolve* (Oxon: Routledge, 2011b), 31–53.

Barsky, Robert F., "Marc Angenot and the Scandal of History," Special Issue of *Yale Journal of Criticism* 17:2 (Fall 2004).

Beck, Ulrich, *Power in the Global Age* (Cambridge: Polity Press, 2006).

Berenskoetter, F., "Identity in International Relations," in Denemark, Robert A., ed., *The International Studies Encyclopedia* (Oxford: Wiley-Blackwell, 2010), 3594–3611.

Billig, Michael, *Arguing and Thinking: A Rhetorical Approach to Social Psychology* (Cambridge: Cambridge University Press, 1987).

Billig, Michael, *Banal Nationalism* (London: SAGE Publications Ltd., 1995).

Billig, Michael, "Remembering the Particular Background of Social Identity Theory," in Robinson, W. P., ed., *Social Groups and Identities: Developing the Theory of Henri Tajfel* (London: Butterworth Heinemann, 1996), 337–357.

Bourdieu, Pierre and Loïc Wacquant, "On the Cunning of Imperialist Reason," *Theory, Culture, and Society* 16:1 (1999), 41–58.

Braudel, Fernand, *La Méditerranée et le monde méditerranéen à l'époque de Philippe II,* 2nd ed. (originally published 1949) (Paris: Colin, 1966).

Brewer, Marilynn B., "The Many Faces of Social Identity: Implications for Political Psychology," *Political Psychology* 22:1 (2001), 115–125.

Broderson, A., "National Character: An Old Problem Revisited," in Rosenau, James, ed., *International Politics and Foreign Policy* (Glencoe: Free Press of Glencoe, 1961), 300–308.

Brubaker, Rogers, Margit Feischmidt, Jon Fox, and Liana Grancea, *Nationalist Politics and Everyday Ethnicity in a Transylvania Town* (Princeton: Princeton University Press, 2006).

Burke, Peter J. and Jan E. Stets, *Identity Theory* (New York: Oxford University Press, 2009).

Chandra, Kanchan, ed., *Constructivist Theories of Ethnic Politics* (New York: Oxford University Press, 2012).

Checkel, Jeffrey T. and Peter J. Katzenstein, eds., *European Identity* (Cambridge: Cambridge University Press, 2009).

Citrin, Jack and David O. Sears, "Balancing National and Ethnic Identities: The Psychology of E Pluribus Unum," in Abdelal, Rawi, Yoshiko Herrera, Iain Johnston, and Rose McDermott, eds., *Measuring Identity: A Guide for Social Scientists* (Cambridge: Cambridge University Press, 2009), 145–167.

Croft, Stuart, *Culture, Crisis and America's War on Terror* (Cambridge: Cambridge University Press, 2006).

Duara, Prasenjit, "Historicizing National Identity, or Who Imagines What and When," in Eley, Geoff and Ronald Grigor Suny, eds., *Becoming National: A History* (New York: Oxford University Press, 1998), 151–177.

Duby, Georges, "Histoire des mentalites," in Samaran, Charles, ed., *L'histoire et ses methodes* (Paris: Librairie Gallimard, 1961), 937–966.

Elbe, Stefan, *Security and Global Health: Towards the Medicalization of Insecurity* (Cambridge: Polity Press, 2010).

Eriksen, Thomas H., *Ethnicity and Nationalism: Anthropological Perspectives*, 3rd ed. (London: Pluto, 2010).

Eriksen, Thomas H. and Richard Jenkins, eds., *Flag, Nation and Symbolism in Europe and America* (London: Routledge, 2007).

Fearon, James and David Laitin, "Violence and the Social Construction of Ethnic Identity," *International Organization* 54:4 (Autumn 2000), 845–877.

Floyd, Rita, *Security and the Environment: Securitisation Theory and US Environmental Security Policy* (Cambridge: Cambridge University Press, 2010).

Fox, Jon and Cynthia Miller-Idriss, "Everyday Nationhood," *Ethnicities* 8:4 (December 2008), 536–563.

Gellner, Ernest, *Nations and Nationalism* (Oxford: Basil Blackwell, 1983).

Hall, Peter A. and Michèle Lamont, eds., *Social Resilience in the NeoLiberal Era* (New York: Cambridge University Press, 2013).

Haller, Max, *European Integration as an Elite Process* (New York: Routledge, 2009).

Hanchard, Michael, "Acts of Misrecognition: Transnational Black Politics, Anti-imperialism and the Ethnocentrisms of Pierre Bourdieu and Loïc Wacquant," *Theory, Culture & Society* 20:4 (2003), 5–29.

Hayes, Jarrod, *Constructing National Security: US Relations with India and China* (New York: Cambridge University Press, 2013).

Herrmann, Richard K., Pierangelo Isernia, and Paolo Segatti, "Attachment to the Nation and International Relations: Dimensions of Identity and Their Relationship to War and Peace," *Political Psychology* 30:5 (2009), 721–754.

Herrmann, Richard K., Thomas Risse, and Marilynn B. Brewer, eds., *Transnational Identities: Becoming European in the EU* (Lanham, MD: Rowman and Littlefield, 2004).

Hobsbawm, Eric and Terence Ranger, eds., *The Invention of Tradition* (Cambridge: Cambridge University Press, 1983).

Hogg, M. A., "Social Identity Theory," in Burke, P. J., ed., *Contemporary Social Psychological Theories* (Palo Alto: Stanford University Press, 2006), 111–136.

Holland, Jack, *Selling the War on Terror: Foreign Policy Discourses after 9/11* (New York: Routledge, 2012).

Hooghe, Liesbet and Gary Marks, "Calculation, Community, and Cues: Public Opinion on European Integration," *European Union Politics* 6:4 (2005), 419–443.

Hopf, Ted, *The Social Construction of International Politics* (Ithaca: Cornell University Press, 2002).

Hopf, Ted, "The Logic of Habit in International Relations," *European Journal of International Relations* 16:4 (2010), 539–561.

Hopf, Ted, *Reconstructing the Cold War: The Early Years, 1945–1958* (Oxford: Oxford University Press, 2012).

Hopf, Ted, "Common-Sense Constructivism and Hegemony in World Politics," *International Organization* 67:3 (2013), 317–354.

Huddy, Leonie, "From Social to Political Identity: A Critical Examination of Social Identity Theory," *Political Psychology* 22:1 (2001), 127–156.

Huddy, Leonie, "Context and Meaning in Social Identity Theory: A Response to Oakes," *Political Psychology* 23:4 (2002), 825–838.

Huddy, Leonie and Nadia Khatib, "American Patriotism, National Identity, and Political Involvement," *American Journal of Political Science* 51:1 (2007), 63–77.

Hughes-Warrington, Marnie, "World and Global History," *Historical Journal* 51:3 (2008), 753–761.

Hynek, Nik and Andrea Teti, "Saving Identity from Postmodernism? The Normalisation of Constructivism in IR," *Contemporary Political Theory* 9 (2010), 171–199.

Iriye, Akira, "Transnational History," *Contemporary European History* 13 (2004), 211–222.

Jackson, Richard, *Writing the War on Terrorism: Language, Politics, and Counter-terrorism* (Manchester and New York: Manchester University Press, 2005).

Kowert, Paul A., "Foreign Policy and the Social Construction of State Identity," in Denemark, Robert A., ed., *The International Studies Encyclopedia* (Oxford: Wiley-Blackwell, 2010), 2479–2498.

Kowert, Paul, "Conclusion: Context and Contributions of the Ideational Alliance," in Shannon, Vaughn and Paul Kowert, eds., *Psychology and Constructivism in International Relations: An Ideational Alliance* (Ann Arbor: University of Michigan Press, 2012), 215–238.

Krebs, Ronald R. and Jennifer K. Lobasz, "Fixing the Meaning of 9/11: Hegemony, Coercion, and the Road to War in Iraq," *Security Studies* 16:3 (2007), 409–451.

Kuo, Alexander and Yotam Margalit, "Measuring Individual Identity: Experimental Evidence," *Comparative Politics* 44:4 (2012), 459–479.

LaCapra, Dominick, *Soundings in Critical Theory* (Ithaca: Cornell University Press, 1989).

Lee, Taeku, "Between Social Theory and Social Science Practice: Toward a New Approach to the Survey Measurement of Race," in Abdelal, Rawi, Yoshiko Herrera, Iain Johnston, and Rose McDermott, eds., *Measuring Identity: A Guide for Social Scientists* (Cambridge: Cambridge University Press, 2009), 113–144.

Le Goff, Jacques, *La nouvelle histoire* (Paris: CEPC, 1978).

Lehman, Edward, "On the Concept of Political Culture: A Theoretical Reassessment," *Social Forces* 50:3 (1972), 361–370.

Mandler, Peter, "What Is National Identity? Definitions and Applications in Modern British Historiography," *Modern Intellectual History* 3:2 (2006), 271–297.

Mandler, Peter, *Return from the Natives: How Margaret Mead Won the Second World War and Lost the Cold War* (New Haven: Yale University Press, 2013).

Margalit, Avishai, "The Moral Psychology of Nationalism," in McKim, R. and J. McMahan, eds., *The Morality of Nationalism* (New York: Oxford University Press, 1997), 74–87.

McDermott, Rose, "Psychological Approaches to Identity: Experimentation and Application," in Abdlal, Rawi, Yoshiko M. Herrera, Iain Johnston, and Rose McDermott, eds., *Measuring Identity: A Guide for Social Science* (New York: Cambridge University Press, 2009), 345–408.

McDermott, Rose and Anthony Lopez, "Psychology and Constructivism: Uneasy Bedfellows?" in Shannon, Vaughn and Paul Kowert, eds., *Psychology and Constructivism in International Relations: An Ideational Alliance* (Ann Arbor: University of Michigan Press, 2012), 197–213.

Neumann, Iver B. and Vincent Pouliot, "Untimely Russia: Hysteresis in Russian-Western Relations over the Past Millennium," *Security Studies* 20:1 (2011), 105–137.

North, Michael, "Virtual Histories: The Year as Literary Period," *Modern Language Quarterly* 62:4 (2001), 407–424.

Özkirimli, Umut, *Theories of Nationalism: A Critical Introduction*, 2nd ed. (New York: Palgrave Macmillan, 2010).

Paxton, Pamela and Anthony Mughan, "What's to Fear from Immigrants? Creating an Assimilationist Threat Scale," *Political Psychology* 27:4 (2006), 549–568.

Pehrson, Samuel, V. Vignoles, and R. Brown, "National Identification and Anti-immigrant Prejudice: Individual and Contextual Effects of National Definitions," *Social Psychology Quarterly* 72:1 (2009), 24–38.

Potter, Jonathan and Margaret Wetherell, *Discourse and Social Psychology* (London: SAGE, 1987).

Reicher, S., "The Context of Social Identity: Domination, Resistance, and Change," *Social Psychology* 25:6 (2004), 921–945.

Schildkraut, Deborah J., "The Rise and Fall of Political Engagement among Latinos: The Role of Identity and Perceptions of Discrimination," *Political Behavior* 27:3 (2005), 285–312.

Schwartz, Seth J., Vivian L. Vignoles, and Luyckx Koen, *Handbook of Identity Theory and Research*, vols. 1–2 (New York: Springer, 2011).

Shannon, Vaughn and Paul Kowert, eds., *Psychology and Constructivism in International Relations: An Ideational Alliance* (Ann Arbor: University of Michigan Press, 2011).

Sjöstedt, Roxanna, "The Discursive Origins of a Doctrine: Norms, Identity, and Securitization under Harry S. Truman and George W. Bush," *Foreign Policy Analysis* 3:3 (2007), 233–254.

Somers, Margaret R. and Fred Block, "From Poverty to Perversity: Ideas, Markets, and Institutions over 200 Years of Welfare Debate," *American Sociological Review* 70:2 (2005), 260–287.

Steenbergen, Marco R., Erica E. Edwards, and Catherine E. de Vries, "Who's Cueing Whom? Mass-Elite Linkages and the Future of European Integration," *European Union Politics* 8:1 (2007), 13–35.

Sylvan, Donald A. and Amanda K. Metskas, "Trade-offs in Measuring Identities: A Comparison of Five Approaches," in Abdelal, Rawi, Yoshiko Herrera, Iain Johnston, and Rose McDermott, eds., *Measuring Identity: A Guide for Social Scientists* (Cambridge: Cambridge University Press, 2009), 72–109.

Theiss-Morse, Elizabeth, *Who Counts as an American? The Boundaries of National Identity* (New York: Cambridge University Press, 2009).

Thobani, Sunera, "Race, Sovereignty, and Empire: Theorizing the Camp, Theorizing Postmodernity," in Bakan, Abigail B. and Enakshi Dua, eds., *Theorizing Anti-racism: Linkages in Marxism and Critical Race Theories* (Toronto: University of Toronto Press, 2014), 280–310.

Transue, John E., "Identity Salience, Identity Acceptance, and Racial Policy Attitudes: American National Identity as a Uniting Force," *American Journal of Political Science* 51 (2007), 78–91.

Urry, John, *Global Complexity* (Cambridge: Polity, 2003).

Vucetic, Srdjan, "Bound to Follow? The Anglosphere and U.S.-Led Coalitions of the Willing, 1950–2001," *European Journal of International Relation* 17:1 (2011a), 27–49.

Vucetic, Srdjan, "Genealogy as a Research Tool in International Relations," *Review of International Studies* 37:3 (2011b), 1295–1312.

Vucetic, Srdjan, *The Anglosphere: A Genealogy of a Racialized Identity in International Relations* (Palo Alto: Stanford University Press, 2011c).

Waever, Ole, "Identity, Communities and Foreign Policy: Discourse Analysis as a Foreign Policy Theory," in Hansen, Lene and Ole Waever, eds., *European Integration and National Identity: The Challenge of the Nordic States* (London: Routledge, 2002a), 20–49.

Wæver, Ole, "Identity, Communities and Foreign Policy," in Hansen, Lene and Ole Waever, eds., *European Integration and National Identity: The Challenge of the Nordic States* (London: Routledge, 2002b), 20–50.

Wæver, Ole, "European Integration and Security: Analysing French and German Discourses on State, Nation, and Europe," in Howarth, David and Jacob Torfing, eds., *Discourse Theory in European Politics: Identity, Policy, and Governance* (New York: Palgrave Macmillan, 2005), 33–67.

Wæver, Ole, "Politics, Security, Theory," *Security Dialogue* 42:4–5 (2011), 465–480.

Waever, Ole, Barry Buzan, and Morten Kelstrup, "Europe and Its Nations: Political and Cultural Identities," in Waever, Ole, ed., *Identity, Migration and the New Security Agenda in Europe* (New York: St. Martin's Press, 1993), 61–92.

Welch Larson, Deborah, "How Identities Form and Change: Supplementing Constructivism with Social Psychology," in Shannon, Vaughn and Paul Kowert, eds., *Psychology and Constructivism in International Relations: An Ideational Alliance* (Ann Arbor: University of Michigan Press, 2012), 57–75.

Weldes, Jutta, Mark Laffey, Hugh Gusterson, and Raymond Duvall, eds., *Cultures of Insecurity: States, Communities, and the Production of Danger* (Minneapolis: University of Minnesota Press, 1999).

Widmaier, Wesley W., "Constructing Foreign Policy Crises: Interpretive Leadership in the Cold War and the War on Terrorism," *International Studies Quarterly* 51:4 (2007), 779–794.

Young, Robert J. C., *Postcolonialism: A Historical Introduction* (Malden: Blackwell Publishers Ltd., 2001).

13

What Have We Learned?

TED HOPF AND BENTLEY B. ALLAN

In this chapter we wish to accomplish three tasks. First, we will summarize the findings of the eight narrative chapters plus Russia with respect to the overarching question of this volume: the future of neoliberal democratic hegemony.[1] We will review and auto-critique the methodological lessons of the volume, and we will elaborate how a large-*n* intersubjective national identity database can contribute to addressing a host of puzzles in International Relations (IR) theory.

I. The Future of Neoliberal Democratic Hegemony

It is useful to think of the chapters in this volume as providing a snapshot of each country's national identity terrain in 2010. On the one hand, this is a very limited accomplishment, for of course what a country's identity is in 2010 might bear little resemblance to the same country in 2000 or 2005. This is precisely the reason why we are embarking on a longitudinal project from 1810 to 2010, although we do not believe identities will change that significantly across short periods of time, say, 20 years. This is an empirical question, and of course large cataclysmic events like wars, economic depressions, revolutions, and natural disasters would be expected to alter the identity terrain more dramatically than in less eventful times.

To recall, we are interested in how and whether Western hegemony, defined as democratic neoliberalism, can persist past the decline of the United States and the rise of China. If not, we are interested in what might replace it. On our conception, Western hegemony is a transnational ideology that is rooted in and supported by domestic identities. The strongest, most robust hegemony would be one universally shared by elites and masses across the nine countries. This would reflect the deep socialization of entire societies, the grounding of hegemony in taken-for-granted common sense. So, the first piece of evidence is what elites understand the identities of their countries to be. The second step is to see if masses share, or contradict, these understandings. For Cox and Wallerstein, and probably most IR theorists, who concentrated on elites, it is elite understandings that matter. So, if we were to find elite consensus in favor of democratic neoliberalism across the nine countries, that would portend a future for Western hegemony. But that would not take into account mass discourse, which our theory contends can become elite discourse if a regime is replaced, or can become part of elite discourse to the extent elites are part of society, too.

If we look at Table 13.1, we can see that Western hegemony has much more elite support than mass support already but that elite support is not consensual.

Let us begin with elite support for democracy. With the exception of Chinese elites, there is consensual understanding that being democratic is a positive aspect of one's identity. The Chinese elite explicitly rejects Western understandings of democracy, while the Russian elite is ambivalent about it. Meanwhile the Japanese elite is silent about it. We might hypothesize here that the Japanese elite is silent because it is already a taken-for-granted aspect of Japanese national identity. But it would only be a hypothesis. Coding absence is very tricky. One way to test the hypothesis is to assess Japanese discourses of national identity every ten years beginning in 1950 to see if in 1960, e.g., democratic identity was

Table 13.1 **A Topography of National Identity and Democratic Neoliberal Hegemony 2010**

	Democracy		Neoliberalism	
	Elites	*Mass*	*Elites*	*Mass*
Germany	+	+	+	
Japan			+	−
China	−		+	+/−
India (E)	+	+	+	+/−
India (H)	+	+	+/−	+/−
France	+	+	−	−
United Kingdom	+	+	+	+
United States	+	+	+/−	+/−
Brazil	+	+	+/−	+/−
Russia	+/−	+/−	+	−

E, English; H, Hindi.

explicitly valued by Japanese elites, but its salience waned over the next fifty years. This would imply it has been internalized as so commonsensical as not to bear mention. If, however, it was barely evident since 1950, we could safely conclude it just is not part of Japanese elite self-understanding.

Elites, with the exception of French elites, also understand neoliberalism to be a positive part of their country's national identity. In India, elite texts in Hindi express ambivalence, while elite texts in English are positive. But notably, in India, Brazil, and China, positive attitudes toward liberalizing policies (openness, free trade, etc.) sit alongside statist or socialist identities. These countries do not share the neoliberal view that the state is an ineffective or illegitimate economic actor. So support for neoliberalism may be ambivalent. But there is no coherent alternative economic identity to rival neoliberalism here. We could conclude nonetheless, that at the elite level, the neoliberal capitalist part of Western hegemony is secure, while the democratic element is at least contested in China, and not fully accepted in Russia.

The masses in all countries save Japan, China, and Russia understand democratic identity to be an important part of their own national identities. While there are no negative understandings of democracy, Russian mass ambivalence toward democracy is directed precisely at Western conceptualizations of democracy. Chinese masses do not think of being democratic as being Chinese. Japanese masses as well do not mention democracy as a salient identity category. But the hypothesis about internalized common sense outlined above for Japanese elites might apply to Japanese masses as well.

The masses in all countries, save the United Kingdom, have ambivalent or negative attitudes toward capitalism, markets, and neoliberalism. This, of course, is a finding of great significance on several counts. First, it demonstrates, as many theorists from Polanyi to Hardt and Negri have argued, that masses experience capitalism and free markets as fraught with negative consequences for going on in the world. It foreshadows the political support any alternative to neoliberalism is likely to garner when offered at home, or as an alternative hegemonic ideology globally. This was Robert Cox's conclusion about US hegemony, viz., that it would be replaced by a socialist or social democratic alternative. What we have in the world today then is an alternative "historic bloc," to borrow Gramsci's terminology, in search of sufficient global material power to bring it into hegemonic dominance globally.[2] Cox had placed his hopes on the Soviet Union, in alliance with the developing world and the Organization of Petroleum Exporting Countries (OPEC), to effect such a revolution. Many had and do pin such hopes on China. But, as we see from the elite discourse in China, there is already acceptance of neoliberalism as part of China's national project. Before concluding that there is untapped mass political support for a global social democratic hegemony, which there may well be, we must keep in mind that 2010 was just two years after the worst global economic meltdown since the Great Depression. This alone could account for the lack of support for neoliberalism among the masses. Again, only a historical longitudinal study across time and space can assess this hypothesis.

In sum, Western democratic neoliberal hegemony is not in a state of crisis, but it surely is not totally hegemonic, either. While elites daily reproduce neoliberal hegemony, their populations struggle against it, and demand it be made more consonant with their own understandings of the good life. On the other hand, Chinese elites stand alone in the world in open opposition to the democratic element of Western hegemony. This poses a huge obstacle to any Chinese global hegemonic project, as they would first have to abandon a fundamental aspect of their own self-understanding. A failure to do so will only perpetuate Western hegemony in the world, especially given the fact that the Chinese elite is co-producing the neoliberal aspect of that order. If China were to democratize, then this too would only reproduce already existing neoliberal democratic hegemony. For this Western hegemony to be replaced, China's neoliberal authoritarian model would have to find resonance among other great powers. Their elites and masses would have to reject their appreciation for democracy in favor of the Chinese alternative.

One of the main promises of a constructivist national identity database is the recovery of significant national identities that would be missed by approaches that reduce identity to pre-theorized categories. We present a few of them in Table 13.2, along with what kinds of international possibilities they imply.

First, there is a group of countries who understand themselves as becoming, progressing, modernizing, and developing: China, Brazil, India, and Russia. And there is a group of countries that understand themselves as already modern and developed, but fear decline: the United States, the United Kingdom, and especially France. Certainly such a distribution of identities in world politics between a group who expects to be the future and a group who fears being the past cannot but affect the nature of world politics. For example, a quick application of prospect theory here would alert us to the fact that the United States, United Kingdom, and France, each of which understands itself as in decline, are likely to adopt risky strategies to maintain their positions against those that are rising.[3] Moreover, all these countries, except Japan, understand themselves as leaders, either globally, as in the case of the United States, or at least regionally.

There is also a group of countries—China, Brazil, Japan, India, and Russia—whose elites and masses understand corruption as a threat to their national projects. In all cases, except Russia, the elites understand the problem as something with which they are effectively struggling. The masses, on the other hand, are less than convinced. Only in Russia do we see elites despairing

Table 13.2 **International Identity Topography**

Categories	Brazil	China	France	Germany	India (H)	India (E)	Japan	United Kingdom	United States	Russia
Political										
Democracy	+		+	+	+++++	++++		+	++	
Rule of law			+					+	+	--
Freedom			+	+		+	+	+	+	
Corrupt	----	-			-	-	---	-	-	--~
Economic										
Capitalist			-			+	+----			
Neoliberal	+-	+-	-	+	+-	+-	-	+	+-	++++
Statist/ socialist	+	+					+			+++
Progressive								+	+	
Developing/ modernizing	+	++++		-	+++	++		++		~~
Social										
Socially divided/ unequal	----	-			-	--	-		-	
Environmental				+			+		+	
Individualist		-					-	+	+-	
Materialist		-							~	
Persevering/ hardworking		+++	-	+			-	-	+-	
Religion						/			+	
International										
Western	+		+							++++
West as other		~								
United States	~	-+	+	+			+	+		
European	+		+	+						++

Notes: This topography is based on raw count tables (in some cases, we have used longer raw count lists than appear in the chapters), normalized as a percentage of total counts, and converted into symbols using the formula in the code book. The one exception to this is for the categories "neoliberal," "democracy," and "United States," which analysts reported to us directly.

E, English; H, Hindi.

at the level of corruption in the society, while the masses have already inter-nalized it as a taken-for-granted feature of daily life. In the United Kingdom, Germany, France, and the United States, corruption rarely appears at any level of national discourse.

Particular bilateral identity relationships emerge between pairs of countries, often marked by differences between elites and masses. Japanese elites, for example, identify positively with the United States, but the masses, while not expressing antipathy for the United States, do not express any affinity either. Chinese elites identify negatively against the United States on strategic grounds, while Chinese masses identify positively with US culture and economic achieve-ments. Chinese elites and masses identify negatively against Japan on geopoliti-cal grounds, but Chinese masses identify with Japan economically. French elites identify positively with francophone Africa, while masses ignore it. Meanwhile, French masses identify positively with the United States and the United Kingdom, while the French elite ignores them both. Both UK masses and elites identify with the United States and the West more generally. Both German elites and masses identify positively with the United States, the West, and Europe, but ambivalently toward France, and negatively toward southern Europe. Both Russian elites and masses identify positively, and selectively, with the West and Europe, but not with the United States. Brazil identifies more positively with Western Europe than any other part of the world; Latin America, perhaps sur-prisingly, is not a significant other for Brazil. The United States, like India, does not identify itself with, or against, any other country.

The findings of the discourse analyses offer an answer to the question of the origins of anti-Americanism in the world. Like many other studies, we find that the United States is hated for what it does, not for what it is. While masses and elites in our nine countries in general identify with a democratic neoliberal United States, the elites and masses of Russia, China, and Brazil, at least, identify against the United States because of its foreign policy.

Finally, there are interesting understandings of the role of religion in the dis-courses of national identity. Most important is the utter absence of any kind of religious identification with national identity in the United Kingdom, Germany, China, Japan, Brazil, the United States, and Russia. In the case of France, there is positive antipathy toward any religious identity, rooted in its strong commit-ment to secularism. Indian discourse explicitly recognizes the danger of reli-gious identity for Indian democracy and progress. Contrary to civilizational hypotheses that reduce civilization to religious groups/affiliation, as in the case of Huntington, the nine countries analyzed here do not understand religion as part of their national identity at all.

II. How to Find National Identities

This volume presents a proof of concept that the method laid out in Chapter Two can produce interesting and usable results. This exercise presents an opportunity to review and critique the method laid out in Chapter Two.

The Ideal Analyst

At the outset of this project we did not know which kinds of scholars would make the best analysts. On the one hand, a professor with a background in qualitative methods would be able to quickly master the coding rules and produce a polished result. On the other hand, why would she want to spend her time doing this kind of "contract" research, rather than publishing her own theoretical research? It would not be appreciated by promotion and tenure committees, and would not be as intellectually satisfying as one's own independent research. Moreover, a professor would have such a huge background of prior theoretical and empirical knowledge, it would be hard to not provide deep interpretations of a country's texts, rather than remain as inductive and atheoretical as possible.

Graduate students raise similar issues. It is not a good use of a graduate student's time if an identity report is not germane to her dissertation. Moreover, she also will have theoretical priors and an interest in expressing herself in print, not just write an empirical report for a collective project. Finally, advanced undergraduates, preferably honors students, would seem to be ideal, as they do not have the store of theoretical priors or the professional needs of either professors or graduate students. On the other hand, they do not have the kind of methodological or disciplinary training of more advanced students or professors, so would need far more guidance along the way.

In practice, it appears that any one of the three kinds of scholars can be ideal. If professors and graduate students are willing, then they are certainly able. And if undergraduates are eager to learn the discursive methods and the theory of social identity being employed, then they are very able, as well. Moreover, in the case of professors and graduate students, the counting procedure can serve as a check against priors and biases to preserve the validity of the results.

The Text Sample

There are two sets of lessons about the sampling strategy. First, do the genres contain rich, overheard identity categories, and do they capture mass and elite discourses in ways comparable across countries? One of the central purposes for choosing a range of texts from elite to mass was to capture the difference between "political" and "social" construction. The former is the elite propagation of a discourse of national identity, while the latter is the everyday re/production of discourses of national identity that may, or may not, challenge or reinforce the predominant discourse on offer from the state.[4] We also expect that socially constructed discourses of national identity are the most likely replacements for the predominant discourse after a change of regime, whether electorally, or more forcefully.

What other genres might be included to achieve this goal? First, a number of our analysts suggested including newsmagazines, but for different reasons. For some, newsmagazines would provide another rich source of identity categories that may be less politicized than newspapers. In the Chinese case, the authors suggested that women are more likely to read magazines than newspapers and so the sample as is may be gendered. Second, to capture more mass views in China, the authors suggested we sample online sources. We are interested in this possibility, but there is no clear sampling strategy that would be comparable across countries. Finally, we could also add popular television shows to better access mass discourses in a variety of countries.

A few reports show that speeches, newspapers, and textbooks tend to uncover predominantly political identity categories. The danger here is that our findings will disproportionately capture the dominant political, ideological categories of a country. For example, one challenge in the US case was overinterpreting progressivism in US society because Obama's speeches articulated Democratic Party positions. But the author, like the author of the UK report, found that contesting political ideologies drew on deep, shared identity categories, although they combined categories in different ways. This leads us to tentatively conclude that, although the sample may be biased toward political discourses, it still tends to capture the core, enduring identity categories of a country. Moreover, for the purposes of a political investigation into international politics, such a bias is acceptable.

Second, are there enough texts to produce valid results? Most analysts reported that the results were likely to be robust to changes in sample size, but many reported that speeches and movies were undersampled. We are sufficiently worried about results being shaped by small sample sizes to think about expanding the number of speeches and movies. For example, one French speech delivered to African states by Sarkozy leads our method to the conclusion that the colonial past and relations with Africa are significant to French elites. Of course, they probably are, but not as significant as they would be if we looked at all of Sarkozy's speeches. Similarly, in the German case, one environmentalist movie drove the counts up and makes it seem as if the masses are highly committed to environmental protection. Of course, Germany is one of the most environmentalist countries in the world, so this is only partially misleading. One solution would be to add a third speech and a third movie. This will not solve the problem but will water down outlier codings like these. The more important redress is to advise analysts to discount these kinds of findings in their conclusions about dominant and challenger discourses, as the analysts have done here. On the other side, we could reduce the number of newspaper articles analyzed to rebalance the results across genres. But despite these shortcomings, the advantage of outlining our sampling and coding rules is that we and our readers are able to make these kinds of observations and correct for them.

Coding Rules

Both we and the analysts are satisfied with the coding rules. They constrain over-interpretation but seem to capture most of what the analysts qualitatively report as central to the discourses of their countries. Plus, the coding rules give some freedom for analysts to bring relevant categories into the topographical table even if they do not break the top twenty identity categories ranking.

One problem however, is that analysts deploy the rules in slightly different ways. For example, some analysts coded instances where capitalism was critiqued as capitalism (-), while others coded it as anticapitalism (+). These kinds of problems are easy to fix. Not all analysts, however, made use of all three ways to code. The code book allows analysts to code a category as positive or negative, aspirational or aversive, or as a significant other. But analysts only used the aspirational/aversive distinction to solve problems. Perhaps this is because the tables only require that they report valence. Future versions of the code book may downplay these latter two coding options to focus on sharpening valence.

Another issue is that the coding rules were difficult to adequately apply to films, in which visual cues may have identity content, but as written the coding rules do not provide guidance. We will add examples of this kind of coding to the book to aid analysts in future analyses.

III. Constructivist National Identities and Quantitative IR Scholarship

As the project moves forward, we aim to engage quantitative IR, first, by translating our findings into quantitative variables that could be incorporated into Correlates of War and other data sets. Our aim is to produce enough reports for enough countries to allow for the creation of a useful longitudinal data set ultimately going back to 1810.

Toward a Quantitative Database

How could these reports be translated into quantitative data? We envision that the topographical tables, because of their basis in raw counts, could be translated into a variety of variables with implications for IR by other scholars. For example, constructivist scholarship hypothesizes that states that share a collective identity, defined as a common understanding of themselves as a "we," are unlikely to go to war with one another.[5] The findings of the long-term project here could be used to test this hypothesis. For example, if "European" emerges as a central identity in German and French discourses after 1945, the data set could provide evidence for the collective identity hypothesis.

Of course, there are other possibilities. For example there is a difference between "collective identity" and "overlapping identity." Overlapping identities are shared in that states understand themselves using the same category. However, overlapping identities are not necessarily collective group identities that posit a "we." So China and Brazil both see themselves as "developing" but do not see themselves as part of the same "we," "developing nations." But this example shows that within the collective identity-peace hypothesis is the assumption that the "we" has relevant peaceful content—we would not expect an overlapping "developing" status to create peace. Some overlapping identities, however, may lead to peace. For example, if both states see themselves as democratic, this could lead to a preference for settling disputes peacefully. Our approach is an improvement over more simplistic identity variables because it allows for this differentiation in content. Moreover, it could generate hypotheses about cooperation among states with overlapping identities on particular issues. So, "developing" might lead to systematic cooperation among states that would otherwise be predicted not to manifest so much cooperative behavior.

Collective and overlapping identities can be quantified in a number of ways from our reports. First, a simple present or absent dichotomous variable could be coded based on whether or not a given collective or overlapping identity category was present in the predominant discourse of identity. This is similar to the exercise we perform for neoliberal democratic hegemony above. Second, the quantitative counts could be translated into ordinal variables via a number of transpositions. For example, the number of pluses and minuses in topographical tables could be added together to yield an ordinal variable that codes both presence of a category and its salience in a given country. These could be disaggregated by mass/elite if that is theoretically relevant to the hypothesis at hand. We must do more work in conjunction with quantitative scholars on these issues.

We suspect that there are problems with the mathematical decisions we have made. For example, we chose to transpose the raw counts into topographical symbols via percentages normalized by genre. We made the decision to create what is essentially a 5-point scale for the topographies because it is easy to interpret, not because it met the standards of measurement theory.

Moreover, at this stage, the raw counts may not be consistent enough across countries to produce reliable quantitative variables. For example, there are simply more pluses and minuses in some countries then there are in others, suggesting that some analysts code a small number of categories intensely and others a large number of categories more thinly.

Toward Quantitative IR and Identity

Imagine a database of national identity reports akin to those in this volume for all great powers from 1810 to 2010 with an accompanying data set compatible with Correlates of War data. What could we do with them? There are many possibilities. We could respecify many quantitative tests for existing theories of war and peace, alliances, conflict and cooperation, enduring rivalries and enmities, norm adoption, and much else.

The normative strand of the democratic peace, for example, expects that democracies do not fight each other because their leaders (and publics) see other democracies and are reassured by their institutionalized ways of managing political conflict at home through peaceful means. Without rehearsing the issues raised in Chapter One, the theory assumes that each country's leaders understand its own country, and others, to be either democratic or non-democratic. With our database, quantitative researchers could for the first time actually code accurately all great powers since 1810 on precisely these theoretical grounds: Are the states that understand themselves and others as democracies less likely to go to war with each other, or not? Now, of course, this would still remain a correlational finding. Case studies would still have to be performed to see whether or not such countries do in fact refrain from military action because of their democratic identities, but at least the correlation would be between a more valid operationalization and measurement of the theory's hypotheses than has ever been achieved before in quantitative work that relies only on Polity IV and Freedom House objectivist indices. We would have the first database of meaningfully democratic great powers, such that any theory that specifies regime type as an independent variable of interest could be assured of having valid measures of that concept for the first time.[6]

While Huntington's clash-of-civilizations account of world politics has been decisively refuted empirically with objectivist indicators of religion, a new database would allow us to go beyond merely assigning religions to countries and actually code countries by how they understand their own religious identities, or reveal whether they even have them.[7] We would also be able to judge whether

great powers in fact understand themselves according to Huntington's civilizational categories. We might find instead, that many great powers understood
themselves as civilized, a shared, if not collective, identity among themselves,
but one which was regularly deployed against those adjudged uncivilized.[8]

One could also explore whether constructivism can help explain the emergence, duration, and end to enduring rivalries. We would hypothesize, mini-
mally, that states enter enduring rivalries because each regards the other as a
hostile Other in world politics. This understanding should persist throughout
the rivalry. Meanwhile, we would hypothesize that alternative discourses of
national identity in those countries do not understand the rivalrous state as a
necessarily hostile Other. When this discursive challenger is empowered by the
state, we should expect an attempt to get out of the enduring rivalry, or necessarily end if both state's identities undergo a transformation. The Sino-Soviet conflict from 1958 to 1988 manifests such a dynamic. The enduring rivalry started
once both states understood themselves as the true vanguards of socialism in the
world. When Soviet identity changed with the ascension of Gorbachev to power
in 1985 to one of a normal social democratic great power, the identity conflict
between Beijing and Moscow was eliminated, and the enduring rivalry ended.

Identity change may not produce an end to rivalry of course. For example, if
Gorbachev's arrival in power had brought with it a discourse of ethnonational
Russian identity for the Soviet Union (and such a discourse existed as an alternative to social-democratic great power) we could hypothesize that a Chinese,
although not communist, hostile Other would obtain, and the enduring rivalry
would not have ended when it did. Diehl and Goertz have created a database of
enduring rivalries from 1816 to 1992.[9] There are eleven great-power rivalries,
each one of which has a birth, life, and death. No plausible general theory has
been applied to all these cases. A national identity database could provide the
empirical evidence to test a constructivist one. Our findings could be easily
translated into a dyadic data set that coded whether or not one or both of the
great powers in these rivalries understood themselves in terms of the Other. But
the database of reports will also provide hypotheses for in-depth case studies
that test for the role of identities in great-power rivalry.

There is a vast quantitative IR literature on alliances: what causes them, and
what effects they have on world politics. A database of national identities could
help refine and test existing theories of alliance formation and effects, as well as
offer a constructivist alternative for them. As a recent survey of the quantitative
IR literature on alliance formation observed, "threat plays a role in every theory
of alliance formation . . . .Yet, large-n empirical support for this relationship is . . .
inconsistent, perhaps because scholars have not yet operationalized the existence of threat in a convincing way."[10] Constructivism operationalizes threat as
hostile identity relations between two countries. This operationalization can

be easily captured by our method's measurements: significant threats should appear as identity categories in the topographical tables.

Lai and Reiter have found that states are more likely to ally with each other if they share a similar language or religion.[11] The presumed causal story behind the observed correlations is that states trust other states that are more similar to them. Notwithstanding what we already noted in Chapter One, namely, that reducing identity or salient similarities among states to ascribed language, religion, or ethnicity is reductionist and invalidating, the database can help test the presumed causal mechanism behind the observed positive relationship between these ascriptions. We can know whether or not great powers understood themselves in linguistic or religious or ethnic terms, respecify Lai and Reiter's model accordingly, and reassess the results. In this case, our proposed overlapping identities or dyadic rivalry data sets would not directly apply because these simple measures do not capture "perceived similarity." However, a scholar interested in testing this hypothesis could use our database of reports to specify their own quantification that could serve as the basis of a test.

Lai and Reiter also find that states are more likely to ally if they share similar political institutions, such as democracies, monarchies, republics, and various types of authoritarian regimes.[12] The presumed causal mechanism again runs through recognizing oneself as meaningfully one regime type rather than another and recognizing other states as either more similar or more different. Our database can provide a more valid operationalization of these variables and allow for a re-evaluation of these findings.

There is a vast, mostly constructivist, IR literature on norm adoption by states. The most common argument is that states adopt norms via a logic of appropriateness: they adopt a norm when it resonates with their identity. There are not yet any large-n quantitative studies to assess this hypothesis.[13] Our database affords that opportunity. For example, if the argument is that states forswear chemical weapons because of a civilizational identity, then we should be able to test that claim. More importantly, instead of relying on the rhetoric surrounding the decision to give up or not use chemical weapons, where ruling elites might say "civilized states such as ours would not use such obscene weapons," we could offer a more theoretically robust test of whether the elites or society of a particular country actually understand themselves as civilized in general, on a quotidian basis, rather than merely at the point of the decision. This would be a more convincing confirmation of the civilizational identity argument.

There is also an argument that norms diffuse from great powers to the rest of the world. Our database would allow for the longitudinal measurement of the relationship between states' identities and their adoption of norms of interest. We could offer a more systematic answer to the question of whether great powers are early adopters of norms, and offer explanations for why, or why not, according to the resonance of those norms with prevailing identities in those great powers. In addition, once of course this database grows beyond only great powers, we could assess whether non-great powers eventually emulate great powers or not. Again, the latters' identities are hypothesized to account for their adherence and nonadherence to these norms.

So, far we have only alluded to the database's potential to test either additional variables, or more valid operationalizations of variables, in existing theoretical approaches to IR. Perhaps still more valuable is the database's ability to allow researchers to fashion their own theories of international politics using the national identity reports' rich collections of potential variables that are revealed in each report's raw count of identities, the predominant and challenging discourses of national identity, and the differentiation between mass and elite sources of those national identities.

If we look at Table 13.2 above, we find a host of identities that are ignored by quantitative measures of identity in IR. What is more, the national identity reports themselves reveal many more that have been later aggregated into what the reader sees in Table 13.3. A few of the more widely distributed identities are as follows: corrupt, hardworking/persevering, modernizing/developing, and socially divided/unequal.

Of course we cannot possibly know now whether any of these are significant beyond the plausibility probe conducted in this volume on democratic neoliberal hegemony. So we cannot know whether these identities have implications for relations among these states beyond the question we asked. Nor can we know if these identities are also relevant to any other country in 2010. Nor can we

Table 13.3 **Identity Relations with the United States**

	Elites	Masses
Japan	+	
China	−	+
France		+
Germany	+	+
United Kingdom	+	+
Russia	−	−
Brazil	−	−
India (English)		
India (Hindi)		

know if these identities have temporal reach beyond 2010. But what we do know is that these identities are salient and meaningful to the nine countries themselves; it is how they understand themselves, and so it is a more valid measure of their identities than any ascriptive scheme that assigns them national identities based on religion, ethnicity, or language. The only identity in the quantitative literature that passes the intersubjective test is democracy.

So far, we have only suggested that a national identity database could be useful in theory testing. But the national identity reports, with their inductive recovery of the intersubjective identity topographies of each country, can also play a role in theory building. For example, we could construct a theory of hegemonic stability that gave central place to the role of its legitimization among great powers, as both Cox and Wallerstein have suggested. Finding out that elites, but especially masses, at least in our cases here, come to associate that hegemony with corruption and inequality at home could undermine the domestic foundations for that hegemony, hastening its demise: still more if they understand themselves as hardworking, but unjustly robbed of the fruits of their efforts.

The mission of theory building also benefits from our division of discourses of national identity into elite and mass levels of analysis. There is the simple empirical reward of knowing what discourses of national identity are challenging the predominant national identity project propagated by the state. This allows us to see potential lines of political conflict within any country. Moreover, we can see what probable changes in national identity are likely to occur if the current regime in power is replaced, and an alternative national identity is empowered. We can also see what kinds of transnational coalitions are possible at the societal level in world politics. More broadly, for the many scholars interested in the connection between domestic politics and foreign policy, the national identity reports offer a new vantage point to gauge what is meaningful to broad masses in each country and how this might constrain or enable their political elites when interacting with other states.

Finally, and perhaps most promising of all, the methodology for recovering national identity travels far beyond great powers. Given the bias that IR theory has for great powers, we deliberately chose to make our project most attractive to theories that concentrate on great powers. But we fully realize, and perhaps should apologize for, the fact that we are complicit in the reproduction of that bias. But our intentions are far wider; we hope that the methodology outlined in this volume will be applied to any and all countries in the world. Just to give yet another, still narrow, example, while there are only 11 enduring rivalries between great powers identified by Diehl and Goertz, they also identify another 52 among non-great powers.

IV. Conclusion

This volume has presented reports on national identity in eight great-power countries using a new method that balances the demands of inductive, interpretivist discourse analysis with the desire to produce reliable and replicable results that can form the basis of a quantitative database. The goal is that the method here can be applied to a wider range of great-power countries through time, back to 1810. The project would produce reports, raw data on identity categories, and topographical tables for these countries at 5- or 10-year intervals. These products could be operationalized by quantitative scholars into statistical variables compatible with Correlates of War and other data sets.

The goal of this data would be to subject constructivist hypotheses about the democratic peace, enduring rivalries, treaty ratification, international organization (IO) membership, identity change, norm adoption, and so on to tests rooted in variables that actually capture constructivist concepts. As it stands, quantitative tests of constructivist ideas rest on reliable but invalid variables like the ethnolinguistic fractionalization index.

But we have also demonstrated the immediate payoff of our approach to national identity by applying our findings to global hegemony. Elite texts in most states identify with the core identity categories of Western democratic neoliberal hegemony. Although neoliberalism lacks support in mass discourse, there is no alternative discourse that can challenge American-led ideological hegemony at the moment. From this vantage point, the prospects for Chinese hegemonic leadership of the great powers is dim, because it lacks a democratic identity, which is strongly supported by elites in almost every other great power. Our reports also produced some unexpected findings. Religion has very little resonance with national identities, providing evidence that no clash of civilizations will emerge. The central identity categories of countries today are domestic political, economic, and social identities—developed/developing, hardworking, socially divided/unequal—rather than international or geopolitical ones.

The reports and method introduced here provide a new and different picture of the international system. We are accustomed to summary statistical representations of the great powers in terms of gross domestic product (GDP), military prowess, debt ratios, and capital accounts. By contrast, here we provide an image of the international system rooted in identities and their cultural background. Part of the value of a database of discursive national identity reports is to portray the world in terms of its cultural and ideological diversity, rather than merely as arrays of statistics.

Notes

1. We have added Russia for this concluding chapter, based on Hopf 2013.
2. This is consistent with Mark Blyth's argument that any systemic change in global political economy requires not just a crisis in the present system, but also an alternative (Blyth 2002). Keohane's argument that high transaction costs lead to international institutional stickiness resonates here as well. While he concentrates our attention on how difficult it is to develop an alternative institution, we focus here, as did Gramsci, on how hard it is to even imagine an alternative in the first place (Keohane 1983).
3. Levy 1997.
4. On the difference between political and social construction, see Smith 2003.
5. Adler and Barnett 1998, Wendt 1999.
6. Of course, this would not assess the empirical validities of those variants of the democratic peace that argue it is institutional constraints that matter. But these have been empirically invalidated because of the greater overall bellicosity of democracies.
7. Giacomo Chiozza, "Is There a Clash of Civilizations?" *Journal of Peace Research* 39:6 (2002), 711–734; and Errol Henderson and Joshua Tucker, "Clear and Present Strangers," *International Studies Quarterly* 45 (2001), 317–338.
8. As was noted in Neumann and Welsh 1991 on European treatments of Russia and the Ottoman Empire/Turkey. In our sample here, only France continues to understand itself as "civilized," but the masses worry that France is a civilization in decline.
9. Diehl and Goertz 2000, pp. 145–146.
10. Brett Ashley Leeds and T. Clifton Morgan, "The Quest for Security: Alliances and Arms," in Sara Mitchell, Paul Diehl, and James Morrow, eds. *Guide to the Scientific Study of International Processes* (Chichester, UK: Wiley-Blackwell, 2012), p. 141.
11. Lai and Reiter 2000.
12. Lai and Reiter 2000.
13. One exception is Simmons and Elkins 2004, who find that common religious identity is associated with the adoption of liberal norms on current and capital accounts and exchange rate regimes across 182 countries. Our database could explore this objective correlation to see whether in fact the countries of common religion understand themselves according to these ascribed religious identities.

References

Adler, Emanuel and Michael Barnett, *Security Communities* (Cambridge and New York: Cambridge University Press, 1998).

Blyth, Mark, *Great Transformations: Economic Ideas and Institutional Change in the Twentieth Century* (New York: Cambridge University Press, 2002).

Chiozza, Giacomo, "Is There a Clash of Civilizations?" *Journal of Peace Research* 39:6 (2002), 711–734.

Diehl, Paul and Gary Goertz, *War and Peace in International Rivalry* (Ann Arbor: University of Michigan Press, 2000).

Henderson, Errol and Joshua Tucker, "Clear and Present Strangers," *International Studies Quarterly* 45:3 (2001), 17–38.

Hopf, Ted. "Common-sense Constructivism and Hegemony in World Politics." *International Organization* 67:2 (2013), 317–354.

Lai, Brian and Dan Reiter, "Democracy, Political Similarity, and International Alliances, 1816–1992," *Journal of Conflict Resolution* 44:2 (2000), 203–227.

Leeds, Brett Ashley and T. Clifton Morgan, "The Quest for Security: Alliances and Arms," in Sara Mitchell, Paul Diehl, and James Morrow, eds. *Guide to the Scientific Study of International Processes* (Chichester, UK: Wiley-Blackwell, 2012), 141.

Levy, Jack, "Prospect Theory, Rational Choice, and International Relations," *International Studies Quarterly* 41:1 (March 1997), 87–112.

Neumann, Iver and Jennifer Welsh, "The Other in European Self-Definition," *Review of International Studies* 17:4 (October 1991), 327–448.

Simmons, Beth and Zachary Elkins, "The Globalization of Liberalization: Policy Diffusion in the International Political Economy," *American Political Science Review* 98:1 (2004), 171–189.

Smith, Rogers, *Stories of Peoplehood* (Cambridge: Cambridge University Press, 2003).

Wendt, Alexander, *Social Theory of International Politics* (Cambridge and New York: Cambridge University Press, 1999).

Appendix

NATIONAL IDENTITY REPORT CODE BOOK

Introduction

This code book lays out an inductive method of interpretive discourse analysis for the recovery of national identity from a sample of speeches, newspaper articles, history textbooks, novels, and movies.

For the purposes of this method, national identity is a set of shared categories that define the nation or what it means to be a member of a nation. That is, how do French people understand themselves as French? What is France?

Step 1: Document List

Our general principles for document selection are to get documents that are widely read and selected in an unbiased manner. We do not want to select documents that talk about identity directly, but rather we want to overhear identity by selecting documents that reveal national identity while ostensibly focused on something else. We also want to capture both elite political discourses and mass common sense, whether these share identity categories or not.

Genres

Leadership Speeches

Choose two leadership speeches by the head of the government/ruling party on a significant day, such as a national holiday address and/or budgetary speech.

Newspapers

Choose the two newspapers with the highest national circulation. If your top papers are all tabloids, choose one tabloid and one "broadsheet" newspaper. From these, for the 15th of each month, read all opinion-editorials (op-eds) and letters to the editor. Separate these into different categories when coding (the idea is that op-eds capture more elite statements, letters more mass statements). If high national circulation newspapers are divided on a partisan basis, say Left and Right, then select these two. Do so even if they are ranked 3 and 4, rather than 1 and 2. For example, in the US case, we would select *The New York Times* and *Wall Street Journal* rather than *The New York Times* and *USA Today*. Or, in the UK case, *London Times* and *Guardian* rather than *London Times* and *Daily Telegraph*.

History Textbooks

Choose two high school history textbooks on your country's national history. Select widely read texts. Start your analysis about 100 years prior to the report date.

Novels

Choose the top two best-selling novels in the country by country's authors in an official language.

Movies

Choose the top two most-attended movies in the country by country's directors/producers in an official language.

Step 2: Coding

In simplest terms you are reading to find the identities of your country. What does it mean to be China or to be Chinese? You are to be as inductive as possible. That said, there are a few orienting principles you should follow.

1. Valence: Distinguish between negative and positive identities. That is, note whether the identity is considered a good or a bad feature of being China or Chinese. So, e.g., in the national identity report on China 2010 you have been given to review, note that a modern China is positive, a backward China

is negative. Neutral identities are those where an identity category is mentioned, but it is not ascribed any particular value. For example, China is vast. Ambiguous identities mean that the text treats the identity as both positive and negative. For example, China's modernization brings progress, but entails environmental costs.

2. Aspirational or Aversive: Is the identity you have found one that China aspires to become, or one it is trying to avoid becoming? So, China aspires to become modern and wishes to avoid dependence.

3. Significant Others: These are the countries, historical periods, ideas, etc., with which China compares itself. These can be historical, contemporary, or prospective. They can be positive or negative. They can be aspirational or aversive. So, China identifies negatively against its colonial past, but positively with Western economic achievements.

You will record the raw numbers of these identities, so as to gauge their frequency.

Keep track of your coding decisions either in one big Word document or in an Excel spreadsheet with coded quotes and coding decisions together.

For example:

"To our compatriots overseas, I want to convey my determination to that which the Republic holds to, with regards to their promises of equality and dignity that was not sufficiently held on to in the past."

Coding: EQUALITY +, DIGNITY+, HISTORICAL OTHER–

"This is absolutely absurd to think that I could be inspired by such a sentiment of nostalgia towards a [colonial] period for which I have, more than once, underlined its injustice and errors."

Coding: COLONIAL HISTORICAL OTHER-

"When the Republicans permanently came to power in 1880, they fought against the influence of the Catholic Church, notably in the schools. By the separation of church and state, the Republic implements secularism that guarantees the free practice of all religions."

Coding: REPUBLICAN+, SECULAR+ HISTORICAL OTHER+

Be careful to distinguish codings of identity categories from themes or tropes in the discourse. Themes or tropes such as extolling the virtues of hard work, invocations of the good life, personal complaints about injustices, or policy proposals are not properly speaking identity categories and can be coded as identity categories only when you think it makes sense to say, "this category is used by people or leaders to define what it means to be French" or the "French nation embodies the virtues of cultural superiority and the pursuit of social justice" and so on. At this point, previously coded themes and tropes can be reconceptualized as identities.

Step 3: Preparing Tables and Analysis

After coding, you will end up with dozens of different identities. You will need to bring order to this list and present the most important categories, as well as synthesize and analyze their relations. There are three substeps to this process.

1. Raw Count Table

First, create a table of raw counts (A.1, A.2) that combine positive, negative, neutral, and ambiguous codings.

Second, produce a table (A.3) that translates the raw counts into percentages normalized by genre. For example, in table A.1, Category x, Speeches should be calculated: $10/13*100\% = 77\%$. Instead of total codings, make a column with an average of the percentages.

Table A.1 **Raw Counts**

Raw Count	Speeches	Newspapers	Textbooks	Novels	Movies	Total Codings
Category x	10	6	3	0	6	25
Category y	3	3	9	7	1	23
Sum	**13**	**9**	**12**	**7**	**7**	

Table A.2 **Example: Raw Identity Counts, France 2010**

French National Identity 2010 Table A.1 Categories	Raw Count	Speeches	Newspapers	Textbooks	Movies	Novels
Cultural center	6	1	3	0	0	2
Egalitarian	10	1	9	0	0	0
Justice	6	1	3	0	0	2
Free/liberty	6	1	3	2	0	0
Modern	4	1	1	0	0	2
Republican	10	1	9	0	0	0
European	8	1	5	0	0	2

(*Continued*)

French National Identity 2010 Table A.1 Categories	Raw Count	Speeches	Newspapers	Textbooks	Movies	Novels
Colonial master (historical)	9	3	6	0	0	0
Africa as a friend of France	7	6	1	0	0	0
Rule of law	7	0	5	0	0	2
Democratic	5	0	5	0	0	0
Respects diversity	3	0	3	0	0	0
Meritocratic/elitist	5	0	5	0	0	0
Old literary	6	0	6	0	0	0
France as German	4	0	4	0	0	0
BRICS*	9	0	5	0	0	4
Pension/aging/ welfare state	15	0	8	6	1	0
Postmodern	4	0	2	0	0	2
Social conflict— rebellious, resistance	54	0	12	40	2	0
Patriarchal	5	0	1	4	0	0
Secular	20	0	8	10	0	2
Catholic/Christian	20	0	4	10	0	6
Homosexuality	3	0	1	0	2	0
Rural, pastoral	10	0	0	0	2	8
Neurotic, overworked urban	2	0	0	0	2	0
Western	9	0	5	0	0	4
Anticapitalist	5	0	1	0	0	4
Civilized	7	0	7	0	0	0
Anti-work	11	0	3	4	2	2
Individualist	3	0	3	0	0	0
Decline	3	0	3	0	0	0
Universal/humanist	3	0	3	C	0	0
United/solidarity	3	0	3	0	0	0
Total	**20.2**	**16**	**137**	**76**	**11**	**42**

*BRICS stands for the emerging economic powers Brazil, Russia, India, China, and South Africa.

Table A.3 **Percentage Counts**

	Percent					
	Speeches	*Newspapers*	*Textbooks*	*Novels*	*Movies*	*Avg*
Category *x*	77%	67%	25%	0%	85%	50.8
Category *y*	23%	33%	75%	100%	15%	49.2

Table A.4 **Top Categories with Valence**

	Raw Count				
	Speeches	*Newspapers*	*Textbooks*	*Novels*	*Movies*
Category *x*	+++++	++	----	−	+
Category *y*	−−/++	++	++	++/−−	

Table A.5 **Example: French Topography**

French National Identity 2010 Topography

	Speeches	Newspapers	Textbooks	Novels	Movies
Republican	++	+	++		
Egalitarian	+	+	+		
Liberty	++	+		+	
Justice	++	+		+	
Rule of law		+		+	
Modern	++	+		+	
Meritocratic/elitist		+			
Secular		++	++++	+	
Democratic		/			
Cultured, Civilized					
Civilized		++			
Cultural center	++	+		++	
European	+/	/		//	
Western		+		++/	
Old literary		+			

(*Continued*)

Table A.5 (**Continued**)

French National Identity 2010 Topography

	Speeches	Newspapers	Textbooks	Novels	Movies
Socioeconomic Values					
Capitalist		–		–––	
Attitude toward work		–	––	–	–––––
Social welfare state		––	++		++–
Pastoral rural, neurotic urban				+++++	+++++
Resistance/ confrontational		+++	+++++	++	+
United/solidarity		+			
Homosexual		/			++/
Respects diversity (aspirational)		+//			––
External Others					
Africa/Francophone	+++++	+			
Germany		+			
Europe	+/	/		//	
BRICS* (competitive)		/		–//	
Historical Others					
Catholic/Christian		–	––//		
Colonial	–––––	–			
Patriarchal	–	–/			

*BRICS stands for the emerging economic powers Brazil, Russia, India, China, and South Africa.

Finally, translate codings into valence symbols (+, –, /, or ~) using the following formula: 1 symbol = 1–5%; 2 symbols = 5–7%; 3 symbols = 8–10%; 4 symbols = 11–15%; 5 symbols = 15%+. If you had – and + codings of the same category, be sure to separate those here. (Note that table below does not use the above figures.)

2. Topographical Table

Next, create a table (A.4, A.5) that presents the categories with valence symbols in clusters or discursive formations. This means grouping categories that you have left separate through bare-bones induction into clusters that you think hang together. Also, note the distribution of categories. Are they equally distributed across all genres of texts? Are they instead concentrated in mass or elite texts? Are the valences the same across genres? Do they only appear in one genre of text, and not in others?

The topographical table (A.4, A.5) should reflect your judgment about what categories are essential to defining national identity in your country. First, include those identities you think most significant, balancing raw counts and your judgment. Second, group categories together into discursive formations (even if loosely). For example, Hopf (2002) groups identities by class, region, ethnicity, and modernity. Third, translate raw counts into valence symbols (+, −, /, or ~) using the formula above.

3. Constructing a Predominant Discourse of National Identity and Its Challenger/s

The final step is to construct and present the predominant discourse of national identity and its challenger/s. This is the most theoretical move on your part, though it should be deeply rooted in the inductive discourse analysis you have performed. Here, fashion what you consider to be the consensual parts of the national identity, as well as those that dominate in the elite or mass texts. This is the predominant discourse of your country's national identity. Next, you construct what you consider to be the primary challenger/s to this identity from what remains.

For an example, see Hopf 2002, pp. 41, 155. In 1955 USSR, Hopf argues that the predominant discourse of Soviet identity features four main elements of the "New Soviet Man": modernity, class, geography, and ethnicity. In 1999 Russia, he finds four discursive formations in circulation: New Western Russian, New Soviet Russian, Liberal Essentialist, and Liberal Relativist. These discursive formations competed with one another to define attitudes toward the Russia past and future.

However, you need not follow this example; we are interested in your inductively recovered findings of the central discourses of identity.

Step 4: Identity Report Draft

Present the findings in a 6,000-word report. When presenting first drafts to the editors it is acceptable to send a version of up to 8,000 words—we like to see lots of quotes, data, and discourses and we can give you feedback on what to

Table A.6 **Example: Chinese Topography**

	Speeches	Textbooks	Newspapers (Op-ed)	Newspapers (Letters to the Editor)	Novels	Movies
Economic Identities						
Moving forward/progress	+++++	+++++	+++	\\	\\	~
Developing economy/catching up	++++	+++	+++	+	+	\
Hardworking	+	+		+	+	++
Sociopolitical identities						
Materialistic		−	−		~~~	−−
Corrupt		−	−	−	−−−−	−−−−−−
Social inequality	\	−	−−	−−	−−−	−−−−−−
Insecure		−	−	−−	−−\\\	\\\
Bureaucracy-oriented consciousness		\		−−	~~~	−−−
Reciprocal courtesy			~		~~~~	−−−
Resilient	++	+++	+			++++
Communism (the CCP formula)						
Socialism with the Chinese characteristics	+++++	+++++	++		−	\
The Chinese Dream (great rejuvenation of the Chinese nation)	++		+		\	
Patriotic	++	++				+
Significant Others						
United States		−	\	\	+	\
Japan (aggressor)		−−				−
Japan (economic model)		\\			+	
The West		\	~	~	+	

keep and what to cut—but the final report will need to be very tight. Here is the outline for the reports:

Introduction

Introduce and summarize your findings to follow. Explain: The predominant discourse of Chinese national identity in 2010 is _____, and its challenger/s are _____. (1 paragraph)

Section 1: Text Selection

Provide the rationale for selection of texts. Go through each of your speeches, newspapers, textbooks, novels, and movies in some detail justifying their selection. (1 page) Provide footnoted sources for the information that guided your choices.

Section 2: Raw Identity Categories

Present the table of raw identity counts (omitting those categories that are insignificant). (1 page)

Explain the table in a short narrative that goes through each identity, what it means, and give examples or quotes from the texts to illustrate. In this section, highlight each identity category in **bold**. (3–4 pages)

Section 3: Predominant Discourse and Its Challenger/s

Present the table of consolidated identity categories/topographical table. Set out the predominant discourse and its challenger/s and explain how you grouped identity categories and why. Central questions to address are:

What are the main elements of the predominant discourse, how much is it distributed across genres, how frequent are its elements?

Now turn to the challenger/s or counter-discourses. What are its elements? How is it distributed? How frequent? How does it relate to the dominant discourse? In addition, lay out areas of elite/mass consensus, showing what is presumably taken for granted at all levels of society; lay out areas of difference between elite and mass, ranging from elite's positive evaluation of some identity and mass derogation of the same, elite's positive evaluation but mass absence, to mass appreciation and elite rejection. Note as well the salience, i.e., frequency and distribution within elite genres and mass genres.

Conclusion (for this volume only)

Summarize how your findings apply to the hegemonic global discourse of neo-liberal democracy. We are interested in how and whether Western hegemony, defined as democratic neoliberalism, can persist past the decline of the United States and the rise of China. So in your conclusion, reflect on the extent to which your findings bolster or challenge this democratic neoliberalism, or how your country challenges or reconfigures democratic neoliberalism. Show how, e.g., the predominant discourse of identity in your country reinforces or undermines this hegemony, and do the same for challenger/s.

The reports will reflect different understandings of democracy and neoliberalism, but we need all the reports to relate to the same "hegemony." For these purposes, democracy refers to i) a political system in which the people rule via elections; ii) a parliamentary or other elected legislative body of representatives makes the laws; iii) institutional checks and balances (rule of law; functioning courts). Neoliberalism is an economic doctrine that promotes: i) faith in markets to solve problems; ii) a negative view of state intervention in the economy; iii) a positive attitude toward liberal economic policies and liberalizing reforms (free trade, deregulation, privatization, openness). But cultural theorists have extended the concept to include corollary beliefs that support and bolster those economic doctrines: iv) strong individualism (Thatcher's "there is no such thing as society"), as expressed in values like individual self-help or individual responsibility; and v) competitiveness valorized as a positive value.

It is important that you use these definitions to differentiate between which aspects of democratic neoliberal hegemony are supported or contested in your findings.

Appendix, Sources, and Bibliography

Include an Appendix with the following: further methodological reflections and supplementary material you think is necessary; a list of the primary sources used; a bibliography of secondary sources if required.

INDEX

Printed in the USA
CPSIA information can be obtained
at www.ICGtesting.com
CBHW051140221123
2064CB00007B/349